My Soviet Youth

My Soviet Youth

*A Memoir of Ukrainian Life
in the Final Years
of Communism*

Irina Rodríguez

McFarland & Company, Inc., Publishers
Jefferson, North Carolina

ISBN (print) 978-1-4766-7759-0 ∞
ISBN (ebook) 978-1-4766-3806-5

LIBRARY OF CONGRESS CATALOGUING DATA ARE AVAILABLE

BRITISH LIBRARY CATALOGUING DATA ARE AVAILABLE

© 2019 Irina Rodríguez. All rights reserved

No part of this book may be reproduced or transmitted in any form or by any means, electronic or mechanical, including photocopying or recording, or by any information storage and retrieval system, without permission in writing from the publisher.

Front cover: *inset* author marching in a Victory Day Parade, May 1986; Ceremony of Inauguration to the ranks of the Young Pioneers, May 1984 (author's collection)

Printed in the United States of America

McFarland & Company, Inc., Publishers
Box 611, Jefferson, North Carolina 28640
www.mcfarlandpub.com

Acknowledgments

To my mom, Olga, the first editor of this work and of all of my undertakings, without whom I would never have become what I am. To my husband and life partner, Robert, who has become so much a part of me that sometimes I cannot distinguish his thoughts from my own. To my stepdad, Oleg, who inspires me with his burning energy and endless passion for music and who is not capable of hostility towards anyone. To my children, Gabriela Anya and Diego Andrei, the main projects of my life, who drive me crazy and make me the happiest person in the world—in turn or simultaneously. In these stories, I also pay back a small part of the debt I owe to my grandparents, Pyotr and Anna, who invested all their thoughts, prayers, worries, happiness and love into me. To all of my family and friends. To my teachers, in particular Dr. Greg Roper of the University of Dallas for inspiring the idea for this book and to Dr. Susan Stewart of Texas A&M–Commerce (TAMUC) for guiding me in my PhD dissertation.

Table of Contents

Acknowledgments v

Preface 1

Propaganda and Life 3

Teachers 15

Culture, Entertainment and Censorship 22

Parties and Holidays 52

More Celebrations and Home Life 67

Military Training and Shadows of the War 82

Community and Town 92

School Fears 110

Exams 121

Joys of Labor at the Soviet Schools 124

More About School 131

Living on Land 148

Extracurricular Activities 157

Death of a Leader 161

Healthcare 168

Bureaucracy	180
Turn to Democracy	188
The News	201
American Afterword	210
Chapter Notes	213
Index	215

Preface

Since I moved to the United States in 1997, I have loved reminiscing about the idiosyncrasies of my Soviet past with other descendants of our "big and happy" motherland, a country that no longer exists. I have also loved sharing my experiences with my new Western friends, often shocking them with the absurdities of our life, which we always considered normal. It never occurred to me to record these stories until May 2018 when I took a creative nonfiction writing class at the University of Dallas with Dr. Greg Roper and four supportive classmates who were better at writing than me. The class was an incredible experience; it awakened my desire to tell the story of my generation of "Homo Sovieticus" growing up during times of political stagnation and the following radical changes in a country of paradoxes. Fear and courage, power and helplessness, tragedy and mirth forever marked the lives of many people like myself.

Most of us are happy the restrictive times of the Soviet Union are over, but we also feel strange nostalgia remembering Pioneer parades, ice-cream that cost eight kopecks, and learning how to shoot Kalashnikov rifles in so-called "Early Military Preparation" classes in school. Nowadays, those times appear to me simpler and somehow purer than the post–Soviet reality. If my tone at times seems affectionate, it does not mean that I wish to condone the horrors of the abuses of power and Soviet crimes against humanity, and, in particular, attacks upon my home country of Ukraine. I simply attempt to tell about my life as I was growing up—my wishes, my fears and my dreams—which probably resemble the wishes, fears and dreams of others like me. I try to describe my life in the strange and paradoxical place known in the West as the Evil Empire, to hopefully make it appear more real and alive to the people who grew up on the other side of the Iron Curtain. At the same time, it is not my wish to monopolize the memories of my generation, nor claim that everybody had the same experience growing up. No two people are the same and the lives of Soviet children, although patterned by the uniform state stencils, took different paths, even more unpredictable since the 1990s.

My interest in telling these stories also arose from the frustration I frequently felt in conversations with people who thought that life in the Soviet Union was drab and uneventful and that everybody wanted to flee it. While we did not have access to advanced technology or fancy clothes, we valued and enjoyed the few toys we had and knew how to have fun—perhaps because we did not have anything in abundance. We did not have videogames or computers, but we invented our own games. We did not know about drugs. We did not travel to exotic destinations, but we enjoyed our four-week vacations at the seaside or state-sponsored vacation centers. We had happy and unhappy moments, just like people anywhere else, and while we had fewer freedoms, we did not necessarily suffer from it. We were free in our own way—free from concerns about medical care and unemployment, free from debt as we rarely had a chance to accumulate any, and free from technological addictions. We were not rich, nor poor. We were subject to the state propaganda machine, but so were the kids and adults of any other country. We lived our lives the best we could and tried to be happy the best we could.

Propaganda and Life

I don't remember seeing any commercials when I was eight. Nothing was advertised. I remember plenty of political slogans instead—on posters hanging above the entrance into government buildings, schools, medical clinics and morgues; inside cabinets, classrooms, libraries, music halls and dental offices; stretched across the streets like Christmas lights during the holidays and greeting us in resorts. We took their abundance for granted and did not analyze their often-paradoxical messages. "The party is the mind, honor and conscience of our epoch!" This conscience quite tolerantly condoned the Soviet control of Eastern Europe and concealed from people the true repercussions of the Chernobyl disaster. "The USSR is a symbol of peace!" which invaded disobedient Czechoslovakia and Hungary. "The Soviet system of justice is the most humane in the world!" This humane system sent millions of innocent people to life sentences or death in Gulags. "Straight ahead towards Communism!"; "The Party is our guide!"; "Lenin's name is eternal!"; "The people and the Party are inseparable!"; "Five-year plan ahead of schedule!" (this sign encouraging accelerated production hung above the entrance to a morgue in our city). Some slogans showcased the love and care of nature expected of Soviet citizens ("The forest is our green friend!"), others gender equality ("Away with kitchen slavery!" or "Glory to Soviet women—active builders of Communism!"), and yet others moral virtues ("We fight drunkenness!" and "Venereal diseases significantly complicate life").

I never thought I would recall them with tenderness, but the images of Marxist-Leninist posters are inextricably connected with childhood memories for me and many other children of the so-called "stagnation period" marked by Brezhnev's rule. Thirty years later, my friends and I laugh after sharing a shot (or two) of vodka as we compare our identical recollections of portraits of Soviet leaders, of *The Pioneer Truth* newspaper, of political information meetings in third grade, and of the tenets of Scientific Communism—the university course everybody had to take whether we grew up in Moscow, Kiev, Tbilisi or Dushanbe.

We were proud of our closely-knit family of Soviet republics—regularly called sisters in children's magazines—and represented in the "Friendship of the Peoples" fountain at the Exhibition of Achievements of National Economy—a Stalinesque theme park built in 1939 that every schoolchild dreamed of visiting. We were proud of our free top-notch educational and medical systems, the Soviet advances in science, particularly in space, affordable four-week seaside vacations, and internationalism. We were proud of the number of medals the Soviet Union earned in the Olympics, many of them gold. We were proud to solemnly stand and hold our right hand bent straight towards the temple in military-type salute to the portentous sounds of the Soviet anthem during celebrations of Lenin's birthday and anniversaries of the Soviet revolution. It was life as we knew it, and we knew no alternative.

"Grandpa" Lenin, with a benevolent (perhaps cunning?) twinkle in his eye, watched our academic struggles from identical portraits on classroom walls. In daycare, we read stories about the four-year-old future leader of the Communist party helping his mom wash dishes, building bird houses with his siblings, learning five languages and starting to conjure plans for the defeat of the exploiting class. We wore the image of his young face framed by blond curls engraved on young Octobrist metal pins and aspired to be like him.

My mom's second grade class, 1950. Mom is second from the right in the top row. It was common for people to adopt a serious and stern look when being photographed. The portrait in the background says, "The people's dreams have come true." Stalinist purges were raging at the time.

Our inauguration into the ranks of young Octobrists in the fall of first grade brought us a step closer to the Communist party as Octobrists were little siblings to Pioneers and Comsomol members.

"Organization of children is the best way of educating future Communists," said Lenin, and early Soviet leaders took these words close to heart, actively starting Pioneer groups, originally on a volunteer basis, on the premises of factories, workshops and clubs. Later, participation in Young Octobrists, Young Pioneers and Comsomol organizations became obligatory. These three organizations made the school's political infrastructure inseparable from the educational one. Each class was simultaneously a Pioneer or a Comsomol unit with a bureaucratic title hardly favorable for a reasonable translation: something like a Pioneer or a Comsomol "detachment." Pioneer unit was divided into smaller units, or "links," each with its own leader, responsible for the successful grades and behavior of its members. If a student was lagging behind, it was the responsibility of the whole "link" to help him or her, visit him at home and provide any extra support.

As an Octobrist, I enviously watched older kids wearing Pioneer ties and could not wait to be like them. Pioneers were "examples to all kids," as the rhyme went, and I longed to show off the proof of my worthiness—the red tie, which would somehow affiliate me with intrepid fighters for the revolution and defenders of our motherland in World War II. Since the breakup of the USSR, our previous customs, naiveté and idealism became easy and trendy targets for mockery. After all, people no longer had to fear a prison sentence for an innocent joke. In the zest of sweeping away the past, however, many of us forgot that there were many noble acts—for example, the fact that early Pioneers worked hard to educate the illiterate population, helped organize orphanages for street children and helped the old and the sick in need. Social work also remained a duty of young Communists during the existence of the Soviet Union, but towards its demise, their roles became mostly reduced to bureaucratic duties.

In theory, you had to deserve the right to be accepted into the Pioneer ranks by exemplary behavior, excellent grades, helping peers and adults in trouble and serving the community. In practice, everybody eventually became one. The only ones who escaped this honor were the kids coming from religious "sects" like Baptists, who were very rare (there was only one family in my school while I studied there). A student could also be expelled from the Pioneer organization for particularly bad behavior or a terrible crime, like going to church (I was deeply affected by a story I read as a child, about a girl who went to church by request of her sick grandma and faced the threat of being expelled. I dreaded the possibility of being thus torn between filial and political duties). I don't remember anyone ever being expelled in our school.

I was a well-behaved student with excellent grades, and my dream came true—I was honored to be inaugurated into the Pioneer organization earlier than others, at the end of second grade instead of third. The sunny afternoon of May 23, 1984, was one of the most exciting days of my early school career. A group of us, distinguished scholars, five girls and one boy from my class and a few other second-graders, assembled in one line in front of the school where most special events took place, wearing honorary "Pioneer uniforms"— white shirts, blue skirts or pants and red pilot hats. We held our new bright red ties and Pioneer pins in extended hands listening to congratulatory speeches by our "vozhatye"—students three grades older who were designated as our leaders, protectors, and guides on the road towards Communism or whatever else the word meant. Red symbolized the color of blood shed by the defenders of our freedom, just like the color of the Soviet banner, and the three ends of the tie symbolized Pioneers, Comsomol and the party. The pin featured a red star with Lenin's face and a fire surrounding it. The fire was not supposed to swallow up the red star or the face, but rather to make it shine brighter at Pioneer reunions around a summer camp fire.

Then we recited the words of the Solemn Pioneer Oath each of us has committed to memory to this day: "I, Irina Chuykova [my maiden name], entering the ranks of the All-Union Pioneer Organization named after Vladimir Ilyich Lenin, promise solemnly in front of my comrades to love my Motherland with ardor; to live, study and struggle as the Great Lenin had called us to do and as the Communist Party teaches us; and to always follow the Laws of the Pioneers of the Soviet Union." We also had to learn and recite those laws developed by the Central Committee of the All-Union Leninist Young Communist League (VLKSM) in the early days of the Soviet Union, to indicate our readiness for entering the Pioneer organization. The laws stipulated that a Pioneer should be devoted to the motherland, to the party, and to Communism; he should be getting ready to become a Comsomol member; he should follow the example of the heroes of struggle and labor; he should honor the memory of the fallen heroes and be getting ready to become a defender of the motherland; he should be the best in studies, work and sports; he should be a guide and comrade of the young Octobrists and a friend of other Pioneers and working youth of all the countries of the world.

The Pioneer law also called us to guard our Pioneer tie as a symbol of our high destination and to protect and guard our sacred Red Pioneer Banner. Nobody thought of the awkwardness of the combination of the word "sacred" with the Pioneer banner, perhaps because the relics of the Communist organization seemed sacred to us at the time. The red banner, a Pioneer horn and a drum announcing the beginning of Pioneer assemblies were kept in a special room called "Pioneer corner," specifically designated for this purpose. During

Propaganda and Life

Top: Reciting the solemn oath at the Young Pioneers inauguration ceremony, May 23, 1984. In the group of Young Pioneers at left, I am second from the right (the tall one). *Bottom:* Older Pioneers, our mentors, or "vozhatye," arranging the Pioneer ties for us, May 23, 1984. I am at center rear.

assemblies and parades, an honorary group of older Pioneer comrades carried them in front of all the students.

Later during the ceremony, one girl from our group, chosen either for her leadership potential or perhaps for being a teacher's daughter, knelt in front of the red banner held by "vozhatye" and kissed it. This marked the final stage of our preparation and "vozhatye" marched towards us, one for each new Pioneer, and tied the knot on our necks. Afterwards, we greeted them in the proper Pioneer way—by raising our hand towards the temple in a Pioneer salute. We also responded in harmony to the honorary Pioneer slogan, solemnly pronounced by the president of the Pioneer "druzhina": "Pioneer! Be ready for struggle for the cause of the Communist Party of the Soviet Union!" "Forever ready!" we answered in chorus. I felt an immense sense of pride. I now contributed to a political struggle for peace, justice, equality and liberty. The only thing I regretted was not living in a bigger city like Moscow where they took the kids to Lenin's mausoleum or some revolutionary museum to celebrate the occasion.

We started preparations to defend the motherland by learning basic marching skills and yelling motivational rhymes that went as follows:

> Leader of the group (standing in front of a group divided
>   into three equal lines): One, two!
> The group (in chorus): Three, four!
> Leader: Three, four!
> Chorus: One, two!
> Leader: Who is marching neatly in a row?
> Chorus: Our pioneer unit!
> Strong, brave! Agile, skillful!
> We love to jump and hop
> Don't even try to catch us!

Or

> (Same first six lines)
> Who is tired? Don't be tired!
> Who stayed behind? Don't stay behind!
> Our mood gets the grade of "5"![1]
> We follow all the laws
> And here goes the song! (Motivational song follows)

Young Octobrists had their own motivational rhymes:

> We are happy children!
> We are children—Octobrists!
> They gave us this name
> In honor of the victory of the Great October!
> We play, we read
> We dream of going to the Moon
> We will keep our strong friendship
> And serve our country!

Nowadays, we laugh as we think back to reciting these silly and pompous rhymes. At the time, shivers ran down our spines as we stood in neat rows hoping to win the honor of being selected as the best marching unit. A couple of times per year the school held exhibitions of marching skills where different units within the same grade competed in the categories of the best marching technique, best appearance, best yelling of the rhyme, best singing, best coordination and other "bests." These exhibitions dispelled the monotony of school routine between holidays and vacations. While such exhibitions remained long in the past in Ukraine, I discovered, perusing the internet, that such events are still very much alive in many Russian schools. My first desire was to laugh, but then I felt a more appropriate urge to cry or at least worry about the dystopian return of the Soviet days.

Each class had its own miniature equivalent of the Supreme Council of the Communist Party, called the Council of the Pioneer Unit. It was comprised of the president of the Pioneer unit, her assistant who also held some bureaucratic title loosely translated as "academic leader of the unit," and presidents of "links." The council held regular meetings with the whole class where they determined ways to improve class performance, praised high achievers and scolded poor students. The homeroom teacher was not to interfere. Although it sounded very official, in reality the meetings of our Pioneer unit were chaotic, underachievers made fun of the leadership and ultimately disrupted the whole deal unless the teacher came to restore order and take proper charge.

We also started holding obligatory "political information" meetings in third or fourth grade, sharing news about Communist party achievements or failures of the capitalist economies for about twenty minutes before school once or twice a week. Pioneer "druzhina" (or the community of all the school Pioneer units) also held occasional meetings where behavioral disruptions of a serious order were discussed, and the culprits explained their behavior in front of nearly the whole student body. Since such large gatherings intimidated even the most audacious troublemakers, the meetings generally went smoothly and did not leave any colorful memories.

All the students, besides the president of the unit and the links, had to carry out some Pioneer responsibility, such as the horn carrier, the drum carrier, the person in charge of political information, and editors, writers and artists for a "wall newspaper." I enjoyed editing the wall newspaper ("stengazeta"). It was a large poster with class news, expressions of gratitude toward teachers, announcements of students' success and caricatures of underachievers or troublemakers. The paper was posted on the wall in the class, but since students would rotate rooms, other classes had access to its often-sensitive information. Such constructive criticism and fun-making was intended to shame poor performers into better behavior and higher academic results. I cannot remember if the caricatures achieved this purpose as they usually did in children's books, but poor performers and hooligans seemed to enjoy and take pride in their infamy. They got used to constant chiding on the school radio, in class and during Pioneer meetings and worked on upholding their reputation. Some became rock stars of sorts whose names instilled fear. After completing nine grades of compulsory minimum education, a few students left school and three classes were combined into two. As a result, our class was to receive an infusion of the infamous troublemakers, whose arrival we awaited with terror. On the fateful day of the beginning of the tenth grade we discovered that the feared brutes acted quite tamely, only allowing themselves occasional harmless jokes, and on the whole were friendly and nice. I even became friends with some of them—every time I return to Ukraine, we see each other and reminisce about the good old days.

Each class unit was named after a revolutionary or war hero. Ours carried the name of a child hero, Lara Mikheyenko, who served as a guerrilla partisan during World War II, or Great Patriotic War, as we called it. She ventured into the occupied territories pretending to be gathering berries or herding animals, and she gathered key facts about Nazi troop locations instead. She was eventually discovered, tortured and executed by the Nazis when she was only fourteen. As we talked about her, I fruitlessly tried to imagine being in her place. With shivers I repeatedly came to the conclusion that I would not be able to do anything remotely similar in valor or self-sacrifice. We read many books about other child heroes like Lara—most were caught or sometimes betrayed and brutally tortured to death. The only story I remember of escaping death by the Nazis also ended tragically—the boy Volodya Dubinin stepped on a mine while helping clean his native city of Kerch after its liberation in 1942. The ironic senselessness of his death after he had survived the worst dangers and battles impacted me and made me clearly see the brutal injustice of war. The political organization of the whole school ("druzhina") was named after a war hero from our own town, Boris Tasuy, who participated in the defense of Moscow and multiple other battles all over the Soviet Union. For his courage and skills, Tasuy was awarded the Order of the Red Star—the highest award—before he fell in battle defending the Kerch peninsula between the sea of Azov and the Black Sea.

Most school events (with the exception of the New Year's party) glorified the achievements of our party in liberating the world proletariat from the enslavement of capitalist exploitation. Most textbooks (with the exception of math) incorporated texts glorifying Lenin's wisdom and foresightedness in making us the happiest and the freest children of the world—and we truly believed we were. I hated the thought of growing up anywhere besides my beautiful, peaceful land which no army could conquer, where we did not have to pay for our education or medical care, and where my family surrounded me with love and affection.

In summer, Pioneers combined their socio-political activities with active vacations in Pioneer camps where their parents sent them to practice sports, have fun, swim, get healthy (a typical expression applied for people going on summer vacation in nature) and meet new friends. I must confess I missed out on this part of the Soviet reality as my parents were too protective and did not want me to go on vacation alone. Being very attached to my family, I never actually wanted to go and was afraid to even think of spending a month away from them. I sometimes imagined myself being different, daring and reckless, venturing on hiking trips and singing at camp fires, organizing games and trying other adventures I never actually undertook in real life. I saw them in children's movies where the camp appeared enticing and romantic. The songs and games by the camp fire fascinated me most, but I also wanted to try sleeping in a tent, which I never did, and tasting the romanticism of simple life in nature. In fact, this desire increased so much with years that living in the United States, I implored my husband who was likewise not experienced in camp life, to try it. The first experiment was not too pleasant, as we did not bring warm sleeping bags for camping in Colorado where it got so cold at night that we ended up sleeping in a van. However, we did not desist and gradually became expert campers regularly participating in camp song festivals for Russian speakers (KSP) in Lake Livingston, Texas—which might be the closest modern equivalent to Pioneer camps, without a political agenda.

I heard conflicting testimonies about how Pioneer camp life actually was. People's impressions depended largely on the location of the camp—if parents could afford sending their offspring to a good camp by the seaside, it enhanced the quality of vacation. Some schools awarded prizes of free Pioneer camp vacations to deserving candidates, often by the seaside. The most craved destination recognized as the absolute best in the Soviet Union was the camp called "Artek" located in Crimea on the coast of the Black Sea. The best of the best students and active Pioneers not only from the USSR but from seventy other countries came to vacation there free of charge by being awarded a special "voucher." Special honorary guests, like Fidel Castro, Indira Gandhi, French author André Gide, Mikhail Gorbachev, American painter Rockwell Kent and Dr. Benjamin Spock, among others, also came to tour the facilities on official visits. My mom was among the lucky ones to receive the award in her childhood, but never went—as it turned out, a bureaucratic error, frequent during the Soviet days, prevented the voucher from being processed correctly.

While the prestige of the camp declined after the breakup of the Soviet Union in 1991, it remained functional and continued to host children, until recently under the jurisdiction of the Ukraine's State Management of Affairs. The socialist welfare system, although weakened by the economic breakdown, continued to completely or partially subsidize most vacationers coming from low-income or large families as well as orphaned, disabled and gifted children. In 2014, the fate of the camp changed again due to Russia's annexation of the Crimean peninsula, after which Ukrainian children could no longer benefit from its beautiful location and educational and medical advantages. Ukraine was forced to move the camp to a resort in Carpathian mountains; I do not know who goes to Artek nowadays.

Dispatching an unfortunate heir to a camp close to his or her place of residence completely eliminated the element of exoticism and fun. This happened yearly to my school friend Lena. When I was walking to the pond by the camp fence in our town, I saw her glance longingly outside like a sad creature deprived of freedom in a zoo. I did not want to be in her place. Nevertheless, many kids enjoyed the Pioneer camps, even if the sea was not close. My stepdad told me of savoring freedom while running around and playing wargames in the woods in a camp near his native city of Kharkiv. He actually liked the benefit of being relatively close to the city: his parents came to visit on Sundays and brought additional sustenance in case state-planned rations did not satisfy his growing appetite.

The most hated part of the camps, by the accounts of most firsthand witnesses, was the so-called "dead hour" or "quiet hour," the two hours after lunch when kids were supposed to sleep but rarely did. Instead, my stepdad recalls, they used this time to plan a variety of ingenious tricks to play on one another: painting toothpaste designs on those few who were sleeping, rubbing rosehip fruit on bed sheets so it would sting when the person lay down on them, or putting a thread with beads under the sheets and pulling it at the moment the victim was getting ready to fall asleep in order to scare him. One boy, too lazy to go to the bathroom during quite hour, peed right from the window of the second floor. Unfortunately, a supervisor happened to be passing under that very window. The quiet hour quickly turned into a loud one.

The Pioneer organization had its own organs of propaganda. *Pionerskaya Zorka* (Pioneer Star), a fascinating morning radio program about life of Pioneers in different parts of the country, featured biographies of distinguished Pioneers, achievements of various Pioneer units throughout the country and parodies on poor and irresponsible students (usually in an abstract form, without concrete examples) interspersed by inspirational songs. *Pionerskaya Pravda* (Pioneer Truth) was the official newspaper of the Pioneer organization. As excited as I was about wearing the Pioneer tie, which I carefully ironed every morning, and as much as I enjoyed reading, I could never bring myself to read an entire issue of this honorable informative publication. It was usually tightly packed with theses of the Communist party meetings, more summaries of Pioneer achievements, simplified news reviews and some stories and riddles for entertainment. After the particularly important meetings of the Communist party, the newspaper directed for fourth- to eighth-graders published the entire text of the party's Central Committee address to the Soviet people, which occupied almost all of the space and did not exactly make for exciting reading material. The magazine *Pioneer* was much better. A thick volume of thirty pages allowed enough space for Communist party addresses, Communist leader portraits, didactic articles but also entertaining stories, challenging crossword puzzles and word scrambles—something that my linguistically inclined mind particularly enjoyed.

We celebrated the birthday of the All-Union Pioneer Organization on May 19 by more marching parades and assemblies, where we listened to endless speeches no one really heard, recited verses and sang songs. The beauty of the event lay in canceled lessons and enjoying the spring weather, as the assembly took place outdoors. The picture of my sixth grade participating in

Celebrating one of the last days of the Pioneers in 1988. Our class had PE just before the assembly, and that's why all of us are wearing jogging pants and none of us are wearing the traditional Pioneer pilot hats. The slogan above the school entrance says, "Following the road of the 27th Congress of the Communist Party means following the road of peace and productivity." I am third from right (see arrow). My friend Larisa is second from right.

this event in 1988 reminds me that we were the last generation to boast Pioneer ties and carry the honorary burden of Pioneer responsibilities. The extraordinary 22nd meeting of the VLKSM dismissed both the Pioneer and Comsomol organizations in 1991. Thus, I could not taste the pride of being a member of Comsomol, the oldest youth division of the Communist party, which implied increased levels of socialist consciousness and military preparation. Comsomol members wore khaki shirts and pilot hats to school and guided their younger peers—all of the eight younger grades—towards a brighter future. Membership in Comsomol was supposedly voluntary, but those young people bold enough not to join could hardly expect to achieve anything in life. Higher education institutions or workplaces required a letter of recommendation from high school or a university with a necessary component evaluating socio-political activity.

I did not decry the disappearance of Comsomol. My pride and illusions diminished considerably during the years of perestroika, which revealed massive bureaucracy and mismanagement of all Soviet political organizations. Nevertheless, the nostalgia of my initial pride remains.

Teachers

We had some nice teachers. They are not the ones that come to my mind when I think of school, however. The nasty, the crazy, the eccentric ones, sometimes a little too obsessed with their subjects, sometimes mean, sometimes short-tempered, emerge from the depths of my memory in vivid detail. First, the stone-faced, frowning, grim principal. She made me think of Stalin. True to the stereotype of the Soviet top-level bureaucrat, this blue-haired lady seemed ancient to us but was probably no more than sixty at the time. On the heavy side, she walked leaning forward and fixing her cobra eyes on everything she sensed as potentially improper or disruptive. Her look seemed even more intimidating behind thick-rimmed glasses. Whenever she appeared in hallways brimming with overly energetic students, all the jumping, juggling, giggling, fighting and pushing instantly stopped, as if by magic. All eyes turned in fear to this symbol of authoritarian power gifted with inspiring terror in students and parents alike. She never taught my class, and I did not have the good fortune of witnessing her pedagogical talent. I don't remember ever seeing her smile, much less laugh. I don't remember her addressing any words of praise to me, even though I had won various awards in mathematics, English and Russian in inter-school competitions called Olympiads. All I remember was her chiding me on the all-school radio for coming to school wearing earrings and having done a perm during my rebellious days in the eighth grade.

An even more memorable figure, because she taught my math class, was the similarly menacing assistant principal (in Russian "zavuch," or the official in charge of the academic work), famed in the whole town for her expertise on the subject but also for her explosive and unpredictable temper. Her name was Yelena Aleksandrovna (all the teachers were called respectfully by their first name and patronymic), but behind her back everybody called her "The Toad." She looked like one—her indefinable age was stuck somewhere beyond fifty, with tiny eyes hid behind droopy eyelids, a squished head that pushed her eyes towards the top and reduced the space left for her forehead, thinning straight hair combed backwards, an imperial walk, a protruding belly, and the invariable green dress. Her voice was the only feature not resembling a reptile. Rather it was a lion's roar whenever she got angry, which was often. She was frequently happy too—especially when you showed enthusiasm for the subject matter she taught with such rigidity and passion. She flipped between those two moods with wondrous ease.

Yelena Aleksandrovna knew her subject exceptionally well, and she firmly believed that all the students should also gain a superb knowledge of math by the time they graduated from high school. She didn't let us consider any alternatives. "You will thank me for this later," she used to say. "You can't get anywhere in this life without math." To inspire us in this venture, she established an "optional" math club. If a student aspiring to get a "five" (the maximum grade equaling an "A") chose not to attend its weekly sessions, the highest grade was out of the question—she found a way to drop it. I remember sitting in one of these sessions in her classroom with tall windows that nevertheless did not let in much light during cloudy winter days, when it started to get dark at three. I would longingly look outside at the adjacent park with melting snow and wonder when the session would be over. It was supposed to end at three thirty, but if we acted particularly uncooperative or if Yelena Aleksandrovna felt particularly enthusiastic, she would not allow us to leave until an hour or so later. Taking into account the homework we still had to do for the following day, this left very little time for anything else. Once a teacher of Russian got sick and her lesson was about to be cancelled. Yelena Aleksandrovna, who happened to find out just in time to prevent such a disaster, enthusiastically snatched the occasion for infusing us with an extra dosage of mathematics. She would not hear of any chance of idleness for our growing minds. We had five hours of math that day. Afterwards, the other teachers noted our unusual levels of eagerness towards their own subjects.

Yelena Aleksandrovna taught generations of families in our town and sometimes mixed up students' names with those of their parents. Many comical situations arose from this confusion. My memory goes back to one of those days when she was in a particularly placid mood. "Borenka! Go to the blackboard!" she called benevolently to the guy named Seryozha whose dad Boris had been her student twenty years earlier. ("Borenka" is a diminutive affectionate form of the full name "Boris" generally used with children or close friends.) "Borenka," oblivious to the directive and pretty much to anything else around him, was held captive by a game of cards with a couple of classmates, his back nonchalantly half-turned towards the teacher. Yelena Aleksandrovna nodded encouragingly and waited a second, considering the possibility that the student needed time to process her request. When she decided his time had run out, she called louder, and less affectionately, "Borya! Let's get up and running!" Same result. Those of us who figured out

At a session of the weekly "optional" advanced math class (*fakultativ*) in tenth grade, 1992. I am in the front at right. My friend Larisa is next to me. Behind Larisa is one of the reputed "class hooligans" all the teachers feared, Misha Salazkiy.

the reason for the misunderstanding waited for the outcome with excited impatience. With each new "Borya" more tension crept into the teacher's voice; she kept repeating the name with increasing volume until velvety redness was gradually swallowing up her face. There remained absolutely no trace of her previous good humor, and she finally exploded in thunder shaking the classroom walls: "Guzenko! To the board!!!" ("Guzenko" was the student's last name, and its employment signaled a radical drop of the teacher's mood to its nadir).[1]

Even if this hapless fellow had in fact been prepared to tackle the trigonometry problem in store for him, the task would still be quite challenging considering the prejudice of the teacher enraged by his early unresponsiveness. Since he turned out to be quite unprepared and irritated her further by his nonsensical rambling, which had little to do with actual trigonometry, "The Toad's" fury grew to the point that she started searching around the room for a possible weapon of revenge. Her eyes fell on the big and heavy broom that a student "on duty" was supposed to use for sweeping the floor during recess and after classes. As she deemed it perfect for the situation, she grabbed it and made a decisive move toward "Borya." While educated in the spirit of utmost respect for authority, "Borya" attempted to follow the rules of discipline in the classroom but his self-preservation instinct prevailed. After taking a couple of cautious steps backward, he broke into steady trotting. The rest of us sat and followed the spectacle deeply fascinated—it was better than the movie theater.

Amazingly, our dignified and stout teacher chased Seryozha/Borya with surprising agility, almost touching him with the broom. His fear and teenager's velocity helped him get away but not too far—he did not want to boast his physical advantage out of respect for the teacher. The race continued in this manner, with both trotting briskly without actually running. Yelena Aleksandrovna periodically screamed at her victim, giving vent to her rage. Our desks were located in three rows, with two people at each desk, leaving little space between the third row and the wall. The tightness presented no obstacle for these joggers, though, who squeezed through that space, completing the circle around the room. They continued their marathon completing at least three circles. Everybody in class, except, of course, the protagonists of this drama, was by that point almost sobbing with laughter. I cannot remember how the scene ended—probably with Seryozha imploring forgiveness and Yelena Aleksandrovna eventually yielding—but it remains a colorful piece in the mosaic of my school day memories. Ever since that day, the name "Borya" stuck to our friend and seemed to fit him more organically than his own. Even my mom several times stopped short of calling him "Borya" when running into him on the street.

Some other teachers I remember mostly by their nicknames. No one knew who authored them or when, but they were passed from generation to generation and perfectly targeted the analogy between the teacher's physical traits and the subject they taught. "Paint Brush" was a tall, extremely skinny lady with long, slightly unkempt dark hair who taught art. Contrary to what one might assume about an art teacher's personality, she was the epitome of imperturbable calm—she would nearly put us to sleep with her monotonous drone and chase away any interest in art we possibly had. "Globe" was a plump and round-faced elderly geography teacher. "Limonka" (the name of the lemon-shaped Soviet defensive grenade) was an elderly history teacher whose body was markedly heavier in the bottom and thinner in the upper part. And of course, there was "Galushka" (Ukrainian dumpling)—the soft-spoken physics teacher whose nickname was only related to her appearance and not to the subject. The chemistry teacher was called "Manka-Vanka" due to the sexual content she infused in her explanation of chemical formulas. "Manka" (diminutive form of the name "Maria") was the code word for acid and "Vanka" (diminutive form of the name "Ivan") the code for alkali. Their mutual attraction produced salt residue. She emphasized with zest that Manka could not have a reaction with another Manka, and her hearty howling laughter still rings in my ears.

Limonka had a curious habit of watering plants in her classroom while students were responding to her extended questions on the reasons of the October Revolution or development of the civil war. Having figured out her horticultural passion, the unprepared students raised their hands just before her arrival to class to show their eagerness to help. If she was in a good mood, she would let them water the plants, and they overzealously indulged in this occupation, prolonging it for as long as possible while the survey went on. They were taking a risk, however: if she was in a bad mood, she would question them on the homework material instead and easily reveal their ruse. Another trick students employed was raising their hand in the beginning of class in hopes of reciting the first paragraph from the assigned reading and getting a good grade before reaching a spot where their knowledge became shaky. Limonka was not easily deceived. "Keep holding your hand up," she would say and ask somebody else. She would later come back to the eager volunteer and question him on the material he had not rehearsed.

Olga Stefanovna, a teacher of Russian language and literature, never taught my class but strangely fascinated me and others by her completely emotionless face, which resembled a mask. It earned her the nickname "Fantomas" (an extremely popular French literary and movie character who wore a latex mask to conceal his identity when committing violent crimes). You could not tell whether Olga Stefanovna was dead or alive behind her mask and whether her eyes were open or closed behind her double-lens glasses. Her former students recall her ruthlessness in evaluating their compositions. "You want a grade of five?"[2] she would say. "Even God's knowledge of Russian does not exceed 'four plus.'" If someone dared to complain about the grade, she challenged them to enter a "line of fire," that is, come to the board at the end of the quarter and face a random assortment of her questions on all the possible topics. Legend has it that once in her youth, a pack of wolves surrounded her in the Kazakhstan steppe where she used to live. Not losing her spirit, she started reciting Pushkin's "Eugene Onegin" and hypnotized them. Not even the wolves could escape her magnetic grip of knowledge.

Nikolai Nikitovich, the music guy, gray-haired and slightly robust but very lively, was extremely enthusiastic about the notes he taught us, the accordion on which he accompanied our songs and also about soccer which often crept into our lesson discussions. When he played the accordion, he would tap the rhythm and sometimes break into dance. The boys knew his love of soccer and often exploited it: They would start praising some player of a younger generation which he clearly despised and thus foment a discussion. I remember one particularly heated argument when Nikolai Nikitovich advocated that the Brazilian legend Pele and the Soviet star goalie Lev Yashin were the best players of all time. Both were retired by that time and the boys did not hold them in great esteem. Our musician took that fact so close to heart that he jumped from his seat panting and screaming arguments in his favorite players' defense while making us girls, the impartial spectators, quite worried for his well-being. On other occasions, he made us laugh by changing our last names in a funny way and dramatizing the songs we were learning by replacing the characters' names with our own. At one point, he represented me as the wife of a class hooligan (a drunkard in the song) whom she greeted with a hoe. Nikolai Nikitovich passed away from heart failure shortly after he retired. I remember him with fondness and shame for our actions that possibly contributed to his condition and for not having appreciated him enough.

The biology teachers ruled over a fascinating room full of tropical plants and glass-covered bookshelves housing a collection of artifacts for study and amazement. Shady plants created a summer-like atmosphere throughout the year. One of them had traveled with us on a train back from a week-long visit to Lithuania—the teacher took such a liking to it that she purchased it in that distant land, although similar species were undoubtedly available in our own city. We had to squeeze our suitcases to allow sufficient room for its thick fretted leaves that took half of the train compartment. When we stopped in the city of Minsk, Belarus, to switch trains, some of us had to miss a tour of the city to babysit the precious plant.

A full-size human skeleton was hiding in the side niche of the biology classroom under lock and key, and we only saw it when appropriate for anatomy class. However, if a teacher would occasionally forget to secure it with a key, the bones would make an appearance in the hallway, assisted by some invisible naughty students. The skeleton grinned, viciously greeting and scaring unwary schoolkids and teachers. In the old school building, it had resided in the attic in a dark, scary corner next to the smelly bathroom, with a steep diagonal passage leading to it. As it was always locked and we never saw the passageway in the bright light, we could only imagine what ghosts kept their secrets in the attic together with the skeleton. We would sneak a peek at the osseous frame irreverently dragged out of its quarters by older students for educational purposes, and the vision would haunt me in nightmares for many a night.

One of the biology teachers, Antonina Antonovna, never failed to hold our attention with her bubbly and engaging teaching manner, whether she was delving into the steps of photosynthesis, analyzing the life cycle of a butterfly or of changes in the human body at puberty, or discussing the details of her daughter's recent divorce or her own philosophy on marriage and sexual harmony. The more sensitive topics were luckily reserved for anatomy classes, many of which were in the last grade and divided into boys or girls only. A model of optimism, Antonina Antonovna would sometimes lose her patience with us. Once, persistent mumbling at the back of the room made her stop in the middle of the sentence she was writing on the blackboard. She turned around, fixed her eyes on the culprit (or whom she suspected to be such) and swiftly threw a humongous piece of chalk at him—all in quick succession so that the victim barely leaned down in time for the chalk to hit the wall behind him and leave a chip in the green paint.

I remember her mention in class once during her frequent digressions that she would never be able to live anywhere except the motherland. She described someone she knew who had emigrated to Europe and was known to aimlessly roam the streets of her new hometown (perhaps Paris) possessed by the feeling of nostalgia. (Patriotism was an important value in the Soviet Union and leaving the motherland out of materialistic or even romantic concerns was deemed close to a sin.) Antonina Antonovna moved to New York shortly after the Soviet Union broke down after receiving a cash prize for her pedagogical work and worked as a home attendant. Eventually, she became a legal resident of the United States and came to visit Ukraine only after twenty years in the United States. She told me in one of our frequent phone conversations that she had missed our school and teaching her subject so much that she asked if she could give a couple of classes while there. She did it with gusto, expertise and little preparation as all the material stayed fresh in her memory all that time.

I also remember a cheerful energetic intern who came to our class for a month in spring of our first or second year. She had not yet been crushed by the weight of administrative demands and pedagogical routine, and she planned every class as a masterpiece. She introduced a spirit of positive competition where each row of students earned points for correct answers. Individual students accumulated points as well, and a certain number of points awarded us a red star glued on the agenda which we proudly displayed to each other and our parents. Class participation increased tenfold. I became so absorbed in earning the points for red stars that I forgot my fear of volunteering. She was our hero. We cried when she left and wrote her countless letters. She responded to every single one of them, and we continued the letter exchange for a year or so. Then she came to visit us during the Victory Day parade—it was a delightful surprise. I can only hope she has kept her youthful ardency, vivacity and dedication to students and the profession, which was truly her vocation.

Preserving a positive spirit for a teacher was not easy with large classrooms, scarce resources and crazy, disobedient and often disrespectful students. A teacher's job is never easy, nor paid well enough. A teacher myself, I recognize it and value the efforts every single one of them put into my formation—as well as the droll memories they helped to create.

Culture, Entertainment and Censorship

We didn't play videogames or watch cartoons on a VCR. We didn't have the requisite devices. We watched cartoons on TV—frequently in black and white. My family didn't get a color TV until I was about seven, around 1982. A home phone arrived around the same time. This offered the possibility of a new and exciting pastime, rather than a practical advantage: Since many people in town still didn't have phones, they paid somebody a visit if they needed to talk. Thus, they combined the talk with social enrichment. If we tried to call a doctor's office, a repair shop or another institution, we ran a high risk of a busy signal or a tone that would ring forever with no result. Administrative clerks or receptionists were too busy to play customer service games. Why should they bother answering the phone at the power station in the event of a (frequent) breakdown? Once they repair it, people will find out themselves. And if the problem is too serious to be repaired today, why bother with unpleasant explanations and upsetting people when their hope can last until tomorrow?

If by some miracle we got lucky and managed to get through to a "customer service" representative, the joy turned out to be short-lived. Customer service consisted in barking some indignant or sarcastic remarks to the customer, such as "Woman, what do you want from me? I don't know any better than you why there is no electricity. We are trying to find the problem." Another variant could be "Woman, if you delay me longer with your questions, the problem will not disappear."

In any case, even if we got through, we also faced the challenge of trying to make out what on Earth the person on the other line was saying behind all the static and crackling noise, which strongly resembled machine guns on a front line. There was yet another exciting possibility—getting through to the entirely wrong place. About once every few days, we received calls from people inquiring if they reached an ambulance, a fire station, a post office or some mysterious family with the last name "Garbuz" (translated into English as "a pumpkin"). Such line crossings also accounted for some unexpected joys: We would unwittingly cut into a phone conversation between two common friends or acquaintances and thus enjoy a three-way conference call—an unheard-of luxury that would never work if arranged on purpose. Cross-connections could naturally have unpleasant consequences as well: We could never share a secret on the phone without fear that someone might, willingly or not, overhear it. Once I called my mom from the United States and cut into her conversation with a friend. In my eagerness to join them I spoke, then increased my volume, then yelled—all without result: They could not hear me while I could hear all the details of their talk perfectly well. On another occasion, my mom discovered an intricate method of improving an illegal bootlegging machine to produce better homemade vodka, all thanks to some guys' chat she managed to tap into.

Trying to place a long-distance call was even worse. The quality of the Soviet pre-digital phone lines was so poor that if you managed to hear a voice on the other line, it sounded as if coming from the deep underground. The quality decreased drastically with distance. A popular joke described a chap yelling desperately into the receiver: "Allo! Moskva? Moskva? MOSKVA?" A guy passing by asked: "Why are you yelling like that across the distance, brother? Couldn't you just use a phone?"

Usually, we could not simply pick up the phone and dial a long-distance number—trying to get through was of no use. We had to "order" a call from the operator who would indicate an approximate waiting time that could range from half an hour to three hours. Having reached the operator, we felt that we already accomplished a small feat as this number also stayed mostly busy, especially at night or during the holidays. The operator would give no exact indication of the waiting time for establishing the desired connection, saying, simply and vaguely: "Wait." It was not altogether convenient when a neighbor came to your house asking to place a long-distance call. It meant she would stick around for the next few hours keeping you away from your duties—a visitor could not be simply ignored and left without entertainment or nourishment. An alternative of going to the post office to place a call afforded an opportunity of long-distance calls with shorter waiting times and less cost, but without the comfort of speaking from home.

Due to the shortage of phone lines, a curious system envisioned two households sharing the same line and similar numbers. We shared a line with our neighbors, which meant that if the phone was used by one household, it stayed silent and was not functional in the other. You could, if you tried hard and had nothing better to do, make out the echoes of your neighbors' conversation. If they "fixed" the phone to eliminate this audibility, a worse problem came in its place and so we preferred not to complain. Once, as a result of something getting "fixed," the phone lines crossed, and the people calling us were repeatedly connected to our neighbors—and vice versa. The phone sharing system practically ruled out the possibility of any leisurely chat with a friend—neighborly courtesy obliged us to wrap it up barely after having started. Naturally, it brought about an even bigger problem if the neighbors engaged in a lengthy chat when we needed to make an urgent call, or any type of call, for that matter. In such cases, we employed tricks like knocking on their door and running away to motivate them to hang up faster. Other times they used some tricks, and as a result we received phone bills for long-distance conversations we never placed. Finally, we were able to pay a fee to be disconnected from the annoying combination and use our own independent line.

The Soviet phone system offered some interesting advantages—for example, you could check the time by dialing 09, verify the train schedule by dialing 08 or enjoy the benefit of the most updated, though doubtfully correct, weather forecast by dialing 01. Sometimes the phone would stop working altogether, and we had to call a repair service, which always took its time to arrive. Strong wind, thunderstorms and especially snow accumulation on the phone cables (quite frequent during Ukrainian winters) were guaranteed ways to break the lines for a considerable lapse of time—the repair service would be less likely to arrive in poor weather. Then the nineties came and everything, including lead phone cables, became a target for theft. Those of us whose cables befell this misfortune had to purchase new ones ourselves or face the perspective of being without phone service for an indefinite length of time.

Before and after the arrival of the phone into our lives, books provided the main source of entertainment. They were valued so much that people like my grandparents did everything possible to find out the approximate day of new arrivals in bookstores in advance. They signed up in special kiosks for a spot granting the right to purchase collected works that would be "thrown out" (according to the Soviet jargon) of the bookstore at a later date. Volumes of collected works were never printed all at once, as Soviet publishing companies teased readers by issuing them one by one over a period of one, two or even three years. The likely reasons for this snail's pace stemmed from the limited capability of printing presses, thorough editing work and, of course, thorough censorship. Although the collected works titles presumed completeness, some works deemed as too risqué for socialist morality or politically compromising never made their appearance. A few years ago, I decided to expand my knowledge of Dostoevsky by reading *The Possessed* which, I was confident, I would find in the home library lovingly assembled by my grandparents over the years. As I did not succeed, I ascribed the cause to a possible loss during the move from Orenburg, where my grandparents lived in their youth, to Yuzhny, where I was born, or to somebody borrowing and never returning the book. I headed to the local library where the same volume, though not checked out, was ironically missing. When I finally bought the modern edition of the book, I realized that Soviet censorship could not allow their readers to possibly become possessed by the desecration of revolutionary ideas after reading this dangerous manifesto.

The night before the next volume was due to appear, subscribers had to gather by the same kiosk where they had initially registered for the special roll call to confirm their availability and interest. Crowds of people waiting for a nighttime roll call which gave them right to purchase a book was the Soviet equivalent of Black Friday. Thanks to this I inherited an eclectic library of collected works by Tolstoy, Dostoevsky, Chekhov, Gogol, Turgenev, Shalom Aleichem, Rabindranath Tagore, Stendhal, Sinclair Lewis, Theodore Dreiser, John Galsworthy, and many others. Lenin, Stalin, Marx and Engels—the most published writers—never made it to our library in spite of their invaluable ideas. High school and university students needed to consult them for successful passage of final exams. Knowledge of Lenin's thoughts on Gogol's novels or the evolution of species was absolutely essential for forming the expert opinion on the subject required for an excellent grade. Luckily, I escaped these requirements as the new democratic wave liberating the minds of authorities in the early nineties made a 180-degree turn towards deriding our old role models. My mom, however, relied on libraries and friends' collections to fill the gaps in her socialist awareness necessary for the proper understanding of all subjects, including biology, physics and math.

People proudly displayed their book collections in their living rooms where they placed wide bookshelves, often custom-made, to accommodate various layers of books in order to save already limited space. They valued reading. Some Ukrainian friends I made living in Kansas brought their books along with them when they immigrated to the United States in the nineties. Kids also knew the value of recycling to keep book production going: several times a year, schools would announce recycling competitions. We brought piles of old newspapers in hopes of surpassing the other class groups in the amount of recycled material and getting books as prizes. We even had a special word for recycled papers: "makulatura." I heard that editorial houses often made schoolkids happy donating them loads of "makulatura" coming from unwanted manuscripts by politically undesired writers, while those writers anxiously waited for the editors' feedback.

A book was usually the most popular prize in school competitions or intellectual games broadcast on TV on Saturday nights. One of the most popular game shows, *Chto? Gde? Kogda?* (What? Where? When?), replaced books with money remuneration during the wealth-hungry nineties forever. The eventual appearance and rapidly growing popularity of personal computers, cell phones and other gadgets played the biggest role in ousting books from people's living rooms and hobbies. My mom recently "inherited" collected works by Dostoevsky from a colleague getting rid of clutter. Mom welcomed him even though she already had one set of his works. We decided my American living room can offer Fyodor shelter. Even though weight limits for air travel have recently made book migration more challenging, at least he does not require a passport and a visa to join me.

I was happy to receive books for a birthday gift (as long as it was not a manual for playing the violin)—good books did not cost much, but just as any other high-quality goods, they were not easy to obtain. Often people who went to Moscow for business or pleasure brought back some particularly rare editions as the city was always best supplied in terms of books, boots, bananas, chocolates, shoes, sausages and pretty much everything else. I still have a few books my school friends gave me for my birthdays, dedicating to me their curved signatures. This tangible mark of their friendship thus remains with me while some of them no longer remain in this world.

I loved reading, as it opened the door to different worlds but also because it helped me see my own life through different, often more excited, eyes when compared to the life of people in some stories. My mom tells me that I started reading at the age of four, and my aunt Galya (whom I call Mama Galya to this day because she is so close to me and my family) recalls the episode when I picked up a newspaper and read the caption "Lee Brezhnev" (I joined the leader's initials "L.I." into a single "Lee"). Mama Galya worked at a library and thanks to her, I never had a shortage of reading material.

One of my favorite moments in school during the days preceding summer vacation was writing down the recommended reading list dictated by our literature teacher Nadezhda Valentinovna. Mysterious and enticing titles like *Running Along the Waves*, *Gift of the Magi*, *Human Amphibia*, *The Last of the Mohicans*, *Three Mousquetaires*, *Topsy Turvy Spring* and others promised a peek into new worlds, countries and universes that would somehow make me a smarter, richer, happier person. I felt the same way about names of foreign countries and cities that beckoned me with exotic customs, buildings, landscapes and people that would help me transform into a different being living a different life. That's why I particularly enjoyed international literature in translation. I loved Tom Sawyer and Huck Finn stories, *The Prince and Pauper*, overseas expeditions of Jules Verne and the bizarre adventures of Alice in Wonderland and in the reverse world behind the Looking-Glass. I "swallowed up" *Robinson Crusoe* particularly fast, although I am not sure how I came to be so fascinated—when I recently attempted to read it for a class, I couldn't progress beyond the first ten laborious pages. Perhaps most of all, I enjoyed the tortuous journey of Dorothy (called Ellie in the Russian version) to the country of Oz and of Underground Kings.

Not a picky reader, I didn't mind learning about the life of people getting ready for the October Revolution and fighting in the civil war or getting inspired by the childhood of little Lenin (whose real name was Volodya Ulyanov). A charming, chubby-cheeked, curly-haired boy did not seem to waste a single day on anything but reading, studying foreign languages, working on community service projects with his siblings, and initiating his plan for uprooting capitalism.

One of my monthly intellectual treats was reading the children's magazine *Happy Pictures*. My mom subscribed to it for ten kopecks a month until I was about eleven. Its twenty or so colored pages featured poetry, folk tales, classical writers' stories in abridged versions, comic book-type stories, riddles and more. Poems and proverbs often carried messages of virtue directed against laziness, cowardice or dishonesty. Propaganda invariably crept into its pages as well: Poems like "Lenin is with us," "I saw a live Lenin," "Glory to Lenin," or stories about Lenin's life filled the first few pages. One story I still remember talked about Lenin's humility and insistence on economizing state resources. He refused to accept any gifts from common people and abuse state benefits to which he was entitled. Instead, he held on to old things, like a cooking pan with holes in it, and asked a comrade to patch it up. The story must have affected me deeply, for I still value frugality and do my best to get the most usage out of appliances, save electricity and water.

Happy Pictures readers were also reminded of the superior moral qualities of Pioneers and Octobrists that value friendship, love reading and drawing, playing and singing, dream of going to the moon and live happily. After the obligatory serious political messages, however, the content gave way to lighter and more entertaining comic book-style stories about the funny adventures of "happy characters" from fairy tales and cartoons, often in other parts of the Soviet Union or other socialist lands.

Just like the marketing customs in the American printing business, each magazine issue was dedicated to a holiday of the month—New Year, Soviet Army Day, International Women's Day, Victory Day, and so on. April was a productive month combining Cosmonauts Day (April 12, the anniversary of Yuri Gagarin's first flight into space) and Lenin's birthday. A page featuring the history of Soviet sputniks would be followed by a picture of a boy lovingly drawing Lenin's name and the date "April 22" on a sheet of paper with an accompanying poem:

> The sun will rise and look into my window,
> It will shine brightly on the portrait on my wall.
> As if alive and wishing me a good day,
> Ilyich will look at me from the portrait.
> I want to become a true Leninist,
> In order to look without shame
> Into Ilyich's eyes.[1]

A page from a 1978 issue of *Happy Pictures* featuring the adventures of its mascots, happy characters, in Cuba. The title above says "Bienvenida" in Russian letters, with the translation below.

Besides pure entertainment, the magazine promoted knowledge of geographical facts and internationalist spirit of friendship among the peoples of the Soviet Union, socialist republics and other socialist countries. Almost every issue included tips about the geography, economy and culture of Soviet republics with maps, national flags and crests, as well as translations of Ukrainian, Moldovan, Lithuanian and Georgian poetry or folklore.

The editors also made sure not to discriminate against the less common languages of indigenous tribes from the Asian part of Russia, such as Kalmyk, Udmurt and Nganasan. The cover of the December 1982 issue is dedicated to the 60th anniversary of the formation of the Soviet Union, showcasing a big circle of kids dressed in national costumes happily dancing around the national crest of the USSR—the sun rising from below the globe framed with a hammer and sickle and yellow spears of wheat with a red star on top.

Such ostentatious displays of internationalism helped hold "the Soviet family" together and kept in check the brewing discontent among ethnic minorities, who only theoretically had equal rights with Russians. Fourteen Soviet republics were considered younger sisters of the mighty Russia, which was leading and guiding them. Their distinguished citizens were occasionally awarded high positions in the Soviet government or in scientific or cultural institutions of Moscow, as if receiving crumbs from the master's table. Moscow higher education institutions, considered the best in the country, also reserved a certain percentage of places in graduate schools for minorities coming from the other republics. However, in general, Muscovites still had the best chance of job placement in their city. Still, the generous demonstrations of multicultural friendship encouraged awareness of the great ethnic and cultural diversity within our "Soviet family" and a friendly attitude towards minorities. Growing up in "the military town" of Orenburg (where families of military personnel lived in closely-knit community) near the Ural Mountains, my mom witnessed this diversity: Their immediate neighbors included Ukrainians, Jews, Georgians, Tatars, Chechens and Russian (Don)[2] Cossacks.

I inherited a passion for reading from my family—my mom and my grandparents spent most of their free time with a book. My grandma, a child of the revolution born in 1917, lived through tough times since the age of twelve—her parents had to hide from the threat of exile to Siberia for having been characterized as "kulaks" (successful peasants suspected of entrepreneurial activity by the Soviets). They sent their kids—my grandma, her older sister and her younger brother—to live with different families of distant relatives who were not exhilarated about their new, uninvited company. My grandma had to clean their house, cook, take care of their kids, while also secretly trying to feed her own little brother who lived with a different family and never had enough to eat. Throughout her whole life she kept the doors of her house and her heart open for whoever needed food, support and care. She did not have a chance to study beyond the seventh grade but this only increased her thirst for knowledge, and she read avidly whenever she could. I keep a distinctly happy image of my grandparents reading in bed at the end of a tiring day occasionally exchanging jokes or my grandma slightly pushing Grandpa if his snoring became too sonorous.

My grandparents held a special place in my life. Just as in many families, partially due to the shortage of living quarters, but also to the strong parental ties among generations, we lived together. My babushka (grandma) took care of me during the day while my mom worked. My grandpa worked as well until he was deep into his seventies but dedicated most of his free time to my entertainment and education. He made various projects with me, helped me solve math problems until I was in the eighth or ninth grade and taught me world capitals and fun geographical facts. For the first few years of my life, I shared a room with my grandparents. Our beds faced each other, each against the opposite wall covered by Persian carpets—a necessary adornment in every Soviet house or apartment. Besides decoration, the carpets also served the practical purpose of keeping the walls warm and were pleasantly soft for leaning during cold winters. On Sunday mornings, I came to my grandparents' bed and made a mini gym out of it by climbing all over my grandparents and falling down in between. I felt cozy and secure.

I looked forward to the evenings when my dedushka (grandpa) would read bedtime stories as I would lie in bed among my stuffed animals watching the exotic garden on the wall in the dim light. My favorites were the stories he made up himself—he had a knack for populating them with eccentric characters and sending them on all sorts of comical

My grandma, Anna Mikhailovna Andreyeva, 1939.

adventures. I loved the tales about a goofy old chap named Ignat who always was forgetting social conventions and his wife's nagging requests. The trouble came when Grandpa would start snoring in the middle of his story, and I would implore him, gradually raising my voice to almost shouting, to wake up and continue. Wake up he eventually would but continued the story by inserting a different character or completely reversed plot. I would have to review the previous narration for him until he would once again fall into slumbers. Then, Grandpa and I would make paper booklets where he wrote down his stories, and I illustrated them—a few of them have survived to the present day.

My grandparents gave up the room which we originally shared for my exclusive usage once I grew older and occu-

Me in my childhood room, July 1977. The carpet inspiring my childhood fantasies is in the background. Many families had the same or a similar one.

pied the living room. There was not enough space in our three-room house for everyone to have a separate bedroom. In the Soviet Union, people did not refer to all of the rooms in terms of "bedrooms" as the American custom goes, for these quarters were frequently used for other purposes—such as an office or a guest room. Couches were converted into beds at night and rooms assumed a properly peaceful and cozy nighttime ambiance. Nevertheless, we lived comfortably in spite of being a bit crowded. We had a front garden and backyard so big that I could not see the back end of it looking out of my bedroom window. Many people in our town of Yuzhny had similar arrangements and many lived in yet more spacious quarters, sometimes with second floors. Originally, when my grandpa built the house in the sixties, the town infrastructure did not allow the installment of all conveniences, such as running water and gas. The family heated the house with wooden logs burnt in the oven and brought in water from the outdoor tap. I hardly remember those times—everything necessary was installed when I was born or shortly after, and I never felt that we lacked in anything essential.

Grandpa tirelessly generated new ideas for fun and sometimes plotted some mischief behind grandma and mom's backs. Once he took me for an ice-cream although they forbade me to eat it—the prevalent theory was that eating cold products made you sick, and I frequently caught colds. Naturally, I didn't have many opportunities for enjoying ice-cream, and grandpa wanted to indulge me. Unfortunately, the theory worked, and I got a sore throat the very next day. Being educated in the strong belief that lying is bad and hiding information equals lying, I told my grandma and mom about our ice-cream adventure. My steadfast honesty brought a lot of trouble upon my poor grandpa's head.

When my mom was little, grandpa's energy and creativity when he was not working focused exclusively on her. They played soccer and hide-and-seek in their tiny one-room apartment, sometimes breaking my grandma's favorite plates. Since the apartment offered little opportunity for true hiding, grandpa pretended to look for mom in absurd places, such as pots and pans, vases and glasses. During mom's childhood, few regular Soviet families had TV, but everybody had radios. At night, mom and her parents, friends and neighbors—both young and old—cozied around the radio set as if in anticipation of a bedtime story. They listened to broadcasts of soccer and hockey matches, using their imaginations to see the events in their minds. They enjoyed music programs, falling under the spell of Tchaikovsky's concerts and Mozart's operas. "Theater by the microphone"—recordings of dramatical productions interspersed with critics' clarifying remarks—continued to be popular well into the eighties. I also remember the kids' program *Tele-babysitter*, with

Grandma and me, July 1977.

a deep and entrancing voice telling us the adventures of fairy-tale and children books' heroes.

The Soviet government took care of the cultural education of its citizens by airing plenty of educational programs and establishing low ticket prices to theaters and museums to ensure that anyone could afford a chance for enlightenment. Mom recalls going to adult theater productions with her parents starting from age four. No relatives lived close to my grandparents' family, they did not know of a custom hiring babysitter, and neither would they consider bringing in someone to watch their child. For these reasons, kids fully participated in most spheres of adult social life back in those times. There were two theaters—Drama and Music Comedy—in the town of Orenburg on the border of Europe and Asia where my family lived after the war. My grandpa worked as instructor at the Orenburg pilot school, which gave the world its first cosmonaut, Yuri Gagarin. Universally accepted etiquette prescribed wearing one's best attire, often home-made, while visiting the theater and bringing along formal shoes in bad weather for change from unsightly boots or galoshes that would spoil the theater-goer image. Those outer-wear items of little elegance would stay in the cloakroom together with coats. No one considered bringing them into the theater room for fear of offending the public eye and appearing couth and uncultured. This was a flourishing period in the history of the Soviet theater—many Moscow troupes went on tour around the Soviet Union and brought frequent performances to Orenburg. Tickets were sold out rapidly, and the house stayed invariably full, even during the week.

Theatre and movie visits with family nurtured my mom's love of literature and music and left lifelong memories of family bonding time. She does not fail to surprise me with her knowledge of Mozart, Wagner, Strauss and Kalman's works, not to mention her literary expertise. The repertoire of tour companies hosted by Orenburg theaters included *Les Misérables*, *Romeo and Juliet*, plays by Chekov and Ostrovsky, historical plays like *Peter I*, *Emelyan Pugachyov*, and *Tzar Fyodor Ioannovych*, along with invariable Communist-themed gems, such as *Ulyanovs' Family*, *Death of the Squadron*, and *In Search of Joy*.

Going to the movies was also a treat, not difficult to afford but often unattainable because tickets would sell out fast, especially for the premier showing. A crowd of unlucky fans often hung around the theater trying to get hold of a spare ticket for a sold-out showing. Surprisingly, movie theaters featured not only Soviet but other Eastern European, as well as many French, Italian, Latin American, and even American, selections. For present-day movie-goers spoiled by the selection of four or five films running at the same time it may be a tad difficult to imagine only one newly-issued movie choice at most city theaters. The repertoire stayed the same over the period of a few weeks. It makes it easier to understand how precious these visits were, however. New films did not come out frequently due to the lack of state funds and quality materials in the post-war days. Deficits of home-produced shooting film made directors recur to the foreign-made materials, allotted in limited quantities, which could be used only in extreme cases of serious blunders. Therefore, actors could not relax and count on numerous takes of the same scene while they perfected their art—they were expected to hit the target on the first try, not having a luxury of mistakes. Film directors and producers had to rely on their skills and intuition to use these disadvantages in the best possible way: create credible special effects and engaging plots and to maneuver between art and censorship.

The fear that at any time censorship could undermine the months- and year-long efforts and end the movie's life by putting it "on the storage shelf" hovered over the directors at every stage of their careers. In the Soviet Union, censorship was an art in itself, and in a medium reaching such a wide audience as movies, this art achieved particular brilliance. A movie had to go through the so-called artistic council of the studio, the state movie council (Goskino), the ideological department of the Central Party Committee of the republic, and finally through the Central Party Committee of the whole country. All these organizations kept a strict watch on the ideological content of the film and the degree of positivity of its message to ensure maximum ideological benefit for the public.

Movies about the war or other tragic events of our history were granted only a moderate degree of depressing content—some movies were banned by Stalin because most of the main characters perished and the story appeared too dark to the leader. Some movies were banned for no other reason that their director or actor(s) were Jewish. In a well-known movie titled *Circus*, a Jewish actor and director sang part of a Russian lullaby in Jewish. He was later killed by the KGB obeying Stalin's direct orders. The assassination was orchestrated to look like a car accident. The scene of his singing was removed from the movie and restored only a long time after Stalin's death. Other reasons for a ban included the authorities' decision that revolutionary or war events were misrepresented in a far too theatrical way or common people were represented (or not represented) in an exceedingly (or insufficiently) idealized way—depending on the mood of the critics. The suspected attempt at satire of the present regime could also ruin the movie or its directors. Frequently the film went directly to storage if it was discovered that the director or an actor had a "wrong," unfavorable history, such as relatives abroad or other undesirable connections. The same thing happened if one of the actors emigrated from the country, as happened with a great comical actor Saveliy Kramarov. He left the Soviet Union in favor of the United States in 1981, which was immediately decried by the Soviet media as a dishonorable act of treason. After a while, his films returned to the screens where they remain favorites of Russian-speaking people to the present time.

The movies were stored on the studio shelves for an indefinite period of time—sometimes for decades—waiting until Stalin's death, Brezhnev's randomly generous approval, or the beginning of perestroika. Other movies, lucky enough to receive approval, could be dismembered and disfigured, whole pieces taken out or changed by censoring decree. Censors sometimes altered the director's ideas and left him little choice if he wanted to see the movie on the big screen. Some movies were placed into a gray category of semi-allowance—not completely banned but also not encouraged, like the films by such renowned directors as Andrey Tarkovskiy and Elem Klimov. The authorities were not pleased with their ambiguous content, unclear messages and absence of optimistic notes. The films would be exiled to a peripheral movie theater and quickly removed from showing. However, the short run sufficed for quick spreading of their fame infused by disapproval of the authorities—they attracted full houses and heated discussions in intellectual circles. To be fair, Soviet film factories made a lot of good movies, many of them—if they could ever find their way past the Iron Curtain—were recognized by prestigious international awards. *Moscow Does Not Believe in Tears* received the Oscar for the best foreign movie in 1981. Its director Vladimir Menshov was not able to savor the award, for, similar to Boris Pasternak who could not travel to Sweden to receive his Nobel Prize in literature for *Doctor Zhivago*, he was not allowed to travel to the award ceremony and learned about his triumph on TV.

During my own childhood, TV firmly established itself as a popular diversion, although its three state channels broadcast mainly the news of the unrelenting progress of the Communist party across the globe. Still, many brilliant comedies were frequently rerun on TV after their debut in theaters and they fascinated us to the point that we still quote their popular lines. They immediately spark smiles of recognition among people from different regions of the former USSR and of different generations. Children and adult movies lucky enough to get through censorship would invariably end in good conquering evil, and the bad character would always be punished, according to the proper rules of socialist realism. This was the main artistic genre highly recommended for use by the First Union of the Soviet writers in 1934. A Soviet literature reference book published in 1988 which I found in my parents' home in Ukraine, explains that the genre prescribed the reflection of the concrete historical reality combined with the ideological upbringing of the working people in the spirit of socialism. At the same time, the book clarifies, this method by no means restricts the writer from the choice of artistic forms, styles or subgenres (as long as they did not contradict the overarching purpose of representing the socialist reality in the most positive light possible).

This illusory artistic freedom was quickly curtailed, however, had the writer dared to use a different genre, especially so controversial and dangerous as the genre of formalism determined by Stalin to be foreign to the true art and to the spiritual needs of the Soviet people. Dmitriy Shostakovich exemplified this dangerous trend with his nonconformist and strange music which, according to Stalin's analysis, "quacks, hoots, pants, and chokes" instead of giving the listener the pleasure of a real melody. The generalissimos wrote in the *Pravda* newspaper on January 28, 1936, that he was offended by this so-called music where shreds of melody got lost in "thunder, screeches, and squeals" in which the artist reflected his own and many people's dismay at the cacophonous Soviet reality. The music that could not be easily comprehended and imitated by proletariats did not belong in Soviet theaters unless the leader's whim, which nobody could change or resist, made it otherwise.

Non-realist painters and writers were similarly subjected to the blame of a bourgeois formalistic ideology supposedly leading to the disconnect of form from content and to the separation of art from life. Following Stalin's lead, all the newspapers published caustic criticism of painters whom he labeled as dabblers, architects who were amateurs according to his resolution, writers supposedly lacking ideological orientation and "false" composers. Thus, any possibility of their further work and creativity was cut off. They would be excluded from the State Union of Composers, Union of Writers or Union of Artists, membership in which was an absolute necessity for artistic advancement.

The rules dictated by socialist realism did not leave any room for doubt in the final victory of Communism and the bright future that unquestionably accompanied it. Proposing an alternative would invite decadence, pessimism, confusion and moral decay characteristic of the literature of the Western world not capable of morally educating young minds. For this reason, our films and proper Soviet literature, while morally uplifting, often lacked complexity. It was safer this way—authorities favored black-and-white simplicity, and to prevent the possibility of censors' doubts, artists often subjected themselves to self-censorship preventing anything that could remotely resemble criticism of our absurd reality.

In the sixties, Khrushchev brought about the period of the so-called "thaw" which welcomed relative freedom of thought and denouncement of Stalin's cult of personality. New freedoms brought new hopes to the people and ushered in the era of the so-called "stadium poets" whose soaring popularity, infused by their new forms of expression, fresh, daring thoughts, and artistic charisma, gathered stadiums full of people to their poetry readings. Bella Ahmadullina, Yevgeniy Yevtushenko, Robert Rozhdestvenskiy and Andrey Voznesenskiy became pop stars and youth idols. They not only read to huge crowds, but also to small gatherings in the intimate atmosphere of private apartments and bookstores. My mom remembers when Yevgeniy Yevtushenko, reading his poetry at the street corner in Kharkiv by a well-known bookstore called Poetry, started to lose his voice due to a cold. Some people living in an apartment just above the spot where he was standing lowered a bottle of hot milk to help his sore throat. He later affectionately commemorated the episode in one of his poems.

Khrushchev quickly repented from his generosity, brutally and ignorantly criticizing writers and artists who dared to go too far experimenting with new styles and drastically deviating from the principles of socialist realism. He severely criticized stadium poets whom he had previously lauded, along with many other talented writers, painters and sculptors. Ironically, Ernst Neizvestny, a sculptor derided by Khrushchev for creating "degenerate" art, later created a tombstone for the leader at the request of Khrushchev's family. Under Khrushchev's rule, a young poet named Joseph Brodsky, who later won the Nobel Prize for literature, was declared a social "parasite" for failure to procure a steady job and confined to a mental institution for his poetry, considered dangerously anti–Soviet.

Leonid Brezhnev, while not so eccentric as Khrushchev, was not capable of scaring many live organisms with his slow temper curiously contrasting with the explosiveness of his predecessor. Nevertheless, he maintained a steady grip on censorship over politics and culture, when, as another dissident writer, Victor Eroveyev, put it, "everything was stifled, squeezed, smashed, squashed and distorted."[3] Many were excluded from the Union of the Writers—the only channel for official publication—and ordinary people kept living with fear of saying something wrong.

As I read the works of many writers persecuted and banned during the Khrushchev or Brezhnev years, I often wonder what could have inspired the leaders' ire. Many do not only avoid satirizing the system or the authorities, but they avoid political subjects altogether. It was probably this very failure to approach the topic of the socialist-capitalist struggle, pessimistic hints or the choice of unusual genres or narrative styles that alarmed the watchful eye of censors. School children and university students of many generations were required to denounce and reprove the decadent mood, civil irresponsibility and artistic faults of brilliant writers like Anna Akhmatova[4] and Mikhail Zoshchenko,[5] in keeping with the decrees of the 1946 Congress of the Communist Party Central Committee. Since the works of these writers were never published in the Soviet Union until the late eighties, the harsh denunciations reached quite the opposite effect and succeeded in arousing the curiosity of the youth in the works so terrifying for the Soviet regime. As a result, my mom and her friends did everything to lay their hands on the self-made copies by the prohibited authors which they illegally borrowed and passed on to one another.

One never knew what and who could be prohibited or criticized next. The fear of censorship and denouncement reached grotesque levels, altered people's minds and forced silence or the use of the code language when approaching sensitive topics, even in the supposed comfort of their kitchens. I remember sitting at a dining table as a child of about six and jokingly referring to Brezhnev as "Lyonya" (the diminutive form of his first name—Leonid, normally reserved for the use among family and friends). The contrast between the intimate form of the name and the frozen numb, almost inhuman, facial expression of the leader appeared very funny to me. However, the reaction of my loved ones puzzled and surprised me—instead of laughing, they hurriedly hushed me, warning me to avoid such a disrespectful way of speaking. While my mom often spoke to me of the brutalities of the Stalin years, I do not recall her criticizing the Brezhnev government in my presence. Jokes and rumors about its members nevertheless circulated in whispers and slowly contributed to chipping away the monolith of their dictatorial power.

Careful satire targeted at the deficiencies and absurdities of the Soviet system started to creep its way into movies in the seventies and eighties. A universal favorite, *The Irony of Fate* (1975) features a group of friends who get so drunk on the eve of the New Year that they board one of them on a plane heading to St. Petersburg. There he takes a taxi to exactly the same address as his Moscow apartment, opening it with his own key, finding exactly the same place with exactly the same furniture, but occupied by an unknown lady. She is the owner the of the flat that he believes to be his own. Another classic, *The Garage* (1980) presents a garage cooperative meeting for natural history museum employees lasting well through the night and into the morning. They have to decide which four members should be excluded from the cooperative since state planning determined that a new highway must take the place of four of their garages.

When I was a child, I looked forward to cartoons or children's movies which aired only at specific times announced in the weekly newspaper guide—since we only had three state channels, the whole guide only took a single page. Fifteen minutes before sleep time at 8:45 p.m. everybody watched the *Good Night, Kids* program, and Friday afternoons we celebrated the end of the school week with *Visiting a Fairy Tale*. Actually, Friday did not mark the end of the school week as for the first few years we also had classes on Saturday, but the last school day was short and the excitement of the upcoming weekend was high.

Everybody's favorite cartoon, still popular nowadays, was a series called *Nu Pogodi!* (Just You Wait!) featuring an awkward wolf chasing a good-natured hare who always found a way to outwit him. The only words in the whole fifteen-episode series were the wolf's exclamation at the end of each episode, "Just you wait!" but the action was funny and clean. You would never see a drop of blood, nor either character driven into brutality by his passions. We could not compare Soviet cartoons with the American equivalents since our TV did not broadcast Western programs until fifteen years later, when I had an opportunity to watch *Tom and Jerry* and *Popeye*. The violent tricks the characters played on each other shocked me. The hare in *Nu Pogodi!* displayed an amazing Christ-like resignation enduring the wolf's abuses and never sought an opportunity for revenge. In fact, in some series he would almost manage to convert the wolf, who would ask for forgiveness but then resume his mischief in later episodes.

I often reflect on the curious paradox of high moral standards applied to the behavior of the Soviet youth combined with considerable opportunities afforded to women by the Communist regime (the right to vote was afforded in 1917; the Women's Department of the Bolshevik Party responsible for promoting women's rights and involving them in politics was established in 1918; and half of the women's population was studying in universities by the 1970s). Soviet pop culture developed in accordance with strict laws of morality and Soviet censorship did not allow nudity or dirty language on TV or in the press. The level of state care about our moral upbringing reached absurd heights. During one of the first open U.S.-Soviet talk shows during perestroika called *Tele-bridge*, a Soviet lady responded to an American's question, "There is no sex in the Soviet Union."[6] In these words, she expressed a widespread stigma attached to the word associated with dirtiness and indecency in the minds of the Soviet public.

By extension, our literature, art and press avoided any mention of anything remotely related to this disgraceful activity. Teenagers received little information about sexual development, filling these gaps through mutual education based on hearsay. Since sex-related topics were taboo, teenagers also received little to no information about contraception, which was difficult to come by anyway. This naturally resulted in numerous early pregnancies, early marriages and subsequent early divorces. After such prolonged "chastity," the rapid Western invasion of graphic nudity bordering on obscenity on our TV screens in the late nineties came as a particularly welcome change to some and a shock to others. Although people made fun of our leaders' asexual, mummy-like appearance and behavior, it turned out they also valued the purity of our pop culture. I remember the universal resentment, especially among older people, when massive amounts of TV trash, like Western soap operas, B- and C-type comedies, horror and action movies, and other light programming flooded our screens. Vulgarity not seen during the Soviet times bothered and unnerved people.

The language of the lowest and most vulgar linguistic register ("mat" in Russian) had previously never made it to the literary works, the press, the

TV or even the informal oral sphere of communication. Using those words marked the speaker as "nekulturnyi" (non-cultured)—that is, not decent, not educated and not worthy of admittance to regular society. They signaled to us "cultured" folks to stop talking to the individual and revert to a proper "decent" shell protected from all the world's filth. I lived in such a shell for most of my youth—I do not remember any of my family members, friends or acquaintances using vulgar or very rude expressions.

When the shell inevitably cracked in my later years, allowing some vulgarity to seep through, for the longest time I had to feign sophistication and pretend I knew what the dirty phrases meant in order not to appear ingenious. I am not sorry for my naiveté. Those were pure and innocent times, which colored my childhood with a shade of sweetness that is becoming more and more diluted and short-lived for modern-day kids. When I return to Ukraine, I have a hard time escaping "mat" on the streets where not only teenagers, but kids who look like they are eight, use it in play. They act proud of their sophistication probably because they feel it entitles them to the membership in the "cool macho" club of modern youngsters. I also hear young girls confidently use the language previously limited to the toughest men—because it must fill them with a strange sort of liberation. I worked hard at keeping the shell of innocence intact for my kids but I had to admit defeat when almost every day, coming back from playing soccer with Ukrainian kids, they would ask me the significance of a new gem of street folklore, bringing me to a standstill. I gave up. On the bright side, my American-born children are integrating into modern Ukrainian society—apparently faster than happened with my younger self hiding in her shell. I trust they will continue to use their natural filters guiding them to leave the specialized vocabulary on the margins as passive, unusable, linguistic baggage.

The junk that invaded our screens in the nineties included an entirely new genre for us–Latin American soap operas. They produced a mass media revolution when all—men, women and children alike—started to adjust their daily schedules to the next episode revealing further endless twists in the fate of the sentimental heroes. The first pearl came from Brazil in 1988. The constantly teary-eyed "Slave Isaura," who for some reason was white, conquered the hearts of the Soviet public with her ingenuity, virtues and faithful love to Fernando, or Pepe, or Jorge—the man who eventually liberated Isaura from slavery and saved her from her vengeful and lustful master. Our people took the series so close to heart that they started calling their modest country huts "fazendas." The following dialogue can still be heard in the streets of Ukraine: "What are you doing this weekend?" The reply: "Going to my fazenda."

Isaura was followed by Mariana from the Mexican novella *The Rich Also Cry* in 1991. It produced an absolute sensation in the Soviet Union by maintaining suspense at the end of each episode, no matter how irritating and silly were the characters' actions, and keeping people glued to the screens for more than thirty daily episodes. The poor servant Mariana and her rich sweetheart Jose Antonio became the main topic of conversations in the buses, trains, subways, doctor's offices, streets and schools. Productivity decreased because people stopped working in the middle of the day in order to catch particularly intense moments of the show. It aired twice a day, and normally busy streets became deserted during the six p.m. showing.

Few people watched TV in the afternoons, but when the romantic drama became too intense, they started adjusting their routine in order to catch some glimpses of the first afternoon show on an office TV if at all possible. Thus, they gained an upper hand in the bus debates about the further development of the action. This happened to our teacher of Russian who could not contain her interest in the culminating events nearing the end of the show. Too tempted by the presence of a TV set in our classroom, she cut the lesson short so that all of us could satisfy our curiosity in the decisive moments of the fate of our beloved Mariana in a cozy, family-like atmosphere.

The Soviet TV audience was also shocked and indignant at the humongous number of commercials that suddenly flooded our screens after the disappearance of censorship and privatization of public TV channels. Screaming and goofy men and women of all ages and often of respectable appearance would interrupt our favorite TV show or an exciting movie, annoyingly thrusting at us cat food, laxatives, condoms, cellulite-reducing devices and other such things which our decency would prevent us from even bringing up in informal conversations. We felt insulted and repulsed. We felt patronized. We also felt deceived by the long-awaited and long-promised variety and high quality of programming expected from the privatization of TV networks. That is not what we imagined from the West. This new generation of programs polluted our TV and substituted intellectual content with cheap soap operas. Some shows seemed to be intended for such simple-minded audiences that they even needed prompting on when to laugh.

After living in the United States for more than twenty years, I am still surprised at how popular TV commercials are here. I rarely find them funny—mostly annoying, especially when they promote delicate hygiene items, or jump out at me repeatedly, as if the producer were afraid that I didn't get the screaming text the first time. My non-market-oriented mind also fails to understand who, besides advertising agents and network officials that need to bring profits to their networks, needs advertising. Who, besides me, knows which product would work best for my particular needs? If I am in doubt or need a piece of advice, I will ask a friend I can trust—not the advertising agent paid for grabbing a slice of my purchasing power.

Life in the United States spoiled me with advanced forms of entertainment—VCRs, DVRs, CDs, and smartphones. What I miss is an old-fashioned phone ring, teasing me with exciting suspense of the not-technologically identifiable voice of a friend, long-lost acquaintance or a stranger looking for the "Garbuz" family. We no longer have a home phone. Telemarketers were the only ones who used to call it for unwelcome, and undesired, surprises.

Food and (Not) Eating Out

We never went out to eat. Soviet restaurant food was the butt of many jokes that revolved around getting poisoned by stale products and sloppy cooking procedures. Therefore, few people visited them, not necessarily because of the prohibitive costs but because of the prohibitive food. To be fair, good restaurants also existed, which were indeed cost prohibitive and sometimes not even open for regular citizens but reserved mainly for the visits of top government workers, international guests or movie stars. There were also special restaurants for writers, composers and scientists. Only a special certificate proving that the holder was an official member of the Union of Writers or of composers or scientists granted access to those sacred sites. We, regular citizens, would sometimes go for a special treat to cafés—bakery-type small restaurants serving snacks, coffee, and a wide variety of mouth-watering pastries. The tantalizing smell of coffee still teases my nostrils at the thought of them. Crystal was the name of the most famous one in Kharkiv, which has become iconic, still preserving its original glass wall look from the 1960s. Decorated with the characters of children's cartoons like *Nu Pogodi!*, it still serves pastries in the shape of those characters that are also popular with today's youth.

In my childhood, I anticipated a visit to Crystal so intensely that I would not eat beforehand, saving space in my tummy for all the sweets I wanted to devour. When my mom would bring me there after a visit to the circus, I would eat a bite and feel nauseous from the amount of sugar hitting my empty belly. Doggy bags did not exist, so I would have to dream until our next visit to Crystal when I would eat all my favorite pastries. Nowadays, when I visit Kharkiv with my children, they love to go to Crystal and eat the ice-cream served in my early days: "Belochka" (The Squirrel)—vanilla ice-cream and whipped cream, covered with melted chocolate and crushed walnuts, arranged in a pretty and neat mound on a silver-colored vase. I love watching the kids tasting a bit of my childhood and making up for all the pastries I had left uneaten on the tables of this magical place.

Since catering was nonexistent, and restaurants were not to be trusted or afforded, people had to rely on their own cooking skills for everyday meals

My grandparents celebrating the arrival of 1951 with close friends. My grandma is in the middle. My grandpa is on the left pouring the wine.

or for parties. These were serious business—hanging out with family, friends and neighbors constituted the main form of entertainment, besides reading. The preparation of food would often take from three days to a week. State grocery stores frequently boasted half-empty shelves, but party hosts performed miracles loading their tables with edible masterpieces from rarely available ingredients which cost more than a week's salary. The secret to acquiring them lay in buying them unofficially, that is, from a friend or an acquaintance working in a grocery shop who had easier access to sausages, cheeses, caviar, canned pineapples, good-quality meat, and even rarities like chocolate butter spread.

The shops stayed empty partly because of the food deficits caused by the inefficiencies of a state-run economy, but also because their employees had the first opportunity of choosing the freshest fish, the least fatty meat, the most appetizing sausage and the prettiest cake. Such delicacies as caviar and chocolate butter almost never made it to the store shelves, although they found a mysterious way to the store workers' and supervisors' tables. These people, caressed by fate and a fortunate choice of profession, frequently bought more than they needed and sold the rest to relatives and friends, often asking a higher price. It was not contested—common Soviet Earthlings could hardly access them otherwise. The remains went to the store shelves but few people risked buying them. I remember sad-looking hot dogs, shriveled potatoes, fly-molested pastries and fish frozen for so long it seemed to come from the Ice Age. People made countless jokes about the exotic "bluebird" from

Soviet grocery shops—chicken so emaciated and antediluvian that it had acquired an unnaturally blue color.

Employees of clothing stores performed the same types of maneuvers with the goods they received through distribution channels, although state clothing factories rarely produced attire worthy of purchase. The commercial sector was thus considered among the most privileged professional field. Its employees were better supplied and usually better off than others, disproving the myth that everybody was equally well off or equally poor in the Soviet Union. Many store employees also had special skills of calculating the change in a way that benefited the seller (who then pocketed the difference) or reportedly fixed the scales so they showed more weight (and, therefore, cost) to the customer who then paid the difference also pocketed by the employee.

While the American shopper can count on finding pretty much anything he needs when visiting a supermarket, we had no such luck. Instead, we went to grocery shops with the pleasure of anticipating a surprise and with the relentless hope of finding a fresh delivery of sausage, chocolate candies, marshmallow treats called "zefir" (softer and more flavorful than American equivalents) or caramel sticks with nuts wrapped in aluminum foil (we called them "little sausages"). Due to the reasons described above, their supplies did not last and lucky discoveries afforded us joys unfamiliar to a spoiled Western shopper. Of course, we could complain about deficits and rudeness of the grocery store personnel in the special "book of complaints" easily available at every store, but we couldn't be certain that anyone but indignant customers ever opened it. If somebody did, it wasn't certain that anyone ever took any corrective measures—or, at least, our inadept eye could not perceive any improvements. It was like a contrivance once featured in a Ukrainian TV show about absurd and useless devices: installed in a Kharkiv supermarket, it represented a mini-traffic light with a green and a red button that customers could push if they were happy or upset about their shopping experience. Sort of like the happy/sad face button you sometimes see in American airport bathrooms. It occurred to someone to check how the device was installed and how marketing personnel used the results of the survey. It turned out the machine was unencumbered of any cables or connections whatsoever. You could lift it and put it back with no harm. Customers could push the buttons to their heart's content, with absolutely no consequences except for venting their feelings.

I must write a few words about the store system. We had very few supermarkets, mostly grocery shops where related food products were divided into different sections of meat, fish, milk, preserves, candy, and so on. Customers had no physical contact with the food until a shop assistant (dressed invariably in white coat and white-crested wreath) advised and served them. Thus, lines formed easily, and a customer, urged by the impatient crowd behind, needed to display some essential purchasing skills—fast reaction and decision-making based on the availability of a certain product or its alternates. If you hesitated, an impatient murmur behind you increased and the shop assistant (you would never see men in these positions, unless it was a meat store) would unambiguously remind you of the importance of quick thought: "Lady, you are keeping me and the line waiting. Decide faster, please!" You could not cheat and combine your requests—shop assistants were assigned to specific sections and would not serve you milk if you visited a meat section. Thus, shopping was an intimidating experience which demanded knack, skills and expertise. The unprepared, the faint of heart, and the shy regularly lost in the shopping battles. For this reason, I did not venture on independent shopping expeditions until I reached university age—and even then I felt my adrenaline levels increase when visiting a grocery shop.

Moscow shops were always the best supplied with exotic high-quality products, like chocolates, cakes, good sausage, cheese, bananas, oranges, lemons and even pineapples. That is why less fortunate residents from all over the Soviet Union, when going on a business trip to Moscow, planned to combine it with shop-hunting. Some people even undertook special shopping expeditions to Moscow, bringing back solid freights of produce for their family and relatives. Such trips required adequate planning and time management for visiting multiple locations, hiding potential prey and allowing sufficient time (sometimes several hours) for standing in lines as well as a sufficient reserve of nerves for possible fights that could break out while waiting or during the purchase. If potential buyers perceived signs of dwindling quantities while the line was still long, they would start pressuring their peers who reached the destination to limit the quantity of their purchase. This would naturally be met with indignation and fights ensued. Fights would also follow if some swift customer suddenly appeared at the head of the line without waiting. When the customer was finally rewarded with a successful purchase, he could count on endless admiration from his family greeting him like Santa Claus. I remember anxiously waiting for my mom to come back from her business trips with rare chocolates we never saw in Kharkiv, and my grandpa once surprised us with a few bundles of bananas, which we had never tasted.

Outdoor food markets offered a great source for buying less exotic, good-quality food—and a slice of private enterprise in a state-dominated economy. Farmers rented space in these open-air markets and sold their produce, which was remarkably more appetizing than the goods at the shop, at higher prices. In smaller places like Yuzhny, where everybody knew one another, such method of food acquiring was particularly popular and efficient since competing farmers wanted to gain permanent customers and would not risk cheating them. Hardly anyone considered buying meat at the shop instead of the farmers markets—meat from state-produced cows, or at least the cow parts left on the shelves, carried more bone and fat than meat, and it was quite inedible. Unfortunately, the markets in smaller towns did not open during the week as they did in the city. Due to the absence of advanced technologies, few imported products and the cold climate, both farmers and shops offered only seasonal food. This meant that in winter we missed cucumbers and tomatoes to such a degree that we celebrated the appearance of the first greenhouse vegetables like a holiday. Lemons and oranges, imported from the Caucases, were so rare and expensive that we could mostly just dream about their taste.

What we could not buy on the market or obtain "underground," we produced ourselves—including marinating cucumbers, tomatoes and mushrooms, and making fruit preserves, wine and even vodka, with the entire family contributing their efforts. In the fall, people would rush to the forests for mushroom hunting—partially to vary their diet but mostly to indulge in a favorite pastime. We got up early and proceeded to a nearby forest by train, bus or car for those lucky enough to have one. A good friend of the family would sometimes take us in her car, and she would choose the most breathtaking places with hills overlooking vast fields and forests touched by many

My husband Robert picking berries in my family's garden in Ukraine in preparation for wine-making under my grandpa's supervision. This photograph was taken a few weeks after our wedding in June 1996, in June or July.

Robert making the wine in my family's home under my grandpa's supervision, June or July 1996.

colors of the fall. We roamed about poking small hills covered by pine needles in hopes of finding red or yellow hats. Later we would examine them together to make sure the harvest would not poison us. We would then choose a picturesque picnic spot and unwrap sandwiches, boiled eggs and tomatoes, and then take out a thermos of hot coffee packed by my grandma. At night, the mossy smell of mushrooms filled the house as we peeled and washed bucketfuls of them for frying, drying and marinating. I have never since been able to find mushrooms whose smell could equal that cozy aroma of the fall.

In winter, we devoured all the preserves and canned goodies, served as sides for main courses of meat, fish or chicken, accompanied by potatoes, rice or very healthy "kasha"—a boiled, salted cereal like buckwheat, millet or pearl barley garnished with butter. In cold and hot weather alike, we also invariably ate hearty soups or borsch as a first course, which Grandma usually made in quantities large enough to last us two or three days. It would be impossible to make soup each day because of the considerable investment of labor and time taken by all the dicing and mincing of vegetables. Borsch, for example, required a large onion, a couple of carrots and beets which accounted for its characteristic color, an entire head of cabbage, a red or green pepper and a few potatoes, all thinly diced. First, however, grandma boiled a beef broth, and only then threw in the vegetables one by one, waiting for the proper cooking of each before adding a new ingredient—doing it otherwise and trying to speed up the process affected the taste negatively, it was said. As we grew up, borsch was gradually becoming such an organic part of us that even many years of living far from our native land could not cure us of the regular habit of eating it. It probably flows in our veins mixed with blood. My husband once observed a Ukrainian lady trying to smuggle a glass jar of borscht through the security checkpoint in an American airport so that she could consume it on the plane. She was desperately trying to convince the officials to try it and ascertain its superb taste and safety.

My grandma cooked and baked most things from scratch, frequently with grandpa's help. They even made pasta and dumplings (vareniky or pelmeni) with a variety of different fillings, such as potatoes, meat, sweet cottage cheese, fresh or jellied fruit, raisins or stewed cabbage. The same fillings could be used in little pies—"pirogi." These were even more challenging since fresh dough made from live yeast needed a lot of tiresome kneading and would not always rise properly. Both my grandmother and my mom said that you needed to develop a special relationship with the dough, talk to it and even sing to it to help it rise better—or it would take revenge if you were cranky or not gentle with it. When it started to rise, grandma had to use it quickly to create cute ovals or circles which seemed to me like little piglets, fill them with just enough goodies so the dough wouldn't tear, and close them up. Sometimes she made open-top rectangles with crisscrosses or braided pieces of dough covering the sweet fillings. Then she baked them in multiple sets since our oven was too small to fit too many pies.

She stored the freshly-baked pies covered with a towel on a bed in my mom's room for cooling. I loved entering that room and going crazy with the smell of freshly baked goods and the sight of the magic bed which, I imagined, hugged all those pies with motherly affection. Grandma finished baking close to nightfall and the room was dark, which added to its mysterious and homely atmosphere. I also loved patting and stroking the pies, which felt warm and almost alive under the towel. Sinking my teeth into the soft and sweet dough, I felt in paradise. Almost half of the dozens of precious darlings would immediately disappear, however, as all the closest neighbors and relatives would receive a portion—in the same way as we would receive portions of their treats whenever they would make something special.

Such meticulous and thorough food preparation took a significant part of my grandma's day, but it was even more serious when we were preparing for a party. Any self-respecting Ukrainian hostess expecting guests would not plan fewer than ten dishes for the first course, at least two hot dishes of meat, chicken and fish usually accompanied by potatoes, and at least two types of desserts that concluded the evening along with tea, coffee, fruit jelly (naturally, home-made), chocolates and an assortment of fruit if the season permitted. The first course of cold dishes would include light snacks of sliced cheese, different types of salami and sausage, caviar (if the host was lucky to find it) spread on buttered white bread, marinated mushrooms, marinated tomatoes, pickles, toasts rubbed with garlic and covered with mayonnaise and salami or sardines, as well as a serious fare of salads.

Extended family, friends or neighbors would assemble a day before or the morning of the party in order to contribute their efforts and dice, peel, crush, boil, stew and fry. The preparation was a holiday in itself, stimulated by the sense of happy anticipation and delicious smells. The omnipresent king of the holiday table was a salad called "Olivier." I am not sure how it got its fancy French name—perhaps in honor of some French chef, many of which were invited to work for Russian aristocratic families in the pre-revolutionary days. It called for particularly arduous and meticulous dicing of boiled potatoes, eggs, meat, carrots, pickles (these were not boiled) and canned green peas, and finally dressing them with mayonnaise.

Another popular salad was called "shuba" (fur coat), or, more specifically, "herring under the fur coat"—I especially miss it, as properly salted herring is not easy to find in American grocery stores. Herring in "shuba" acquires a peculiar flavor not always appreciated by non-Ukrainians, as its saltiness mixes with sweetness of boiled beets, the zest of pickles, and the powdery texture of boiled eggs, all arranged in layers on top of herring and mixed with the same invariable mayonnaise. Fashion trends have brought and carried away other varieties of salads but these two, "Olivier" and "Shuba," have outlived any fashion, political or economic turbulence, and will probably remain on the Ukrainian table forever.

Pure unmixed herring in sunflower oil, decorated with raw onion rings, is another Ukrainian table constant—it goes well with vodka, accompanied by a piece of rye bread. And I almost forgot about salo, which very few non-Ukrainians can appreciate or even tolerate—raw salted pork fat or bacon without meat, served in slices and eaten with rye bread with the same ubiquitous accompaniment of vodka. Traditionally a part of the peasant fare, the product long ago became everybody's favorite—I had always taken it for granted until leaving Ukraine and realizing how much I craved it. Monuments have been created to it, and songs, verses and anecdotes have been dedicated to this "Ukrainian drug." A museum of salo featuring ingenious sculptures made from this unusual construction material recently opened in the city of Lviv in western Ukraine. The museum houses a restaurant of "salo-art cuisine" boasting forty different types of salo in "salo sushi" menu with exotic options and no less exotic names, like "Peasant Glamour," "a la French,"

"Non-Traditional with Prunes," and "Japanese Dream." More artistic culinary options of "Venus's Breasts," "Van Gogh's Ear," "Monroe's Lips," salo models of some other body parts and chocolate-covered salo might also incite curiosity, if not appetites. Other modern restaurants also add glamorous desserts made with sweet cream out of salo. A popular joke features a Ukrainian presenting salo to a customs official inquiring about drug possession. In fact, American customs officials seem to be well familiar with salo by now, as this is the first food item they try to verify in the luggage of Ukrainians coming into the country. A popular song says that a Ukrainian can never have enough salo. When my parents ask me what I would like to eat when I come back to vacation in Ukraine, herring and salo always make the top of my list.

A peculiar dish called "Holodez" could compete with salo for the most exotic, enigmatic, if not repulsive delicacy for the Western taste. It translates into English as "aspic," or, as my children call it, "meat Jell-O." The last time I asked my daughter what she would call it, she referred to it more explicitly as "disgusting." My husband has never brought himself to try Holodez in twenty-two years of our marriage and my children hide when they see signs of its upcoming appearance, but most Ukrainians adore and crave it. It is made for special occasions due to the particular complexity of the process, in large quantities that do not fit in a fridge in hot weather. Thus, most people reserve it for winter tables when food can be stored on balconies or unheated hallways. Holodez requires special cuts of meat with plenty of cartilage favorable for producing a glutinous substance when boiled for six or seven hours in a huge saucepan. Chicken feet, ox tails, and bone marrow all contribute to produce the best results, but better-quality beef and chicken are also welcome. It is extremely important to separate the meat from the bones after boiling, which can take a good amount of time and patience. The meat is then divided among twenty or so plates along with crushed garlic for spice and gluey liquid. Its smell and vapors fill the house with holiday spirit, and the smell of crushed garlic still brings me the feeling of anticipation of a feast. The high number of plates is explained by the guests' hearty appetites and the hosts' desire to reserve some leftovers for themselves for it disappears from the tables with astonishing speed. When my parents visit me here in Texas, we sometimes make Holodez if we can find the proper cuts of meat. Needless to say, we have to find time when my husband is out of town.

While my grandma made all of the above dishes with extraordinary skill and dexterity, she was the absolute master of baking. I admired her patience and persistence rolling out different types of dough and baking close to twenty thin layers necessary for two different cakes, "Napoleon" and "Mishka" (little bear), each prepared in plentiful amount for family and friends. She would work on them the whole day and then lay them to cool and rest until the following day, when she would labor on two different creams for filling and chocolate frosting. The process concluded with covering five or six layers for each cake with cream and adding frosting and walnuts, crushed by hand, on top. I could not wait till this stage since I had the immense pleasure of licking the remains of the cream from the bowls. Grandma would also make my favorite eclairs by baking the shells, making the butter cream which I adored, and laboriously filling the shells with the cream. Huge quantities of dessert were also necessary for endowing all the guests with some goodies without which, according to the custom, they could not leave the celebration. Modern time-saving appliances and ready-made ingredients for desserts have brightened up the lot of women preparing for parties, but they have also destroyed part of the rudimentary charm of baking, without which no cake tastes as it should.

Parties and Holidays

In the Spanish classes I teach, we discuss the notion of religious syncretism: early Catholic priests in Latin America gradually introduced Christian beliefs, combining them with indigenous customs. To facilitate the evangelization process, they focused on similar characteristics between Catholic saints and pagan gods and between Catholic and pagan celebrations. In its early days, the Soviet powers undertook a reverse process which could be called secular syncretism: It attempted to eradicate Christian celebrations, weaving some of their crucial elements into the newly atheistic society out of fear of resistance and gradually secularizing them. Thus, the major winter celebration shifted from Christmas to New Year's, the New Year fir tree took place of the Christmas tree, and the red star decorating the top of the tree came to symbolize the star on the Kremlin tower as a Communist symbol rather than the heavenly celebration of the birth of Jesus.

In fact, early Soviet authorities originally eliminated Christmas trees altogether as evidence of bourgeoisie prejudice. Guards and militia patrolled the streets on Christmas Eve, peeking into the windows to check for illegal holiday preparations. In 1935, the trees got a chance at rebirth in Soviet homes as the politician Pavel Postyshev proclaimed that this pre–Christian symbol could bring great joy to Soviet children. The authorities agreed there was no great harm in the tradition as the Christian nature of the holiday was mostly erased from the children's memories. This proclamation also welcomed back Grandfather Frost—the Russian equivalent of Santa Claus, previously considered by the Soviet powers as an ally of the priests. He came accompanied by Snow Maiden (Snegurochka)[1]—a Russian folk character who became associated with Grandfather Frost's granddaughter since the end of the 19th century. When I was a child, these two figures were as essential for the New Year holiday spirit as Santa Claus and his elves are for the Christmas fervor of American kids.

Our school vacation lasted for two weeks starting from the end of December, and the New Year fir tree party, with games, songs, dances and gifts, led by Grandpa Frost and Snegurochka, composed its integral element.

My grandma's older sister, Anastasia, dressed up as Snegurochka (Snow Maiden) for a party at the kindergarten where she worked, probably around 1938 or 1939.

Universities, factories and other institutions organized such parties for the kids of their employees. The newly rehabilitated and secularized Grandpa Frost and Snow Maiden welcomed kids to the first New Year fir tree when the first Soviet Palace of Pioneers opened in my native city of Kharkiv, in the building of the former Home of the Gentry, in 1935.

Since the return of the fir tree, no child could imagine a New Year celebration without the festive ceremony of its decoration just on the eve of the holiday, to not allow the spirit to get stale. The wide oval table in our living room got covered with tree decorations as we unwrapped them from old newspapers one by one, greeting each newly emerged toy as an old, dear friend ushering with her a host of memories. We then carefully selected the perfect place on the tree for each. Still now, I try to hold off as long as possible on the installation of the Christmas tree as I fear the festive mood will wear off if we get it in early December. I prefer to keep it alive long into January, when most of American society starts getting ready for Valentine's Day. These days, as my kids increasingly gain the right to vote in home issues, I start to lose mine, and the tree cheers our living room much earlier in the season. The frequent Texas December heat also diminishes my festive mood with inappropriate summer-like air. I long for biting frost and deep crunchy snow for sledding and snowball fights. Instead, I get a hurricane of dry leaves and, occasionally, the strongest resemblance of a winter blizzard—a thick, viscous fog.

The gifts Father Frost brought us on the night of December 31 were very modest by American standards but no less important for us than gifts were for American kids. On the morning of January 1, I woke up barely controlling my excitement and trying to guess whether Father Frost fulfilled my desires diligently indicated in the letter I had sent him. I ran to see whether he filled the shoe I left under the fir tree. I kept my belief in miracles until the advanced age of nine or ten—and in communication with Father Frost, I never forgot my manners, indicating that I would understand if my wishes exceeded his possibilities and he couldn't grant all of them. My mom has kept some of my humble letters with a wish list that included a book, a box of paints, a game or a new dress. When at the age of nineteen I spent my first Christmas with an American family, the tower of gifts in the living room left me agog: My modest childhood presents that fitted almost entirely in my boot could not compare with the pile of gifts that blocked the view of my host family's Christmas tree. I felt an acute embarrassment for the tiny Ukrainian souvenirs I brought for their kids—all that my family could afford for me to share with my American friends.

The New Year's party normally started around 9 p.m. with "seeing off" the old year. It meant saying toasts for leaving everything bad in the past and bringing everything good into the new year. Toasting, which necessarily involved subsequent drinking—the number two national sport of Ukraine after chatting—required the initiator to get up with a full glass of champagne, wine or vodka and pronounce a minimum two-minute speech. A decent New Year toast requires a brief foreword, the main point being wishes for someone in particular or everyone in general, and clinking glasses before drinking bottoms up. A brief intermission of heavy appetizers would be followed by another toast for, as a Slavic saying goes, "there's only a short interval between the first and the second shot," and yet another, since, according to another proverb, "the second shot flew by like a bird, and beckoned the third one with a wing."

Somewhere after the third toast, the order of ceremonies would generally disintegrate into a happy chaos that could take the party in many unforeseen directions—simultaneous toasts at different parts of the table, singing, yelling, dancing, dressing up as Father Frost and the Snow Maiden (occasionally with men taking the role of Snegurochka), exchanging symbolic gifts, sledding, snowballing and, sometimes, fighting. Once at a friend's house, we put the stereo outside and danced the night away in spite of the frosty wind and deep snow around us. Another time, we went sledding in a ravine after which my sleds disappeared forever. Nobody could remember their fate. One common denominator united all the New Year parties and all the parties in general: heavy eating. People would cook for days getting ready for the event, starve the whole day of the party to save space for the delights and then gorge on multiple rounds of abundant appetizers, sides, main courses and after courses. We could take a break around eleven p.m. to recharge our batteries, to get our second wind before welcoming the New Year at midnight, and then renew our gorging efforts until three, four or five a.m. To have more excuses for toasting, we would welcome the New Year according to the different time zones in the Soviet Union—starting with Siberian time and ending with our own.

The New Year parties often included an element of masquerade, where people would dress up as Grandpa Frost and Snegurochka, as well as other folk or pop culture characters. We also participated in masquerade parties in school. As there were no party factories, the responsibility for making costumes fell, as in every other case, to the parents who had to stretch their creativity to great lengths to find a fun and practical idea, and then to cut, paste, sew, glue, paint and knit. Once, I wore my mom's dark-red velvet robe with

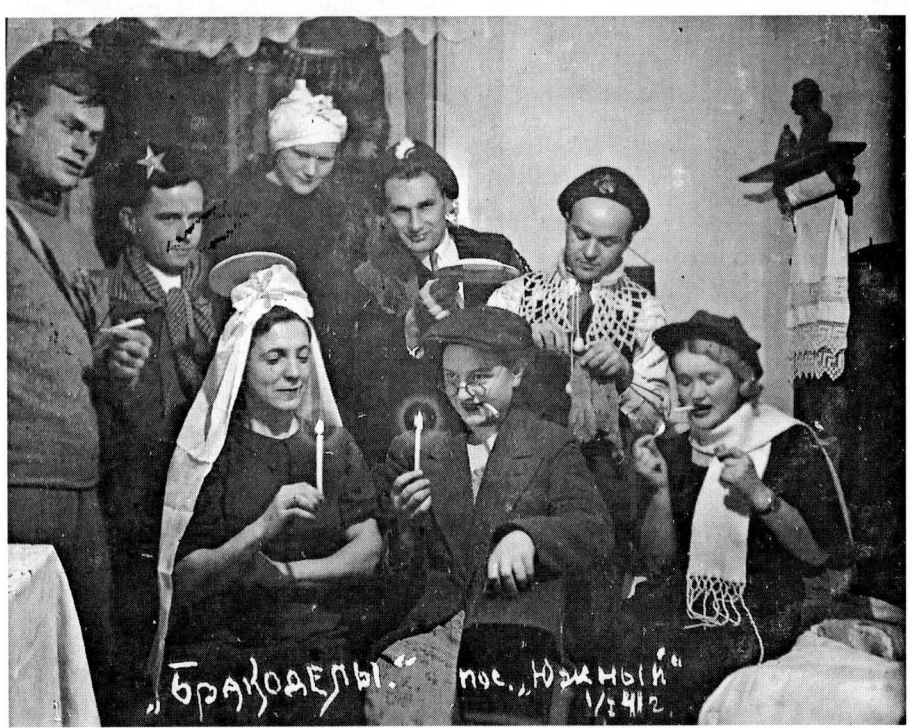

My grandma and friends celebrate the arrival of 1941 with a masquerade skit they called "Matchmaking." My grandma is at the top in a white hat.

broad white and pink stripes on the front, representing Yaroslavna—the Kiev Rus princess. The robe was so long it reached the floor, with broad sleeves that made it appear so pompous, it was appropriate for 1980s stage performance but not much else. I can't remember how mom got it, but it still lies in her drawer in the apartment with no usage after my "utrennik" (a word for kids' school activity literally meaning a "morning event").

The Soviet state, not honoring religious traditions, punished people for going to church by demoting or firing them from official positions or kicking them out of the Communist party or Comsomol. This was a great disgrace and a serious obstacle for career advancement. Communist leaders took turns standing guard by churches and taking note of any transgressors from schools or universities. In my mom's childhood they were afraid to even think about celebrating anything resembling Christmas. However, centuries-old traditions, such as Christmas carol singing at people's houses and preparing special Christmas dishes, lived on, as well as some folk traditions rooted in pagan times, such as divinations[2] on the night of Christmas Eve. The state terror altered the tradition of Christmas caroling, and the songs giving glory to the birth of Christ reappeared only in the nineties when believers were no longer considered pariahs. In my childhood, Ukrainian verses purged of Christian elements and focusing on good tidings to the family, already filled the houses, mostly in the countryside, on the night of January 6. (January 6th is the Christmas eve according to the religious, Julian, calendar. The official civil calendar was switched in the Soviet Union from Julian to Gregorian in 1918 but the religious calendar remained Gregorian. As a result, the Russian Orthodox holidays are celebrated 14 days after the same holidays in the Western churches.) Kids and adults of all ages, familiar and unfamiliar to us, would stop by to show off their art and ask for food or money in return. These requests would often come in jocularly harsh terms, such as follows:

> Shedryk-vedryk, give me a varenyk [a Ukrainian dumpling]
> A bit of kasha and a ring of sausage.
> And if you don't give me the sausage,
> I will smash your house to pieces!

The New Year celebration inaugurated a whole string of unofficial winter holidays with peculiar traditions born from the fusion of ancient folk rituals and Christian beliefs. Ukrainians have been particularly ingenious in creating occasions for celebration when the state would not give its blessing. The shift of calendars from Julian to Gregorian in 1918 offered such an occasion for honoring the New Year twice. Old ways die hard, especially in Ukraine, and people could not let an excuse for a party slip away, thus celebrating the New Year on its regular eve, continuing on January 1, and then again on January 14, according to the Julian calendar. By then, school was back in session, work in full swing, so why not take a break with vodka, good food and merriment before the state allowed us the next official break in March? The old New Year celebration would involve the unique ritual of so-called "seeding." In the morning, a male visitor threw seeds of wheat (or any other available cereal) all around the house to bring good luck and wealth to the hosts. Old folk beliefs admitted no gender equality and attributed bad luck to female visitors who could not count on a warm welcome that day.

The Epiphany, on January 19, marked the arrival of the coldest weather, somehow considered propitious in Ukraine and Russia for taking a dip in nearly frozen waters to commemorate the baptism of Jesus. People plunge themselves in the cross-shaped holes carved in the ice to cleanse themselves of spiritual and physical impurities. While they used to do it hiding from the authorities, the ceremony is well established now with priests blessing the faithful "walruses" and makeshift cabins provided for warming up and boosting the body with hot kasha and tea. The health benefits of cold water have long been heralded in Russia and Ukraine, where people like my mom dump buckets of nearly freezing water on top of themselves in any weather including severe frosts when bare feet stick to the snow and steam rises from the body. Yet more adventurous characters not only momentarily plunge but also swim in ice water as part of their exercise routine, while regular folks walk around them curled in layers of fur and wool. Known as "walruses" in Russian, these people claim that the cold water restores their nervous and immune systems, improves blood circulation and smooths wrinkles. I am not sure about all of these, but I can definitely attest to feeling refreshed and cheery after dumping a bucket of cold water on myself amidst tall bushes and flowers in my Ukrainian garden during the July heat.

My mom just before dumping a bucketful of cold water over her head in our Yuzhny garden in the winter of 1998. I followed her example for one year before moving to the United States.

In some villages of western Ukraine, people celebrate the Malanka holiday on the eve of the old New Year since the Saint Melania feast falls on January 13. Saint Vasyl follows on her heels on January 14 (in the Orthodox and Catholic traditions, almost every day celebrates a new saint), and for this reason they sometimes call the old New Year "the meeting of Malanka and Vasyl." I confess I have never heard about Malanka until coming to live in Texas where the Ukrainian community commemorates it with banquets and dance parties fueling patriotic pride in descendants from Ukraine and their children or grandchildren. Shamed by my ignorance into researching the tradition, I discovered that during this feast, one of the biggest and loudest of the year in southwestern Ukrainian villages close to the Romanian border, people acting as Malanka and Vasyl, sometimes cross-dressed, lead processions of other random characters, such as devils, goats, bears and gypsies in improvised costumes along snowy streets in the evening. They stop by people's houses, sing and act out funny skits, and eat and drink through the night. Some celebrations have been known to last for more than two days.

The Ukrainian dance ensemble of Dallas named Zorya celebrating Malanka in 2017. My son is second from right in the front row. My daughter is third from left in the middle row.

Parties and Holidays

During winter vacation and for the rest of the winter we spent a lot of time outdoors. Winter air was proclaimed by health experts to be particularly clean and devoid of germs so even babies were taken outdoors in freezing temperatures, wrapped in multiple blankets, coats and scarves. I got a sturdy multicolored wooden sled with metal runners and rails for back and shoulder support as a prize for getting vaccinated at the age of three. Just about every child I knew had a similar one—Soviet mass production ensured that children all over our eight million square miles would not envy each other's material possessions. We all had similar sleds, beds, desks, books, shoes, track suits, coats and dolls. A sled was a necessary tool for the utmost winter fun—bursting through the crisp, cold air on a fast ride down a hill, feeling the biting wind on the cheeks, and sometimes swirling backwards on the ice made us forget all of our worries. Sometimes we went skiing in the backyard or along the neighborhood streets on our identical skis that would attach to our warm woolen winter boots called "valenki." When we grew up, we extended our ski expeditions to the outlying fields and even risked occasional hills, where I broke two skis due to my recklessness, or, rather, inadequate skills.

My friend and relative Roma (front) and me skiing leisurely along the Sovetskaya (Soviet) street where I lived, 1982. My friend Olya (back) did not have the equipment and pretends to ski.

My friend Oksana's house stood on the edge of a ravine on the outskirts of the town. With no danger of cars driving around, we would race to the bottom of the ravine to our hearts' content until darkness. Many other kids would do the same, and we felt the community spirit come alive. Although it was bitterly cold, we would be drenched with sweat after multiple hikes uphill taking into account the heavy fur coats our babushkas forced on us in the perpetual fear that we would catch a cold. (Other well-known reasons for catching a cold were drafts if you left several doors in the house open in summer, and drinking cold water in any weather, especially hot, since the change of temperature was deemed particularly dangerous.) In childhood photos taken in winter, I look like a head of cabbage thanks to multiple layers of tights, pants, undershirts, sweaters, a coat and a belt supporting all of this mass. The clothes weighed more than I did; they made walking difficult and clumsy, and my face was hardly visible behind at least two hats—one woolen and one fur.

On February 23, the day of the Soviet army, we automatically congratulated all the men since they all had to serve the obligatory two-year term in the army once they turned nineteen. In school, we prepared gifts for boys, such as books about the Soviet army, small bags of stamps (stamp collecting was a popular hobby) or one soccer ball for all with the girls' signatures. We

With a snowman my grandpa built for me, 1981.

would also prepare "morning parties," where we recited poems and pronounced speeches dedicated to Soviet heroes. Sometimes we would stage skits where boys would dress up as soldiers and girls would represent military nurses wearing white kerchiefs and red crosses on the front.

On International Women's Day (March 8), the roles reversed: it was now the girls who received the gifts of plush bears or bouquets of flowers. Since the Soviet Union relied on the domestic growth of flowers, we hardly saw them during the long winter and truly appreciated their appearance as the aromatic inauguration of spring. In reality, warm weather, if it did come in early March, would not spoil us for long and return only in April or even later. We often spent spring break walking on top of snow hills on the level of the fences pretending to be giants—the snow layers had accumulated and packed so hard that we didn't sink. Then we deliberately tried to break the top layer, which was often slightly melted, to see if we would fall through snow holes. The excitement from the fall signaled that winter was finally yielding to spring.

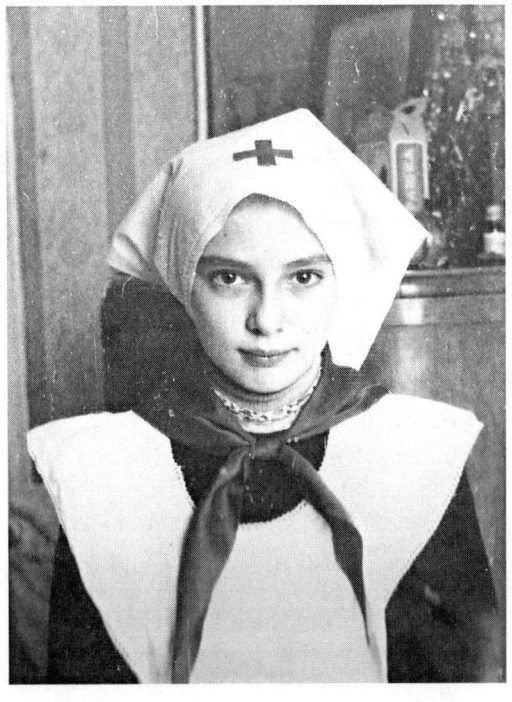

Me wearing a kerchief of a military nurse for a school event in honor of the Soviet Army Day on February 23, 1985. I was in the third grade.

The Eighth of March, celebrating women and spring simultaneously, also had socialist beginnings—curiously, in the United States, where, it seems, most people have never heard of it. Its earliest celebration was organized in 1909 in New York by the Socialist Party of America, which many Americans try to erase from their memories. Even more curiously, the country with the history of strong feminist movements and struggle for equal rights has ignored the holiday recognized by the United Nations and by most countries as honoring women. Soviet propaganda also did its part in distorting the history of the holiday as it usually ascribed the honor of starting the tradition to the German revolutionary Clara Zetkin and diminished or silenced the American origins. Only recently researching the tradition, I discovered the truth about Zetkin who merely supported the establishment of the annual celebration proposed by her fellow revolutionary Luise Zietz, but somehow got the most credit in the annals of Soviet popular history.

International Workers' Day or Labor Day, which we celebrated on May 1 together with most of Europe and Latin America, also originated in the United States—the country seemed to be quite a popular hang out for socialist activists at the turn of the century, although it did a good job of suppressing the memory of those days. This time, the honor went to Chicago where a strike for an eight-hour working day was followed by a scuffle with police and many deaths in 1886 (called Haymarket affair), initiating the movement for workers' rights. In the Soviet Union, the first Bolshevik leaders headed by Lenin took most credit for this deed—they used the demands for workers' rights, bread and education for all as main reasons for inciting the revolutionary struggle. (The young Soviet state was, in fact, very effective in combatting illiteracy as the percentage of literate population rose from 28 percent in tzarist Russia to 75 percent by 1937).

City employees marched in columns along the city streets as part of May Day demonstrations with the obligatory euphoric air—most of them were forced to participate by their HR departments.[3] The militia closed off the central city square and adjacent streets not only to car traffic, but also to people who could get through only if they were officially part of the demonstrations or if they showed an internal passport[4] indicating their residence in the central area. City officials and most honored employees occupied the most prestigious positions on the main square tribunes. My mom once overheard a little girl ask her parents who was standing on the tribunes, and after learning it was the best workers, followed up with another inquiry: "What about us? Are we the worst workers or are we just bad?"

Some employees would be privileged to carry socialist slogans stating, "Peace! Labor! May!" or "Proletarians of all the Countries! Unite under the banners of the Leninist Communist International! Straight ahead towards new victories!" as well as portraits of the greatest individuals of the socialist world—Lenin, Marx, Engels and the members of the Central Committee of the Communist party. If such an honor was bestowed upon you, you were bound to stick to the demonstration process to the very end, without the freedom to leave like the mere mortals reaching the tribunes. You were entrusted by the party to return the sacred socialist images to the workplace safe and sound.

I never participated in May Day demonstrations mostly because living in the suburbs considerably complicated the logistics of transportation to the city, especially with children. My mom and grandpa had to follow strict instructions from their organizations on where to congregate and start the procession. Since finding the right spot by eight a.m. implied wasting a good amount of time and nerves, particularly considering various street closures, they preferred not to take me. I desperately wanted to go. I longed to be with the crowd walking along the streets lined with freshly blooming trees, recognize familiar faces among the demonstrators, wave to the people and the cameras and celebrate with the community. I personified the spirit of collectivism, ingrained in Slavic cultures and solidified by the steady extermination of individuality during the Soviet rule. This spirit urged me (and still does) to partake in the joy of the community spirit and join parties, demonstrations, marathons and other gatherings. I was not alone—when the frail Soviet state stopped requiring participation in these events, many people previously complaining of the socialist obligations started experiencing post–Soviet withdrawal pains which included nostalgia of the fervor-filled Communist holidays.

Instead of joining the demonstrations, I joined other non-official workers who, with the arrival of warm weather signaling perfect conditions for yard work, emerged outside with spades, pitchforks and rakes. Although the original purpose of May Day was to honor the workers by giving them the day off, in the Soviet countryside it worked the opposite way: people took advantage of the day off to catch up on the garden work. We dug, took out the weeds, planted new flowers and vegetables and painted fences. The look of the moist and seemingly breathing soil after many months of snow and gray slush inebriated people whose senses had become numbed by long winters. Thus, shedding heavy clothes and working in the yard gave true pleasure, raw excitement at the possibility of touching the soil, hearing the birds, smelling the first tulips and dandelions in bloom and enjoying the fresh aroma of young grass.

Another harbinger of spring was the sight of the whitewashed trees, which I miss in the United States—people covered the trunks with white paint starting from the ground up in order to kill worms and parasites. Contrasting with dark trunks which appeared even darker from the moisture of the melting snow, the white accentuated the intense greenness of leaves and grass. The sight of neighbors across the fence, engrossed in similar projects, enhanced the feeling of communion with people and nature. At the same time, it also stimulated a peculiar competition—the game of keeping up with the neighbors' progress. If they finished shoveling their yard in preparation for planting before you did, it afforded a shameful reputation of disorganized landowner on your head, and there could be no question of focusing on other projects until you brought your yard to decent conditions.

There was also fun—after yard work or in lieu of it (in which case one was branded as a lazy bum by the neighbors), people sang, played accordions or guitars, walked around the streets in noisy groups, participated in official parties frequently held in city parks, and, of course, ate and drank. An integral element of the preparations for any holiday and building up the anticipation was writing greeting cards. We sent greeting cards to relatives, friends, co-workers and even casual acquaintances to congratulate them on the occasion of the New Year, Soviet Army Day, International Women's Day, May Day, Victory Day and the anniversary of the October Revolution—everything non-religious. The design combined folk elements with Soviet symbolism—a cosmonaut in a rocket ship bringing New Year gifts to bears and bunnies, a cosmonaut carrying a fir tree and New Year greetings or Father Frost with Snow Maiden riding a Soviet spaceship instead of the reindeer.

As no imagination could stretch far enough to invent new wishes every month, the first few lines followed a generic pattern and included wishes of good health, success in personal and professional life, sunny weather, a spring-like mood and clean, peaceful skies above the receiver's head. The remaining space on the card offered room for actual creative exercise where you could fit a brief summary of your life's recent happenings. Modern one-click technology left these epistolary exercises in the distant past. My grandpa usually wrote so many of these greeting cards that he would mix up the addressees and frequently sent cards to the wrong people. Confused recipients would later inform us of the blunder but we never found out the full extent of it since some people lived so far away that we never actually saw them. We met some of them on vacation, and we maintained the many-year-long friendships thanks to the greeting cards and letters. Unfortunately, we never saw some of those friends again, especially if they moved abroad—we eventually lost touch forever.

Summer offered no official holidays, which did not matter if you were a schoolchild. The freedom of our three-month-long vacation was disrupted only by rain which often came in long spells and prevented us from going outdoors and brought boredom. Modern-day kids would probably not think of rain as much of a bother, except when it interrupts their soccer game or other sporting activity. In my days, rain presented a serious obstacle to fun. The non-existence of Xboxes, PlayStations, iPads and cell phones and only three TV channels with limited children's programming left us little choice but to rely on our own creativity when affected by the weather. It regulated our lifestyle but we would not succumb to its disruptive fits. We stubbornly went outside even in mud and drizzle, trying to submit the forces of nature to our will and hoping to defeat them with our resolve. It was exasperating to wake up and see nature win over our will once again, dashing our enthusiasm with the fifteenth day of downpour. Grasping a tiny ray of sunlight through the thick veil of clouds was better than receiving a long-awaited gift. In sunny weather, we practically lived outdoors and came in only to watch a movie or a cartoon, eat, and sleep. I read outdoors as well—the tall, thick-crowned trees formed a canopy above our backyard—and lying with a book in the shade of this enchanted forest on an old cot was delightful. Some of our friends even slept outdoors at night when it became too hot—I was always fascinated by the idea although my parents were not.

Kids from the entire block, ages five to fifteen, played together in the evenings, with older kids taking care of the younger ones. Sometimes, older boys would beat up defiant youngsters but one of the more mature girls would typically interfere. We played hide-and-seek, tag, soccer, dodge ball, spoiled telephone (or just "telephone" as it is known in the United States), a game called "gigantic steps," "break the chain," and simply ran around until it got dark, around ten. We enjoyed similar pastimes to any other kids in the world—had picnics by the river, swam, walked in the woods and rode our bikes all over the town, often without adult supervision. Relatively calm suburban traffic did not bother us.

We loved climbing trees, especially those that bore fruit we could pilfer, like mulberry—a grainy, tender, succulent oval resembling a blackberry, with the sweetest juice that left inky, unwashable stains on our hands and clothes. Perched on some high, bench-shaped branch hidden behind the leaves, we enjoyed spying on people walking down the street. We also observed the street scene, less conspicuously, from the top of the fences surrounding our

My friend Oksana (left) and me having a snack at the bench in our backyard, 1979. I am wearing a wreath of natural flowers—weaving wreaths was a popular summer activity.

My friends Oksana (left), Kostya (center) and me, drawing with chalk on the street in front of my house, 1979. There was relatively little traffic at the time of our childhood, and we could play quite freely on the street.

front yards as well as the back. Climbing on top of the fence and peeking down held a special fascination of conquering the border between the private and public life without crossing it—we stayed in the middle and got the best view of both worlds. In the afternoons, our parents made us help with chores—picking berries form our own yards, cleaning or washing dishes, pulling up weeds.

They also encouraged or sometimes forced us to practice school work—math or reading—in order not to loaf around too much and get behind before the new school year. The socialist dogma implanted a high sense of duty into our minds (or at least our parents' minds) and it did not allow us to spend long intervals of leisure without pangs of consciousness. Thus, in the beginning of summer vacations, not letting myself slack up, I prepared my daily schedule which included fifteen minutes of morning exercises, forty-five minutes of piano practice, one hour of reviewing textbooks for the new school year, one hour of chores and two hours of reading. I recently found a copy of the tightly-packed daily activities plan from summer of 1986. But then, as my husband has always said, I am weird.

More Celebrations and Home Life

When I first participated in a birthday party in the United States, I realized in amazement that the birthday girl was actually *celebrating*—not cooking, baking, shopping for supplies, laying the table or washing the dishes. Her friends did all that. Well, at least they bought some drinks, chips and veggies along with the birthday cake and brought all of this to her home. After the short session of hors d'oeuvres and cake, the guests along with the host proceeded to party elsewhere—to bars or dance clubs.

A Ukrainian birthday girl could not afford lounging around on her big day, nor for several days leading up to it. (The situation was slightly different for Ukrainian men but even they contributed their chopping, grinding and peeling efforts to family celebrations.) She would be stocking up on provisions and cooking a minimum of twenty hearty and light dishes to make sure the table stayed covered until the guests had various helpings of all of them. Ukrainian guests would be mortally offended if they were only offered chips and veggies followed by one lonely cake, and news of this disgraceful act and scanty, ridiculous fare would quickly spread all over town. Neither could one consider skipping the celebration honoring the most important day in one's life as caring friends and relatives would affectionately remind you of its proximity and of their imminent visit, whether you were happy to see them or not.

My mom likes to say that everyone but the birthday girl celebrates her birthday. The whole night, she continues serving new dishes, taking away empty plates and washing them several times—after appetizers, after the main dish and after the dessert. The guests stay at the table for several hours, sometimes getting up for dancing or smoking in between. Thus, they have a good opportunity to leisurely savor the treats—and not hunt for them around the house, as my mom feels she must do when she comes to parties in American homes. She also hates having to hunt for a place to sit where she can balance the plastic plate on her knees, trying not to spill or drop something while cutting the meat.

After years of severe persecutions of the faithful who were trying to preserve sacred traditions during the Soviet times, a host of religious holidays returned to our legal reality. In those times, priests were required to share information about the religious ceremonies they performed with authorities who in turn investigated who had dared to request these services. The culprit then faced the danger of being excluded from the Communist party (membership was necessary for promotion in many positions) or even being fired. We could hardly judge the priests: Theirs was probably one of the trickiest occupations during the Soviet times. Lenin proclaimed religion to be the opiate of the people and began one of the harshest and cruelest campaigns in history against it. Multiples churches were bombed, burnt and pillaged, and multiple priests were tortured and executed. Those who survived in the subsequent years were subjected to the severe control of the party organs. The KGB searched the homes of the priests and regularly called them in to be questioned at KGB headquarters, from where they were not certain of coming back.

Preparing the tables for a birthday celebration, 2008.

In a recent TV program about the greatly respected Moscow Orthodox priest and Biblical scholar Alexander Men who was brutally murdered in 1990, his widow told stories of how the family used to hide prohibited books by

Solzhenitsyn and other possibly "unsafe" writers in a pile of charcoal outside the house. While Soviet propaganda was widely encouraged, religious propaganda was punished with minimum three years of imprisonment, and there were possible repercussions for the family. Men was also expelled from the Irkutsk Agriculture Institute, where he had studied before deciding to dedicate himself entirely to religion, for his Christian beliefs. It was a particularly dangerous balancing act for priests to stay true to their spiritual integrity while trying to keep their churches open, tend to their small flocks and obey the authorities.

Many people, like my grandma, still baptized the newly born in concealment since they did not consider any future possible without such a blessing. To arrange the ceremony, grandma's lady friend who worked in the church asked the priest on her behalf not to register it officially so that my parents' employers at state universities would not find out about this subversion. Grandma also tearfully promised the holy father she would not let him down in her turn. My own father never found out about my baptism.

Soviets even invented new temples for the realization of important life acts previously celebrated in churches: grand wedding palaces for registering marriages and newborn palaces for registering births. These temples were equipped with elegant interiors, the finest samples of Soviet furniture and primped but lifeless priestesses of bureaucracy. They pronounced their same-patterned congratulatory sermons so many times in one day without variation that they did not even bother to conceal looks of boredom on their faces. While at the start of my own wedding ceremony I was ready for the icy official reception, my groom, who expected everyone to radiate happiness on our special day, was taken aback by the stony expression and imperious timbre in which the lady in the last-century outfit commanded us to kiss each other and be happy. We took our time, mostly because we wanted to savor the first kiss of our married life, but also to irk her. The duration of the kiss obviously exceeded the standard prescribed by the official guidelines—the lady started to shift awkwardly and attempted the beginning of her next homily. Our guests' applause submitted her into silence until we properly completed our first kiss as husband and wife.

The stone-faced bureaucrat was hastily and anxiously approaching the end of her duties when my ingenuous groom presented a new obstacle unprecedented in the annals of the Soviet bureaucracy. When the moment came for signing the most important document of our lives, he took his own pen out of his pocket, declining the official Soviet graphological instrument (although the wedding took place during the early post–Soviet period, I am certain that the pen was from the Soviet Union). Robert brought a Montblanc Meisterstück gold-plated pen presented to us as a wedding gift by a close

Robert signs the marriage license with his special pen as the wedding palace official throws a displeased look at the audience, June 8, 1996.

family friend from Argentina. He held the idea of signing the marriage act with it very dear to his heart, even though he could not read a single word on the document. To the lady, on the other hand, this licentious action represented the utmost subversion of the sacred protocol. Like most Soviet bureaucrats, she could not deal with alteration of the official rules. She threw a fiery glance at her assistant, barely containing her fury, put back the rejected pen, and finished the speech through clenched teeth.

Bureaucratic intricacies distracted me from the description of our reborn Christian celebrations such as baptism. It offered a chance to gain new relatives—godparents of a baby technically share the responsibility of bringing up the child—and cement a special type of relationship between the parents and the godparents. Parents and godparents call each other "kum" (male form) or "kuma" (female form) often endearingly as a greeting. While Spanish-speaking countries have an equivalent word for the same type of relationship—"compadre" or "comadre"—the English language lacks such a term and a concept. With few immediate relatives, my family and friends formed an intricate network of "kums": I baptized the daughter of our good friend Olya who later baptized my own daughter. However, since she had not been baptized herself, the priest performed a simultaneous ceremony of her own baptism, with my mom and my husband becoming her godparents (my husband is thus her godfather and kum at the same time). Olya's husband Vitaliy later became my son's godfather, and my friend Tanya his godmother. My relative (and the son of my own godfather) Roma became my daughter's godfather.

Other families who did not baptize their kids still elected nominal godparents for them, and thus the term "kum" never fell into disuse. Ukrainian folklore has produced many facetious songs and anecdotes about "kums" flirting with each other and kum visiting his kuma when the husband is not home. That said, Ukrainian folklore hardly spares anyone—a typical wedding song (and an obligatory dance for mother and son-in-law) presents a mother-in-law who treats her son-in-law so well that, after quarrelling with his wife, he decides to marry her mother instead.

In the time of my childhood, many families also secretly celebrated Easter which was not imaginable during my mom's youth. My grandpa, required to be a member of the Communist party as a military man, could

My daughter's baptism in the Orthodox church in Ukraine, 2006. Godfather Roma, at left, is holding her. Godmother Olga, who was simultaneously baptized in the same ceremony, is second from left. My husband is second from right and I am on the right.

not come near a church. My mom, first an interpreter at the State Intourist Agency, and then a university professor, likewise could not afford to display her faith. Her job was particularly sensitive and stressful for she was under continuous KGB watch for Soviet political correctness (in other words, she could not say anything that could remotely tarnish the image of our great motherland). My grandma, a homemaker, was the only one who attended mass and observed the Orthodox rituals faithfully. She never missed a chance to bake traditional Easter bread to share with family and friends and take to the cemetery and leave on the tombs of the loved ones for the Remembrance Day, a week after Easter.

Baking Easter bread took a whole day and a lot of physical effort—Grandma spent the morning combining the ingredients, kneading the dough, waiting for it to rise properly and then catching the right moment to shape it into a hundred tin molds of different sizes, starting with the shot glass size and ending with almost a bucket. She baked all those "kulich" for the rest of the day, well into the night. They always came out perfect—soft, yellow from egg yolk, sweet, with raisins inside. As there was never enough space on the kitchen table, she took them outside to cool and then decorate with icing and sprinkles—my favorite. The icing dried into a hard, glassy surface which cracked on the teeth and turned into a sweet powder. We continued eating Easter breads for about a month, and they preserved their special flavor even as they were getting dry. We also gave away many to friends and neighbors—and they did the same in keeping with the community spirit of sharing. It was said one had to try twelve different breads during the Easter season.

On the night of Easter, my Grandma took some breads to the church to be blessed, along with eggs painted with onion shells, sausage, salo, cheese and other essential treats. Easter services started around ten p.m., then people carrying lit candles would circle the church three times following the priest in a special procession. The mass then continued until four a.m. when the priest would come outside to bless the food—people stood with their baskets around the church waiting for him. Only then could the strict Orthodox forty-day Lent be broken, and people could eat, starting with the egg and Easter bread. The last three days of Lent were the strictest as hardly anything except for grains and produce was allowed, and only the very few, most devoted believers could go through with such a trial—the rest of the fasters (which in those days mostly consisted of old ladies) tried their best.

If birthday and baptism parties required a lot of food and preparation, nothing could beat heaps of comestibles on the wedding tables where multiple courses continued to be served throughout the day and well into the night. At least, that is how it used to be during the weddings I attended in my childhood and during my own wedding soon after the break-up of the Soviet Union. More and more people prefer a Western-style wedding now, with only one round of food and fewer traditions, many of which have been discarded as traces of old times. I have seen some of these events at restaurants—beautiful couples, elegant guests, expensive-looking food, romantic music, but not much fun. Sometimes the music selection at these modern weddings is baffling, probably because people do not understand or do not analyze the English lyrics. At a recent wedding celebrated at a restaurant where we dined, they played Gotye's "Somebody That I Used to Know"—a song about a couple breaking up.

I hope the old folk-style weddings do not disappear in the face of the pressure of the Western traditions, and my kids get to participate in some of those—like my neighbor aunt Valya's wedding in the early eighties. People from the entire block, both close and distant relatives and friends, filled our neighbors' backyard for a two-day celebration. Aunt Valya later confided that neither she nor her groom knew who some of the guests were. The whole afternoon and evening of the first day was dedicated to the main celebration, eating, drinking and wedding games. The second day of the wedding in the countryside was usually reserved for a masquerade when people dressed up in folk Ukrainian costumes, with cross-dressing, singing farcical songs, more eating and drinking, and more dancing well into the night.

Because of the challenge of finding space for more than a hundred people at home, neighbors brought along their tables, benches or chairs. Everybody

The children's program at neighbor aunt Valya's wedding, 1980. My grandpa, singing, is on the right. I am second from right.

sat in the yard, and the bride's dad built wooden floors to provide the appropriate dancing space. The Soviet restaurant industry did not offer catering or take-out options, and the bride's mom, with the help of family and friends, cooked and baked for days to prepare enough food. People happily consumed it, said toasts for the bride and groom, drank, danced and ate and drank again before playing wedding games. No wedding was complete without stealing the bride's shoe and stealing the bride herself. The best man (or the witness, as they call him in Ukraine) had to pay for allowing the disappearance of the shoe by drinking a glass of vodka, singing or dancing. The payment required by the stealers (some nimble guests) often included a flirty element when both witnesses, male and female, usually chosen from various still-single friends, had to dance together on one chair or take clothes pins (which the guests had put on strategic locations of their attire) off each other while dancing blindfolded. Then the bride herself would disappear. It was up to the groom to pay for her disappearance. She was usually led to a hiding place during some dance while people were not looking, and the groom would have to successfully execute a series of tasks as a redemption cost.

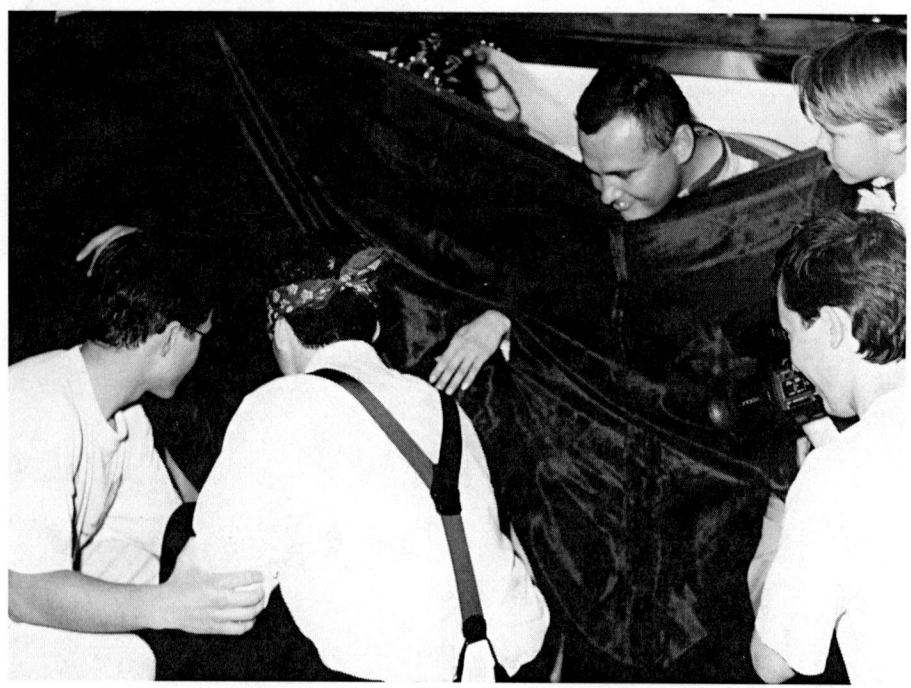

Robert, blindfolded with his back to the camera, is trying to match my hand with my foot as Vitalik, whose foot had been switched with mine, looks down from behind the curtain, June 8, 1996.

At my wedding reception, my blindfolded husband had to identify my hand and foot as myself and a few other girls and one burly man were sitting behind a curtain with holes through which we stuck our hands and feet. To add to the challenge and confuse the groom, my own foot was switched with the guy's. Robert found my hand pretty fast but as he tried to feel the matching foot, he pulled back in shock, discovering something big, hairy, and rough. As my husband does not lack a sense of humor, he reacted quickly to the trick and grabbed the guy's foot again tickling it. After some help from the witness, he was able to establish the proper identity of my foot and hand.

Robert had already endured various trials on the morning of the wedding, when he arrived to pick me up at my parents' house—my maids of honor along with an eight-year boy in a tuxedo blocked the entrance, demanding a "ransom" payment from him in actual cash and decipherment of a riddle. The riddle consisted of finding the lipstick imprint of my lips on a piece of paper, mixed with a few other imprints. For an extra challenge, the girls had asked my grandpa for permission to paint his lips and then had him kiss the paper—this did not fool my faithful groom, who confidently pointed

My husband-to-be Robert haggling over a "ransom" for the bride at the entrance to our Yuzhny home. My friend Lena and my relative Vanya are blocking the entrance. Lena is holding a sheet with "the lips trial."

to the imprint of my lips! The payment consisted of a massive stack of "coupons"—the Ukrainian currency at the time of transition to a capitalist economy and extreme inflation when prices were changing every day.

When he finally got through the lines of defense, Robert and his witness (my cousin) made it inside my parents' house, where we received my mom's blessing and drank a glass of champagne. It was only ten a.m. and another toast followed shortly at eleven when we finally made it to the wedding palace. Champagne on an empty stomach is a time-honored method of easing soon-to-be newlyweds' nerves and ensuring that no doubts arise at the last moment. A ceremony at the Russian Orthodox church followed the civil marriage—and the priest's congratulatory speech was a lot more sincere and affectionate than the mechanical words of the official whose profession was to greet the newlyweds.

The only minor inconvenience was the length of the ceremony—about an hour of standing and listening to Old Slavonic chanting with occasional mention of our names reminding the groom he was at the right place. The witnesses bore the biggest burden—they had to hold wedding crowns that weighed several pounds over our heads during most of it. A video recording shows a few guests starting to yawn. They had to wait a bit longer—according to the tradition, after the ceremony and the greetings, we drove to the main

Witnesses Sasha and Lena holding crowns over our heads as we listen to the priest at the church ceremony, June 8, 1996.

city sights to take pictures and walk around accepting congratulations from strangers. The main photo sights included Lenin's monument on the central square, the large monument to Taras Shevchenko, the most celebrated Ukrainian poet and the fighter for independence (the site where Robert proposed to me three months earlier), and the monument to the motherland and the fallen World War II soldiers where newlyweds typically left flowers.

By three p.m. we made it at last to the café where the guests who, in contrast to us, were prohibited from drinking or eating prior to our arrival, were eagerly waiting for us in a crowded hallway. The master of ceremonies (called "Tamada"), bubbling with energy and good humor, pronounced a few greeting rhymes signaling to the guests to throw grains of wheat and rye on us to bring us happiness and health. The tradition also required the parents to greet us with bread and salt (a symbol of hospitality in Slavic countries), and we had to feed each other pieces of bread dipped in salt. As I wanted to make sure to give proper welcome to my new husband, whose family could not attend the wedding, I broke a big piece of bread and shoved it into his mouth. It took him a while to master it, especially without any liquid. The liquid followed in proper order (that is, after we were done with the bread) and, not surprisingly, it was another toast of champagne

According to the Ukrainian tradition, I am feeding my husband bread dipped in salt as he is trying to cope with its large size.

which by now added to our euphoria. The parents tried their best not to be greedy and to fill the glasses to the brim, and somebody mentioned we had to drink it all, to not leave any drops "for tears." Hungry, nervous and half-drunk, we painstakingly kept working on the champagne for a while longer until we could break the empty glasses into small pieces and proceed to our seats. The guests, worn out by the long wait and kindled appetites, followed. The wedding reception lasted the whole afternoon and went well into the evening. It included multiple courses of food interspersed with dancing, toasts and games. The toasts were typically followed by the chorus yelling "Gorko!" (meaning "bitter") which signaled kissing time for the couple. "Bitter" refers to the taste of vodka which needs to be purified and sweetened by a kiss. Sometimes the guests would also count in chorus to measure the length of the kiss. My godfather, who got a bit drunk after a long period of abstention during the official ceremonies, even helped us by putting his arms around us and patting our backs for extra encouragement. Other guests, also slightly inebriated, happily participated in the games. Two of our friends (our future "kuma" Olga and "kum" Vitaliy) represented the goddess of beauty Aphrodite and the god of the wedding Hymenaeus—they changed into Greek-looking tunics and wreaths, brought "the torch of love" and read a "decree" commanding us to engage in proper behavior during our marriage. Naturally, it dictated the husband to be caring and protective, and the wife faithful and submissive.

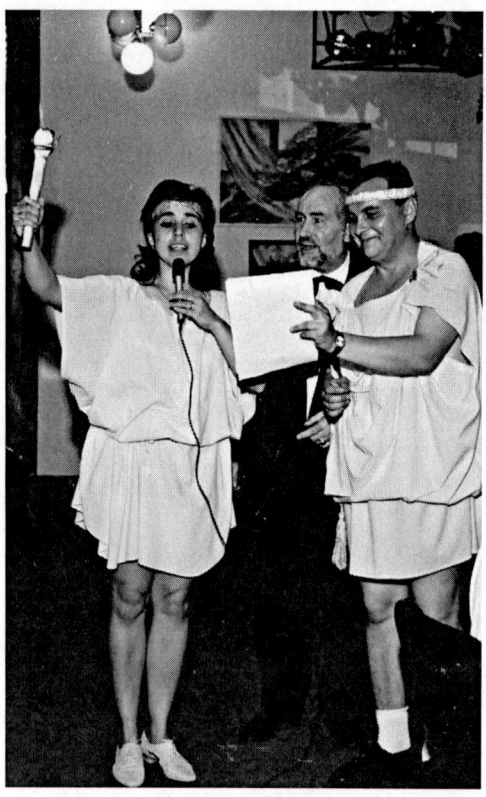

Friends Olga and Vitalik (our future "kums"), dressed as Aphrodite and Hymenaeus, reading the "wedding decree."

Uncle Vitya and his wife Aunt Lena represented storks bringing us a baby girl, while another couple represented a stork bringing a baby boy. The two storks competed against each other bringing us their "baby": a blue or pink pacifier on a plastic chain that was to be tied to a bottle of amaretto to be opened after the birth of the baby. Each couple had to stand in the appropriate "stork" position: they lifted the opposite legs and waved the opposite arms in a bird-like fashion. On a signal, they skipped towards us on the other legs. Although bets seemed to be against the older couple, they turned out to be much more agile and reached us a lot faster (though cheating at times and running instead of skipping). Thus, they sealed the prediction of our first-born being a girl (which ended up being the case).

Before then, I had never questioned or wondered about the abundance of children-related games at Ukrainian weddings (there was another one at ours requiring guests to guess a number of future children). It was my husband who realized and pointed out how much importance people attached to the children question. He said he could not imagine playing such games in an American wedding—couples made their own choice whether to have children, and prying ahead of time, even jokingly, could be considered rude. When you got married in Ukraine, it was automatically assumed that you would have children—the sooner the better. Many of my classmates had children right after school graduation—and some of them became grandparents while my own children were starting elementary school. The situation is changing nowadays as many couples choose to have children later in life but few decide not to have children at all.

As important as it is for Ukrainian families to have children, their average number has decreased drastically in the 20th century, following the revolution. While both my grandparents came from large families of five or more children, they had only one daughter—possibly because they married shortly before the war. My father likewise was an only child and so was my aunt Galya (my mom's cousin), my aunt Asya (also my mom's cousin), Aunt Asya's son and my stepdad. Most of my friends and classmates had one

Mom and me at aunt Valya's wedding, 1980.

sibling and many were only children. I can count on the fingers of one hand the people I knew who had three kids—and nobody I knew had more than three. Parents were pouring all of their love, care and attention on those few offspring, however. I remember my mom organizing my playtime—we shaped fruit and veggies out of Play-Doh, made pretend food with it, built doll houses, read, walked and sang together. Ever since those early days, my mom has been my best friend. She now plays baseball, football and other games with my son and helps my daughter solve math problems.

Grandparents frequently lived together with parents and took care of the grandkids while the parents were working, thus eliminating the need for daycare. They would pick up the kids from school, cook lunch, supervise homework and organize educational activities. One of our relatives, Grandma Lyolya (whose exact degree of relationship is so complex, it is too difficult to specify), learned French together with her grandsons and dictated French texts to them besides helping them with Russian, history and math. My own grandma was always busy with housework and the invention of new treats, and so my grandpa read and invented stories, built projects and thought of new games with me and my friends. Before New Year, we constructed fir tree decorations, such as a house out of cardboard—my grandpa placed a tiny light bulb in it and connected it to the string so it looked like the house had a light inside. Since he loved geography, we studied the world map and he told me stories about jungles, deserts and piranhas. While he never crossed the borders of the USSR, he dreamt of traveling and educated himself about amazing facts from world geography and culture. Thanks to him, I learned most of the world capitals and

Grandpa with me (left) and my friend Elya after the Victory Day Parade in 1984.

acquired a thirst for seeing new lands. I dedicate every new trip I make to my grandpa thinking how happy it would make him to know that I am realizing his dreams. My mom's and grandparents' endless love for me made my childhood home an oasis of happiness and safety where I forgot about school worries and felt that every day together with my family was a holiday.

Military Training and Shadows of the War

When you wear a gas mask, it makes you look like an elephant. A grotesque, thin elephant, with a long trunk but no ears on the oval, smooth gray rubber-covered face, too narrow for an elephant, and big round eyes protruding under the plastic cover. Breathing in a gas mask becomes heavy and laborious, especially if you run. Seeing clearly behind plastic is not easy either; you have to be careful where you step. But the biggest challenge is putting it on—stretching the rubber for an opening big enough to squeeze in your face, smoothing out the folds which stick to each other, and perhaps trying a bigger size. You have to be careful—if the mask is too big, it will fall off and let the noxious fumes penetrate your system. It would probably be futile to look for a different size in a Soviet school military training class— you grab what is available from a pile of thirty-some gas masks which are not really sorted by size or by class. The same set of masks passes from one class to the next. Needless to say, nobody worried about disinfecting them before the next class tried them on. You can't afford to be squeamish with a threat of the Third World War hanging over you. Fitting your nose in the right hole is tricky as well—it gets caught in the folds, which prevents breathing altogether. A panicky feeling descends as you envision the possibility of never finding the outlet for fresh air and perishing in the attempt before a chemical attack strikes.

We experienced no chemical attacks, but the fear was always there in our hearts and in the air of classrooms where we were frequently reminded of the possibility of the Third World War and the danger of attack by our Cold War enemy—the United States. We had to be ready. One more way the school administration ensured our alertness, besides practicing putting on gas masks, was through the presentations of various attack scenarios—mostly chemical and nuclear attacks—represented by a monstrous mushroom of clouds of dust, illuminating the dark sky and our nightmares afterwards. It was the early eighties, and no PowerPoint slides were available to support the presentation. Sometimes, colored photos enhanced verbal images, but it was our imagination that did the most powerful work in making the scenarios come alive. That's what happened to my friend Lena, who had a panic attack in the middle of a lesson in the second or third grade.

I was sitting next to her and saw her first. She started rubbing her eyes and then lowered her head to the desk not making much sound. Only her shoulders and two tight black braids were shaking slightly. "What is it, Lena?" No answer. The presentation that had caused the sorrow had happened earlier in the day and I could not guess the connection. The dusty mushrooms must have been eating their way into her brain all that time until finally exploding in the images of the worst imaginable catastrophe that would destroy her loved ones, her friends, herself and even her unloved ones—like the teacher who had imparted the hateful talk. Everything, including school and homework, became precious to her in that moment of child's revelation of the fragility of life.

Tears kept flowing without explanation, and even the most incorrigible troublemakers, the girl-haters who pursued Lena and the rest of us on other occasions by pulling our hair, calling us names and tripping us, became subdued by the depth of her grief and a vague sense of guilt. Her mom worked as a math teacher at our school and only when she was summoned to our classroom did Lena feel secure enough to admit her fears—of the nuclear explosion or of a chemical attack. She did not really know herself, nor could she put into words the realization of terror planted by images of the destruction of life.

The fears of war appeared so much more vivid to all of us because of the proximity of another calamity—World War II, in the Soviet Union better known as the Great Patriotic War. It took the lives of more than forty million people and an almost inhuman effort of many more men, women and even child fighters—soldiers and underground partisans—to compensate for the blunders of the government which had not prepared the country for the Nazi attack. In the 1930s Stalin and his cohorts had executed the cream of the army for imaginary crimes and made a disgraceful non-aggression pact with Hitler. It opened the road for the Nazis to attack Poland and proceed to the border with Ukraine. On June 22, 1941, at four a.m., they bombed Kyiv, the capital of Ukraine. It was a Sunday, and recent high-schoolers, full of hopes, had just returned from graduation parties. Soldiers stationed in and around Kyiv, like my aunt Galya's dad, were thrown unprepared to the defensive lines like meat to wild beasts. Aunt Galya could never find out where and when exactly he perished. Every May 9, during the Victory Day holiday in the Soviet Union and now Ukraine, Russia and other former Soviet republics, she cries as she mentally goes back to the first victory celebration, when she could not find her father among the soldiers returning from the front. The World War II Museum in Kyiv commemorates many soldiers like him and many civilians—mostly women, children and the elderly who survived or did not survive the brutalities of the enemy determined to erase the Jewish and Slavic races from the face of the earth.

My generation grew up with the echo of the sounds and the vision of the scars of the Great Patriotic War. Monuments, books, movies, songs and stories about the war surrounded us everywhere and made us feel its shadow very close. The house in front of ours—where good friends of the family now live—became the site of the Nazi headquarters in our town during the occupation. The town and the surrounding areas were frequently bombed, and walking around the woods, we would come across large holes in the ground left from bomb explosions. About 860,000 people lived in the city of Kharkiv in 1941 when the Nazis attacked and only 200,000 were left by the end of the war. Many went to the front, others were hanged, shot, or gassed, and yet others were driven to concentration or labor camps. City buildings provided bomb shelters, and some of the signage indicating the way towards them have been deliberately maintained as a reminder of those dark days. An awkward structure painted with cartoon characters appears to make an integral part of the playground in front of our apartment building in Kharkiv. Its original destination was to provide the entrance to the underground bomb shelter. Many of those have been preserved in case of future disasters that could turn out even more tragic. Tombs of unknown soldiers spot the countryside and the woods of the former Soviet Union, where the battles took place. One of those, always covered with fresh flowers in summer, stands in the forest just outside Yuzhny.

Before every vacation, we listened to the presentations about proper precautions when finding unfamiliar objects in the woods or fields surrounding our town. Mines and grenades exploded and still explode from time to time in these former areas of war actions, injuring or killing children who inadvertently pick them up. When we visit Ukraine, our neighbor Seryozha often takes my husband to the nearby forest with a metal detector in search of lost artifacts from the war. They have found plenty of machine gun shells, Soviet belt buckles, and even musket balls used centuries ago. The unexploded grenades also turn up in the big cities like Kharkiv or Kyiv. One of our popular childhood games was fighting the fascists—we imagined that trees were our enemies, for no one wanted to play their part.

Victory Day, celebrated in the Soviet Union on May 9, was one of the most important holidays of the year. The Soviet citizens felt immense pride in their forefathers for having stopped the steady eastward advancement of the Nazis and for having reversed the course of the war with victories in Kursk and Stalingrad in 1943. I was proud of my grandpa, an air force flight

Military Training and Shadows of the War

Me in 1981 with the cannon from World War II that helped liberate Yuzhny. It was placed on the outskirts of the town. I am holding the popular cartoon character "Cheburashka."

navigator who contributed to the cause. In Kharkiv, the big city located fifteen miles from the town where I lived in my childhood, we also celebrated (and still celebrate) August 23, the date of its liberation in 1943, with fireworks and concerts. The Soviet army liberated the city twice—the first victory in February 1943 was followed by a counterattack from the Germans, who again surrounded Soviet troops. It was finally and definitively liberated in August. My mom remembers the dark pictures of destruction she witnessed in Kharkiv as a child a few years after the war: skeletons of the former apartment and university buildings, factories and monuments, destroyed roads that would take years to rebuild and piles of trash and debris. Three hundred thousand people died in battle, in Nazi camps or from hunger during those horrible years. The images of the war seen in books, museums and movies caused me to have childhood nightmares when I would see our backyard in rapidly advancing flames or fear being torn away from my family.

Every year, on May 9, our town of Yuzhny celebrated Victory Day in the local park (called Victory Park) by the tomb of the soldiers fallen in the battles for Yuzhny and by the monument to the fallen heroes shaped as a figure of a mourning mother. War veterans stood on the specially erected tribune,

First grade Victory Day parade, 1983. My class marches as the rest of the schoolchildren watch and wait for their turn. I am on the front right.

pronounced and listened to speeches and watched the reenactment of the victory parade organized by our school. We stood guard by the tomb of the unknown soldier. We also marched on the square in front of the mourning mother monument—an imitation of a true military parade, vying for the title of the best and most coordinated marching unit, the best costumes, the best chanting of Soviet boot camp-type cheers, and the best singing. Nikolai Nikitovich, our music teacher, walked briskly by the side of each class, accompanying our singing by playing the accordion.

We rehearsed for a month polishing our marching and singing skills. We had to be ready: The whole town would come to watch us before heading to the official ceremony of the victory commemoration and the informal festival in the park. We loved the rehearsals taking one or two class periods, and we loved participating in the actual parades, especially when we could show off dignified pilot or marine costumes made by our parents. Once I was so excited on the morning of the parade that I started running around our backyard and slipped on the fresh dirt, which was wet after a spring shower. The excitement quickly turned to despair when I saw my white shirt with the consequences of the fall. Fortunately, my mom had a spare white shirt, and my grandma performed miracles to speed-clean the skirt, which also bore the consequences of the fall.

One year the teacher (and perhaps the parents, who opted for more easily manageable materials) decided on using the costumes of Soviet cosmonauts. We simply hated the cheap, tight-fitting cotton jogging suits that made us look malnourished and equally the tight-fitting hats with wires sticking out on top and ears sticking out on the sides. We resembled misplaced aliens rather than cosmonauts. I begged my grandpa not to take photos of our group. My favorite year was the seventh grade when we vaunted honorary blue suits, blue pilot hats and white strings of the participants of the military-sports game called "Zarnitza." The closest translation of the term means "remote flashes of lightning after the storm is gone." The name could have two interpretations: flashes of faraway war explosions or sparks of the revolutionary movement foreboding the disastrous thunder which eventually brought our mighty empire to ruin.

The purpose of the game, organized all over the Soviet Union, was to inculcate us with patriotism and proper preparation for army service. Only two people from my class—my friend Larisa and myself—got the honor of participating with the other, more deserving group. In April of that year, we went to the regional event where we competed against other schools and won first place. In order to win, we staged an imitation military camp in a forest, hid from the enemy and appropriated the flags of the other competitors and "killed" as many of the enemy militants as we could. "Killing" involved tearing off their shoulder stripes—we collected and counted them to present as evidence of our trophies.

We also competed and earned points in the categories of general sports preparation, assembling and disassembling rifles, providing medical care for the pretend "wounded" (bandaging the wound, assembling the stretcher and carrying the wounded from the battlefield, and so on). None of the above were my forte, and I was chosen to be a messenger. Larisa and I spent many an afternoon learning Morse

(From left) Larisa, me and our friend Elya dressed in Zarnitsa military uniforms on Victory Day 1987.

code and messaging each other flag signals, and we became quite a coordinated team. I believe we enjoyed this messaging system more than modern kids enjoy texting—the gratification from deciphering the signals was definitely greater. With great emotion, I recently found a photo of our "Zarnitza" group marching victoriously in a book about Yuzhny written by one of its eldest residents, V.A. Lomakhin, in 1993. What an honor it was to receive a special mention in the parade! We felt like war heroes marching in the parade on Red Square, with all eyes and cameras fixed on us. After marching, we took turns to stand guard by the tomb of the fallen soldier.

When we made it to the ninth grade (two years before graduation), methods of disaster preparation became more sophisticated. Weekly classes called "Early Military Training" ensured that both boys and girls became responsible fighters ready to defend ourselves and others. We had to wear khaki military shirts on the days we had class. Some students preferred to wear them every day out of pride for our big and mighty motherland. The training was led by a middle-aged former military official with a complicated last name, Skolozhabsky, and a much easier nickname, Gibbon, due to the heavy lower jaw and the overbite that made him look a bit like a monkey. He rehearsed nuclear and chemical war scenarios with us, analyzed types of chemical agents, explained what could be done to prevent or neutralize the toxic effect, reviewed regular weapons and, of course, helped us to put on gas masks. "Why are you laughing, girls?" he would ask with exaggerated graveness that only made us laugh harder. "Chuykova [in Soviet schools teachers called us by our last names], you will need these skills one day, and if you don't know how to do it properly, you will be sorry!"

The goal was to put on the gas mask in six seconds. Few could master the skill. We did not enjoy the feeling of rubber on the skin of our faces. We sweated profusely wearing them. And then we were assigned to refine our gas mask skills at home. My friend Lena, who now became less sensitive to the military training procedures, and I practiced the task while walking home from school. We actually enjoyed intimidating passers-by with our trunks and felt strange pride in being entrusted with such serious military equipment. At home, I kept practicing and impressing house guests and neighbors until I mastered the art and could impress Gibbon himself. He was a serious and comical figure at the same time, the comical effect hiding in his seriousness with which he stuck out his jaw talking about the subject matter which, in the early nineties, was quickly losing its menacing urgency. Or perhaps our teenagerly nonchalance made us laugh at his stories of military life and warnings of danger that made him appear stuck in the heat of the Cold War.

We knew we would most likely not put on gas masks, nor shoot Kalashnikov rifles. By the time we ripened for that perilous art in the last year of high school, our skepticism and insolence ripened as well. Perhaps exactly

Our "Early Military Training" teacher showing us the structure and function of the Kalashnikov rifle, 1992. I am in the center, at right. Larisa is beside me.

this attitude of insolent carelessness prevented me from memorizing the steps of the rifle assembly and preparation for shooting. All I can reconstruct from my shooting days was walking to the shooting range across the school square and lying down with rifles in our long winter coats (the place did not provide heating) for the right shooting position. Fire! Fire! All that followed appears in a blur, except for the pretty clear half-instinctive awareness of the fact that I never hit the target.

The nuclear danger did come, but not from our arch enemy. Ironically, it sneaked up us from the heart of our own dear motherland. It was ever more perfidious because of our naïve belief in the grandeur, safety and protection of our state. The authorities speculated on this belief cheating us into nonchalantly watching the fiery spectacle of the Chernobyl explosion in 1986 and into marching in May Day demonstrations just days after the release of deadly amounts of radiation into the Ukrainian and Byelorussian air. Our glasnost-minded government acquiesced to informing the public about the accident, but refrained from superfluous details about the extent of the damage. We had to grope our way through the screen of ignorance. People desperately checked with physicists and other specialists who could have at least some insight into nuclear science. Some physicists we knew assured us there was no danger—whether due to their own ignorance or out of fear of saying

Victory Day parade, 1984. Waiting for our turn to march, wearing our marine outfits. I am second from the right, the tall one, and the only one smiling. The unwritten Soviet photo-taking protocol dictated subjects refrain from smiling.

the truth, we can only guess. A good friend of my mom, however, who visited Chernobyl several times to help control the consequences, told her at once this disaster was a hundred times more powerful than Hiroshima.

To be on the safer side, we drank drops of iodine and covered our mouths with handkerchiefs on the way to school. We laughed away the danger as our young, naïve brains could not perceive the harm associated with the strange term new to most of us—radiation. A girl from Pripyat, the young town built especially for Chernobyl workers, came to our class for a month while her family looked for a place to relocate and she stayed with relatives in Yuzhny. The romantic aura of a heroine immediately surrounded her; everyone wanted to sit next to her and be her friend.

No one could have guessed that the peaceful energy so glorified by the Soviet slogans became a deadly weapon turned against the country's own innocent victims. In its twilight years, the empire dealt another fateful blow to its citizens who already endured too much inhuman suffering both from war enemies and its own peace-heralding leaders. The disaster and the grief that followed further corroded the faith of the people in the Soviet state machine and was one of the final straws that broke its back just a few years later.

The Victory Day parades in Yuzhny stopped around the same time our enthusiasm for military training and the grandeur of our country dwindled, in 1989. The new school was built, which took some space from the little old school square. Perhaps more important, the Soviet Union was heading towards its demise and our patriotic spirit started to lag in the face of an unstable future. The parades never came back to life, but Victory Day commemorations continue in Yuzhny and everywhere else in the former USSR. I cherish their memory when the whole town comes together to celebrate victory, sacrifice, memory and community.

Community and Town

The spirit of reliance on the community has held together the society of eastern Slavs since the beginnings of their state in Kievan Rus. In times of trouble or happiness, people knew they could seek help from each other, find a friendly ear for expressions of grief or good news, work and eat together, and, of course, live in the same house with generations of relatives. Reliance on worker solidarity also paved the way for the Socialist Revolution of 1917. Their masses helped realize the dreams of the poor, but crushed the comfortable reality of many innocent rich. Possessed by the desire for retribution and nudged by revolutionary leaders, the proletarian masses took away many estates from the aristocrats and converted them into orphanages for poor children, public hospitals or communal living quarters. At other times, blinded by fury, they simply destroyed or burned aristocratic nests as hateful symbols of bourgeois power.

After the revolution and still after World War II, when atrocious bombings destroyed so many buildings, many Soviet families lived in so-called communal flats due to a lack of residential space. My mom and grandparents shared an apartment with four other families; all of them had separate living rooms and bedrooms, but they shared one kitchen and bathroom. An equal amount of space was allotted for each family on the kitchen table, and each section held a kerosene-fueled stove. The kerosene would light up very quickly, making those stoves quite dangerous, but these arrangements afforded a bit of independence to each housewife.[1]

My mom does not recall any inconvenience or quarrels caused by the constant close contact with others. Instead, when she talks about her childhood in Orenburg, her face lights up with nostalgia for the days she calls the happiest of her life. The communal apartment promoted a lifelong friendship with people of diverse backgrounds who lived like one big family sharing holidays, joys, grief, household duties, weekend walks, visits to the theater, and much more.[2] When the family moved to Ukraine after Mom's high school graduation and built a house all for themselves, it seemed terribly lonely for

Sunday picnic with friends from the communal apartment at the Urals River, 1952. My mom is holding the accordion. My grandma is lying down.

her. Her nostalgia was relieved by letters that kept coming from her Orenburg friends almost every day for the next few years.

The communal spirit was also apparent in constant visits that friends, relatives and neighbors paid one another for no specific reason other than saying hello and lingering for an hour or two or longer. In the cities, people lived in a more isolated way, but in small towns like Yuzhny where I grew up, one never felt alone. It is true even nowadays when advances in technology bring lifestyle changes to all the remote corners of the world. We also owned an apartment in Kharkiv, the second largest city in Ukraine about twenty kilometers from Yuzhny, but we only stayed in it occasionally. My mom got it a year after I was born. She did not buy it—no one bought or sold apartments in the Soviet Union where private property practically did not exist. People were "awarded" apartments, completely free of charge, as merit for service at a pubic organization. This wonderful benefit had a tiny problem: You had to wait for your turn in a virtual line for a number of years, sometimes an entire lifetime. Some people got their reward for waiting only at a ripe age. In 1958, the Central Committee of the Communist Party allowed the formation of "living cooperatives" where people had to pay for their apartments, thus acquiring them much earlier and receiving a permanent right to them with no possibility of it being revoked. However, living cooperatives did not become too popular, for who would want to pay for an apartment if one could get it for free? My mom got lucky since Kharkiv State University built a few apartment buildings when she started working there, and this fact accelerated the distribution process. Mom got the apartment after only a few years of waiting, and all she had to pay was a monthly communal service fee of a very nominal seven rubles a month, which amounted to five percent of her salary.

However, when my parents got divorced, almost immediately after Mom got an apartment, my father claimed half of it, and she was forced to exchange it for two one-room flats.[3] One room was not spacious enough for my grandparents, my mom and myself, even taking into account my family's history of co-habitation, and we continued living in our house in Yuzhny. We used the Kharkiv apartment during the summer and occasional stays when Mom worked late. I loved the exotic feeling of the city's continuous hustle and bustle, crowds of rushing or strolling people everywhere, and ubiquitous cafes and shops. My mom and stepdad later exchanged their separate apartments for one three-room place in the center of the city, very close to their place of work, but by that time they had grown too fond of their snug suburban home and garden to move back to city life permanently. They continue to stay there only occasionally. Our new place in Kharkiv is wonderfully airy, convenient and full of light, but when I think of "a Kharkiv apartment," my memory invariably goes back to the crowded room on Crimean Street. Its tall ceilings and smell of lacquered furniture and Mom's perfume symbolized for me the prestige of city life, over which I hoped to reign one day.

It is our Yuzhny home, however, that personifies true community spirit, which I miss. It is Yuzhny where my kids prefer to stay when we visit Ukraine, thanks to stronger ties among people, the friends they easily make in the neighborhood, and the fun they have playing in the town stadium. They never get tired of the surprises presented through constant encounters with people we know or people who know us and in the number of spontaneous visits we experience in a single day. A neighbor might drop by whenever she notices our family having a meal or an evening tea under a terrace roof outside and join us for a few minutes or two hours. A friend comes over to say hi. The family doctor stops by to check up on us and stays for tea. Sometimes even the cell phone does not prevent a spontaneous visit, since the visitor leaves no time for finding an excuse if you are not in the mood for hospitality. The conversation may go somewhat like this:

> Hello, dear. Where are you?
> I just got home from work and I am getting ready to unwind.
> And I just got to your house and I am standing by your fence right now. Will you let me in for a cup of coffee?

A "cup of coffee" is more of a code for "a shot of vodka" accompanied by a hearty snack, without which no coffee would be complete. Such a conversation leaves the host no possibility for maneuvering out of hosting and culminates in a two- to four-hour reunion leaving both the host and the guest in no condition to continue their normal daily activities.

Before I head to Ukraine for my two-month-long vacation from my university teaching job, I dream of using it wisely and catching up on reading, writing and studying. When I plunge myself in the world of Ukrainian small-town life, I find all my time suddenly draining into a black hole. "When in Ukraine, do as Ukrainians do," I tell myself after making the same realization year after year: While I remain faithfully Ukrainian at heart, I am also well adapted to the efficient American lifestyle allowing minimal wasting of time. In Ukraine, I have to readjust and try not to get frustrated at the necessary activities of talking, eating and sitting around. When my parents are at home, every meal becomes a ritual where my aunt who lives across the street and an elderly neighbor, Aunt Nina, often join in ("Aunt" is a common unofficial form of address to all the older women one knows well, not only one's relatives). When we finish a three-course breakfast of eggs, sausage, sweet cottage cheese, salty regular cheese, caviar and honey, it is almost time to start cooking lunch, and so the routine continues.

In my childhood, when few families had phones and those lucky ones who did experienced constant breakdowns and bad connections, people dropped by constantly with a request to use the phone. They also used the occasion as an excuse to catch up on the latest news, explain the reason for the call, the history leading to it and analyze all the possible consequences. Pouring out their heart, they would also require your total attention and get offended if you tried to combine listening to the story of their lives with cooking dinner. Not all the visits were welcome. Even if they were, the visitors overstaying their welcome would almost urge you to ask if they had anywhere else to go or remind them that it was time to hit the dusty trail again. However, the social etiquette required the hostess to serve the visitor cookies, tea, or something more substantial if he happened to barge in during a meal. The same etiquette dictated the visitor refuse a couple of times, and the host keep insisting until the convinced guest indulged the treat with no further resistance. Not aware of the cultural differences, initially I followed this etiquette when someone offered me treats in the United States. I quickly learned not to refuse if I really wanted something. There were no second chances.

I remember some days when my grandma would not be able to accomplish a single thing the whole day because one person would leave, another would enter right on his heels, and the chain continued until nightfall. In many cases, though, a sudden ring of the doorbell held a promise, a mystery—not of a solicitor asking if you needed a new roof, but of a surprise visit from a dear friend, possibly from afar, whom one had not seen for a very long time. In winter, when I sat at my desk next to the window, the sound of the visitor's steps on the snow enhanced the sensation of mystery and happy anticipation of company. Such was a memorable ring of the doorbell one gloomy winter afternoon when I, about thirteen years old, was at home alone with Grandma. An unfamiliar voice from the hallway made my grandma first stumble with hesitation and then cry with delight. It was my mom's childhood friend from Orenburg, one of the kids who had lived in the communal apartment, now a tall and well-built man who happened to be in Kharkiv for a business trip. He found our house in Yuzhny by the mailing address and by asking people on the street. My family had not seen him for twenty years. That evening, filled with recollections and laughter, made it seem like they continued living next to each other all those years.

The community spirit was somewhat damaged during the Stalin years when the government encouraged spying on neighbors and even on one's own family under the constant suspicion of possible treason. In spite of this, it could not disappear completely, especially in small towns, where everybody knew everybody and remembered the entire history of the oldest residents, frequently the first settlers of the place. When my grandma was very young, somebody denounced her parents as potential "kulaks" (well-to-do peasants considered enemies of the people, although they usually acquired their wealth thanks to hard work). When the family faced the distinct possibility of deportation to Siberia, a well-wisher warned them, and they were able to escape in time.

The town of Yuzhny (or *Pivdenne* in Ukrainian, translated into English as "Southern"), where my grandparents' families settled in the early 20th century, was built for railroad workers. The railroad was called "Southern," and therefore the town was named in the same way. The railroad was located at the bottom of the hill where lay the center of the town. Going down to catch an electric train to Kharkiv, we could hardly see the station behind tall reeds and voluptuous crowns of trees in summer and behind caps of snow in winter. In spring, the station literally drowned in marshes, swollen by waters of the melting snows running down the hills in bubbling and happy rivulets. I savor the happy memories of going down to the station in any weather, looking forward to tasting life in the exciting big city. In my childhood, visits to the city were not so frequent—only for the occasions of visiting the circus, going to a theater or taking fun rides at Gorky Park. For my mom, who moved to the underdeveloped Yuzhny in her youth, the station served as a reminder of being shoved into the province while she longed for the hustle and bustle of the city. Numerous times she told me of her formal white shoes being stuck in the fall mud by the station. She had to wipe them with a tiny napkin to restore some of their glory before resuming the trip to Kharkiv.

Most Yuzhny residents worked in Kharkiv and took a thirty-minute electric train ride there and back. Living on top of the hill made for a steep

Mom in front of Kharkiv State University where she was a student, and later a professor of English, 1965.

and strenuous walk back home from the train station. The regular perpendicular network of Yuzhny streets and their numbering system resembled that of American cities. Streets that ran parallel to the railroad line had regular names (such as Komsomol, Lenin, Marx, some other revolutionary hero, October, and so on), but people referred to them more frequently as "the 1st," "the 2nd," "the 3rd," and so on. The numbers increased as the streets ascended. Perpendicular streets were also named "the 1st," "the 2nd," "the 3rd," but the specifier "perpendicular" was added to avoid confusion.

The fact that we could compare Yuzhny to New York was one reason for us to take pride in our small town. There were others. For example, the belief that a lush cherry orchard on the outskirts of the city used to belong to the aristocratic Alfyorov family inspired the writer Anton Chekhov to write the eponymous play. Chekhov was known to spend his vacation near Yuzhny and he mentions Kharkiv in that very play as the destination the family travels to after the sale of their estate. Another interesting fact about Yuzhny is that it is the hometown of Yuri Knorosov. Not many people (in the Soviet Union or in the United States) have heard about this humble ethnographer who played a pivotal role in deciphering the Mayan script without visiting the land of this great civilization. "I am an office worker," he said. "In order to work with ancient texts, you do not have to climb the pyramids." A memorial plaque dedicated to Knorosov hangs in the hall of our school, and two monuments to him have been erected in Cancun, Mexico. On a recent tour to Chichen Itzá, our guide's lecture explained Knorosov's contribution to humanity.

Besides these important claims to fame, Yuzhny is simply a picturesque place: lush orchards and flowers of all the colors of the rainbow behind fences, more flower beds and benches in front of the fences where old babushkas[4] used to congregate and analyze the appearance and history of every passer-by. A central park (which my grandpa helped plant decades ago) sits on the highest point of the hill at the heart of our town. Two ponds on the other side of the hill are encircled by a ring of weeping willows which throw their brushy reflections on the calm waters. On one side of the pond, there was a grove of birches—these bright northern trees letting in plenty of sunlight through their tiny leaves and creating their own light by their white thin bark. My mom and I loved to come to that grove even when the pond became abandoned and dirty when the municipality no longer had the means to take care of it after the fall of the Soviet Union. We would sit on the slope at sunset and watch the stillness of the water and the darkening blue forest on the opposite bank. We would conjure up the images of a different, lively pond just a few years back.

In my childhood, members of our community and numerous vacationers came here to swim, laugh, sing, barbeque, jump into the water Tarzan-style from a "tarzanka"—a type of swing tied to the branch hanging over the bank—and glide along the banks in boats rented from a nearby station. According to a romantic Yuzhny tradition, high school students concluded their graduation parties by walking to the pond to see the sunrise. The boat station fell quickly into a decrepit state when the Soviet Union broke down and never came back to life. A few wooden planks still dangle in the water as a souvenir of those days. The pond became privatized, or, as we used to say, "grabbatized"—annexed by the newly rich who had typically accumulated their wealth by not very honest means, profiting from purchases of decaying state property and offering bribes to the new municipal government that helped them get around the legal ways of registering the purchase.

The government had no right to sell the state property, but such was the kleptocratic nature of the economy in the newly-independent states that there was no law that could rule over the new owners of the land, the rich and the powerful. On the banks where we used to walk, they built huge mansions with tennis courts and swimming pools barely distinguishable through the few chinks in six-foot-tall brick fences guarded by fierce dogs. Residents of the entire street leading to the pond were resettled in order to provide space for the houses of nouveau rich "New Russians" or "New Ukrainians," as they came to be called. They offered people monetary compensation, but no option of staying in their old houses. These mansions became a sore sight and topic for the residents of the town, who could hardly access their pond since in many places "No Entrance" signs and bars prevented passage to the previously public beaches.

My grandparents saw those beaches become the party spot of the town in the first part of the 20th century—in photos, they are young, happy and wrapped in coats and scarves, in handmade sleds going downhill by the banks still devoid of any vegetation (the trees were planted in the fifties). The pond transformed itself into a skating rink during winter. In summer photos, my grandparents and their friends look equally happy and busy with picnics, songs and games. In one photo, they pose on a tall watchtower later destroyed during the war and never reconstructed. They recalled Yuzhny with hardly any streets or fences, as a mixed forest/field providing vast opportunities for my grandpa's mischief. Once as a child he and his buddies lifted the outhouse standing in the backyard of an evil-tempered neighbor and carried it off to the other neighbor's backyard. On another occasion, he and a friend climbed into an unsupervised steam engine and somehow managed to start it. When the engine began to move and they realized they didn't know how to stop it, they became a bit nervous. Fortunately, they found a way to drive it into a dead end and left it there.

Sledding on the pond in the winter of 1940. My grandma is on the sled at the right, in the front with her legs stretched out.

Born in 1914, when Russia entered the First World War, and orphaned at the age of four, grandpa never spoke of his origins. Perhaps he did not know. Perhaps he was afraid. In those terrible years, people tended to conceal a privileged background, which could bring a terrible fate not only upon themselves, but upon their own children, who could be refused entry to the universities in the best case or imprisonment, torture, and death in the worst. Some were forced to change family names or renounce their parents, declaring that the motherland was their true mother and Lenin their true father. Many family histories were lost forever. Grandpa's brothers and sisters inherited a vast library from their parents—an indication that he came from a well-educated family. Left alone, starting from an early age he had to work for other people. He often endured their abuses for not properly tending to the flock of geese or disregarded his duties by mingling in a game with other kids.

Love of learning and discipline guided grandpa throughout his life: In those times, full of obstacles and limitations, he became a self-made man. He could not attend school but a teacher living nearby helped him prepare for the exams covering the material of the first three years of school. He dreamt of becoming a geography teacher but could not afford the luxury of this option when the USSR faced a distinct prospect of war with Germany. Instead, he conquered many other nearly insurmountable heights. After graduation from high school, he was drawn into obligatory military service. His excellent performance and discipline helped him become selected for study in the infantry military college in Odessa and later for pilot school in Orenburg. Grandpa eventually became an instructor at that school, but in spite of his success he was never able to fly beyond the Iron Curtain and realize his dreams of traveling to faraway places.

Hardships and pressure had not killed grandpa's zest for life and endless humor—he was the life of the party and continued playing pranks on family and friends until an advanced age. In the middle of some celebration, he would sneak away to a neighboring apartment and use their phone to call one of his friends, celebrating at his family's home. "What are you doing?" he would ask in a severe and fierce tone. "Have you forgotten?" "Forgotten what?" the half-drunken friend would ask in a trembling voice, suddenly panicked and not recognizing grandpa's voice. "Have you forgotten that you have to be at your workplace right now?" Grandpa would continue bullying the friend in this manner until the guests finally realized what was going on. On another occasion, during a May Day demonstration, he stepped aside and stared intently into the rows concluding the march, arousing his friends' curiosity. "What are you looking at?" they inquired. "He's winking!" he observed, ambiguously, continuing to gaze into the crowd. Another friend with a stern expression on his face chimed in. "Yes, indeed he is blinking."

Soldiers playing chess, probably around 1934 or 1935. My grandpa is on the left.

After much impatient nudging, grandpa finally revealed to the others the identity of the naughty object of his attention: "Karl Marx on the slogan is blinking!" During my husband's first visit to Ukraine, my eighty-something-year-old grandpa even played jokes on him—one morning instructing him to "Get up!" in clear English. On another occasion, my husband caught a small fish in our pond which he proudly brought home to cook. Upon seeing this tiny bounty, grandpa quipped, "I'll have to cut its head with an ax!"

In my childhood, the hillside leading to Yuzhny ponds was occupied by two vacation centers and eight Pioneer camps sponsored by various Kharkiv factories. Children of factory workers, other Pioneers from all over the Soviet Union and, some people said, even visitors from Cuba and the German Democratic Republic played, swam, practiced sports, watched movies in the open-air theater, read and practiced knitting, sowing, wood-cutting and building projects in multiple supervised activity centers. All over town we could hear the happy sounds of the Pioneer horn announcing wake-up and meal times. At night, we could hear the music from their dance parties and would feel jealous of their (relative) freedom. We feel nostalgic about those summer sounds and bustling centers, most of which fell into complete ruin. Mom and I ventured into their territory a couple of times since they closed. Dismal terror seized us and brought back memories of post-war destruction to my mom: piles of bricks from ruined walls, the best preserved already stolen, dark holes in place of windows, sports bars rusting away, overgrown trees and grass taking over the benches of the movies theaters. On the other side of the pond, we contemplated the big carcass of the metal star with fire—a Pioneer symbol—rusting away and getting swallowed up by the bushes until one year we could not see it any longer. The only survivor of the post–Soviet chaos was one of the vacation homes, privatized by some beer company and converted into an exclusive center for the select rich. We can no longer see behind its polished tall fences, and all we hear from the former dance grounds where the Yuzhny youth mixed with the vacation crowd is silence.

A stroke of luck supported by the enthusiasm of the town residents finally fell on our beloved pond in 2013. The municipality raised money to clean the pond after many years of abandonment and brought sand to make a new beach. Local volunteers called on the community to clean up the banks, set up a volleyball court and build changing rooms. The pond now once again attracts the whole town in summer and resembles the happy place of my childhood.

In my childhood and youth, October Street leading from the train station up towards the town center was the liveliest street in town as a human river poured out of the electric trains and headed home, gradually splitting into fast and leisurely walkers who then branched out onto side streets. I loved being part of this stream—it was second best to the demonstrations that I never managed to experience firsthand. The same love of community bred the Yuzhny tradition of using the same two train cars when taking a train to work and back. It made it easier to find friends and "electric train acquaintances," release professional stress in happy chatter, find company for a game of cards and, of course, discover new romantic companions. Naturally, you could gain them by trying different train cars as well—such maneuvers enlarged your romantic horizons. Thirty minutes provided plenty of opportunities for flirting, joking, laughing, getting to know each other and scheduling dates.

If the train ride did not offer any opportunities for socialization, you could use the time wisely and do your homework or read. Getting out a book could be a trick if you wanted to avoid talking to an undesirable companion. One risk of going alone, especially on dark winter nights, was dozing off and missing your stop. It happened a few times to my grandpa and stepdad who found themselves in remote corners of the Kharkiv region and had to wait for trains in the opposite direction, which did not come frequently at night. If they were lucky and missed only one stop, they opted for a brisk walk home. Taxis did not reach our rural parts until recently when affordable Uber-type services spread out into the most distant parts of our civilization.

The train ride, which may seem to a busy American like an annoying inconvenience and waste of time, afforded us a daily dosage of entertainment and stress relief, that is, unless we missed the train or it was canceled. Then we braced ourselves for a twenty- to sixty-minute waiting time and looked for more—hopefully agreeable—acquaintances. Once the train arrived, we also had to bear the additional inconvenience of a cozy squeeze with fellow travelers. In winter, hanging on one foot between the other bodies with hands stretched out in different directions was a bit cumbersome. In summer, it was a bit nasty as open windows provided the best and the only source of air conditioning. Because of the universal terror Soviet citizens had of drafts supposedly causing colds, this source of comfort was also frequently cut off. Even to this day an attempt to open a bus window on a hot summer day will be met with a directive to close it by a middle-aged woman.

Closer to the breakup of the USSR, train cancelations became more frequent. One day, so many trains were canceled that two friends and I opted for the next available one (and probably the only one in the following couple of hours), which took us to a completely different station. I cannot remember if we found another mode of transportation or walked back but I surely remember playing many card games, laughing and thoroughly enjoying ourselves on that journey that took a good part of our day. Nowadays, a lot more people own cars and use them for daily transportation. Many others use buses, which get to the city faster and stop at many points in town. Many others, however, turn back to electric trains because of frequent bus breakdowns and extremely crowdy conditions which do now favor reading or talking. Although it was not the fastest, nor the most convenient method of transportation, I miss electric trains. They made me feel part of the big whole, a grain of sand among many others sharing their lives with me for a small part of the day, and the trains never let me feel alone.

True need of companionship also immediately brought strangers together in long-distance train journeys where people traveled in closed or open-door compartments of four people (two sleeping on lower berths and two on upper). A small table between the berths immediately united travelers who shared their sausages, cheese, roast chicken, cutlets, pies, and, of course, vodka. A night of communion sprinkled with vodka and frequent songs with guitar accompaniment could result in life-long friendships or, at the very least, the sharing of life stories. On one trip, after a long chat with a companion, we discovered that he was a neighbor of one of my English professors and a son of the lady with whom my mom toured Hungary twenty years earlier. Recently, my family traveled in an open compartment since all of the private ones were sold out. A neighbor from the side berth, just across from us, unnerved my husband with intense continuous staring. Robert feared he pondered the possibility of stealing our stuff. I finally persuaded him the guy was simply looking for companionship or perhaps satisfying his curiosity at encountering foreign-language speakers, still not frequently seen in that part of the world.

Slowly improving living standards have made car ownership possible for many more people in recent years. Cars have also helped eliminate physical and emotional human touch, without which a ride to work becomes a simple necessity and not a celebration of community spirit. Cell phones and the Internet have also contributed to the transformation of life in the former Soviet Union, especially in the cities where even close neighbors do not know or hardly greet each other. The impersonal breath of technology has also contaminated life in smaller towns like Yuzhny where old babushkas no longer patrol the streets guarding local morals and casting expressive, disapproving glances at the girls whose skirts they deemed too short. We used to call the babushkas "our local militia" or "our X-ray" due to their penetrating stare. They would immediately spread the word around the neighborhood if they happened to notice anything wrong. Such violations of the local order could include a young girl walking hand in hand with a new boyfriend or, God forbid, committing a terrible moral crime like kissing under a tree. The girl's parents or grandparents would be notified with miraculous pre-cell phone speed even before she reached the door of her family home. Somehow our feministic society harbored paradoxical gender prejudices, as girls were expected to be the guards of high morality while boys got away with holding hands, embracing or kissing, with no harm to their reputation.

Most of those old-timers whose families lived on our street for generations and felt almost like family have passed away and their children have sold their family estates. The children of new residents often prefer videogames to playing outside, and their laughter and screams no longer rule the streets like ours did thirty years ago. But the community spirit has not died away: Local shop assistants know all their customers and greet us happily when we come back to pick up groceries after a year's absence. Many of my classmates still live in their childhood homes and their kids go to the same school we went to. Our neighbors and friends share with us their harvest of cucumbers, zucchini, tomatoes and apricots. We have a door in the wire fence between our front yard and the yard of our closest neighbors to facilitate communication and daily visits for salt, bread, eggs or for chatting and sharing a meal. We also share pancakes, pies, doughnuts or even portions of soup whenever something comes out particularly well. The doorbell rings, and we find aunt Valya or aunt Sveta standing there with a plate of pies or freshly made soup to treat us. As it is not proper to return an empty plate, we fill it with our own delicacy once we make something tasty—thus we take turns treating each other. When my mom broke both of her hands in one unfortunate accident, the neighboring ladies took her under their constant care. They stopped by several times per day to bring her food, warm it up, help her change and do anything else she needed.

Nighttime is most popular for "posidelki," a word formed from the verb "to sit," which implies prolonged sitting around and talking. Our roofed patio provides a hospitable spot which attracts neighbors and friends, sometimes until two in the morning. On some such occasions, we have had spontaneous parties with fifteen or more people. During our visits to Ukraine, the number of visitors progressively increases as the date of our departure approaches. When the sad day arrives, relatives, neighbors and friends come to say goodbye, sometimes with pies, cases of beer or vodka, and always with warm hugs that make us realize they truly care. They stand in front of our house, waving till the taxi leaves, bringing tears to my eyes. Before taxis made it to Yuzhny and we used to have to take the electric train to get to the city, they would accompany us to the station, helping us with the luggage and bringing champagne for a "pososhok," a final good-luck toast.

When I go to a local supermarket, library, beauty salon or pharmacy, I run into people I have known since childhood. It would be sacrilegious not to exchange a few warm greetings and a bit of news with them. In summer, the local pond becomes the main hangout, attracting kids and adults who spend leisurely afternoons swimming and sunbathing or simply drive by for a quick dip between household chores. On the positive side, sometimes

Family and friends accompanying us to the electric train station before our departure to the United States after vacation in Ukraine, August 1999. Back row, from the left: Robert, Vitalik (our kum), Uncle Vova, my stepdad Oleg, Aunt Galya (Mama Galya), Aunt Katya, Grisha and Valera (my schoolmates). Front row, from the left: Olga (our kuma), me, Mom, Misha (the former school hooligan), Valera's daughter Ksusha and wife Sveta.

someone offers us a ride and we avoid a three-kilometer uphill walk home. On the negative side, the book I usually bring to the beach in the hopes of catching a few moments of calm always seems to stay unopened.

Since everybody knows the summary of everybody else's personal life, I catch up on residents' marriages, divorces and deaths. Social media has reinforced the informational saturation even further, to the point that people know each other's recent pastimes and can guess each other's plans. "You must be going to Tanya's birthday party!" a neighbor comments upon seeing me, dressed up, heading indeed to my friend Tanya's place, as her birthday was earlier announced on Facebook. "I saw you had a great time in London," another acquaintance who apparently has seen our recent photos offers. Most residents know that I live in the United States, and few have means to travel there. Thus, I am inundated with the same questions time and again: Do I live in a house or an apartment? How big is my house? What is the weather like? How large is my backyard and what grows there? How much does the milk and meat cost? How much money do I make per month? How much do I pay in taxes and insurance? How much does gas cost? How much does the heating cost in winter? Since my home economic skills have always been very poor and I gratefully let my husband manage our finances, I disappoint people with my lack of pragmatism and use it as an excuse to continue my interrupted itinerary.

I try to snatch brief leisurely moments for reading in between sitting, chatting, eating and housework, which may take much longer than in the United States due to temporary water or electricity outages. I realize how important it is to relax and talk to friends and relatives I don't see for most of the year and look back at those moments with nostalgia during my hectic life in the United States. At the same time, I cannot help feeling some guilt for the loss of my productive potential in this slow-paced routine that used to be my reality. When I travel to Ukraine, it is as if I fall out of one life and jump into another. Both of them enrich me and sadden me in a strange way: Coming back to the place of my childhood, I find people who have grown older continuing the same routine forever, and I see many places I loved fall into ruin. As the retro FM radio station plays music from my adolescence, I relive the excitement of my young dreams and get a vague feeling of anxiety. Perhaps I realize that I am growing older as well.

Yuzhny's effective network of human relations maintains the informal homegrown economy with a personal touch. One can find a home-based business for any need, and the provider will deliver the service at no cost and treat you to a bit of conversation and gossip to boot. A cobbler passing by your house will pick up your shoes in need of fixing and deliver them when they are ready—a simple phone call settles the matter. A milkman, the profession now defunct in most countries, still brings us fresh milk—although my husband, accustomed to American ultra-pasteurized products, claims it has a tangy taste and too much fat. A personal beautician will come at the agreed time to pluck and paint your eyebrows. A hairdresser comes to aunt Galya's place to cut her hair since she often does not feel well enough to go out. If your car needs a new part, give a call to a neighbor working in auto parts, and he will deliver it on his way home from work.

Once, as I was walking to the playground with the kids, a car slowed down and a guy looking vaguely (but not exactly) familiar leaned out. "Will you be taking the eggs?" he asked quite unexpectedly. Puzzled but reluctant to offend him, I said, "Yes," just in case. "Okay, I will bring them in half an hour." It took me about ten minutes and a phone call to my mom to figure out that the gentleman was the husband of a lady who was selling us the eggs from their hens. In a similar way, we get deliveries of sausages and cheeses, chicken and rabbit, fruit and dumplings. In August we get fresh honey, sometimes with honeycombs, produced by bees that people cultivate in special places called "paseka," located in flowery, ecologically clean meadows suitable for honey production. On summer mornings, we also discover surprise gifts of fruit, vegetables or other produce on our porch—caring neighbors and friends share their bounty with us, less industrious and agriculturally dexterous, without disturbing our slumbers.

Several local mani-pedi artists compete with each other—but sufficient demand ensures enough nail work for all. Several unofficial taxi drivers can come at any time to take us to our desired destination. Several teachers specializing in different subjects can tutor my children in need of intellectual stimulation. A highly efficient dentist—also my friend and "kuma"—can even tend to me at midnight and then drive me home if I do not find myself in the adequate state to walk after the treatment. When we wait for the bus to or from Kharkiv, several cars pass by and offer us a ride—the Western prejudiced attitude towards hitchhiking has not reached these parts, and this service is one of the most successful of all. Sick and tired of overfilled buses careening wildly at every turn, people happily hop into cars to pay a fee established by silent agreement by the town residents—sixteen hrivna versus an official bus fee of fifteen (equaling sixty cents versus the official fare of fifty). A pair of pants in Ukraine will have a much longer lifetime thanks to affordable tailor shops where skillful masters will replace a zipper, widen the waist or cover up a small hole.

The biggest demand hits the construction business—things frequently break or fall apart in the houses built thirty or forty years ago or in the new houses hastily built. Construction or repair workers who usually train themselves by constant practice and by watching YouTube videos realize their worth and take advantage. For almost a year my mom has been interchangeably pleading with and threatening one of them, a guy named Sasha. He fixed the roof of her house a few years ago, but still needs to come back and finish the installation of gutters, for which she had already paid him. It is customary for construction workers to abandon their projects halfway and never return if they suddenly discover a more financially promising offer of work. Sasha owes work to at least a couple of other people we know, but dedicates all of his efforts to a big house in need of remodeling recently bought by an oligarch.

Thanks to this highly developed customer service system, we accumulate new acquaintances and share tips about other services or news of the town. When I take a bus from Yuzhny to Kharkiv, I am likely to meet another acquaintance and again it would be improper (or indecent, according to the Russian-Ukrainian turn of the phrase) not to dedicate part of or the whole thirty-minute journey to talking. Decency is a very important concept in the Slavic world, and the word "decent" does not only refer to the moral code of behavior, but also to appropriate social norms and respectful attitude towards others. Taking out a book I packed in hopes of reading during the ride and ignoring the old acquaintance would be indecent. I obligingly chat away while abandoning the reading material for better moments to come. Sometimes I seize some such moments at my kids' tennis class until their instructor decides to join me for a friendly chat.

While the tradition of calling people simply to chat has become practically extinct in the United States, it is well and alive in Ukraine where chatting is a national sport. In the United States, wishing people a happy birthday also has become reduced to maximum efficiency—people are content to receive a Facebook greeting or a text message. Sometimes these messages abbreviate the greeting to a simple and efficient "HBD." Such a message will be taken as more of an insult in Ukraine where people expect a phone call or a visit. The protocol also dictates that a brief greeting must include the expression of best wishes for good health, good fortune, vast knowledge, a springtime mood and a clear, peaceful sky above the head of the birthday person and his relatives. A leisurely talk of no less than twenty minutes covering the most recent (or not so recent) developments in each other's lives and the lives of one's relatives is more appropriate, especially if the talkers have not seen each other for more than a week. My kids' guitar teacher interrupts her lesson every time a phone rings to listen to birthday greetings or other important news. My mom tells me that on her birthday, her three phones (two mobiles operated by different carriers and a landline) do not stop ringing. She spends practically the whole day talking. This is not so bad, as all the attention assures her of being surrounded by love and care, but it is not so easy for planning the day's activities.

Everyday life in Yuzhny does not foster ideal conditions for focusing on a research project or private family time. Yet, I am happy that the coldness of technology has not supplanted human communication here. I feel life's crazy rhythm slow down, and my mind takes a break from constant racing. My spirit and soul renew themselves in the healing company of sympathetic and cheerful people always ready to come for help, for tears or for laughter. Most important, I feel that my beloved town has managed to preserve its community spirit and has remained the same friendly, gossipy and familiar place of my childhood.

School Fears

I was afraid of school when I began the first grade. I felt like I was entering a zoo, squeezed in a tight space between the dark hallways of a seventy-five-year-old building, with classrooms on both sides preventing any sunlight from seeping through. I don't remember the electricity ever being on—the antique structure probably did not foresee it. Instead, wild beasts aged seven to seventeen lit up the place with their energy before and between forty-five-minute-long lessons, jumping, racing, pushing and tackling each other and anyone who got in their way. No "bubble in your mouth," "Talk in your inside voice," or "Walk in a line" admonitions so efficient in American schools could be remotely successful here—I can imagine the mirth of my fellow students had they heard similar nonsense. Nothing short of a roar would stop them; strong voices must have been the number one requirement in the job description of Soviet teachers and top administrators.

Our educational system combined elementary, middle and high school levels, and students from grades one through ten studied together in one building. Newer school buildings housed younger and older kids on different floors or in different wings, but our vintage building had no such capacity. To alleviate the stress on the building and the teachers, our student population was divided into two shifts: the first half attended lessons from eight in the morning until one or two in the afternoon, and the second one came in from one p.m. through seven at night. The youngest kids from the first two grades were grouped, for some inexplicable reason, in the first shift together with the oldest kids from the last three grades. Those high-schoolers seemed incredibly grown up, strong and menacing as they stampeded along the tall and scary hallways in wild throngs, smashing everything and everyone in their path. Some older guys were fond of terrorizing young and vulnerable victims easily targeted for mockery and abuse. I don't think I ever fell in the ranks of the victims myself, but I vividly recall the crazy fear I felt at the sight of those brawny teenage bullies.

School Fears

First grade class picture, with our old school building in the background, 1982. I am in the top row in the middle. My friend Lena who had a panic attack after the presentation of a nuclear war scenario is top right. Serezha (Borya), chased by the math teacher Yelena Aleksandrovna, is fourth from the left in the middle row.

Sometimes, when a teacher had to leave the classroom for a short while, she would pick one of the older bullies named Vasya to sit in and proctor our work. Such supervision was essential since the moment the teacher left the classroom, rampant chaos started to reign. Boys chased each other around the classroom, jumping over the desks and pulling girls' braids; girls yelled at them and vainly tried to restore order; both boys and girls hit each other with textbooks, schoolbags and other objects of considerable weight; and only lonely figures tried to catch a moment in the craziness to review their lessons. Vasya's "proctoring" entailed administering a couple of clips on the back of the head to the most inveterate hooligans, and this example would serve to calm the others. Thus he brought quick and efficient results where even the most control-eager girls and teachers often failed.

One morning during the first fall in school my fear of high-schoolers reached its peak. We had to leave our regular classroom to go to PE, and high-schoolers occupied it during that hour due to the lack of space in the building.

The kids that were frequently sick could get a medical note to be excused from PE (a subject that sprouted another significant cause of terror in my early school years), and I was among the frequent possessors of such a document. Since I was an extremely shy and indecisive child, my mom or grandma, both of whom were well aware of my fears, would come to pick me up and take me for a walk until the next class. One fateful morning, my mom was running slightly late and my teacher forgot to watch me before her arrival. My childish mind, not allowing any room for excuse or error, led me to pack my things and venture on a walk home alone (something I would not normally do), crying bitterly all the way, deploring my fate of an abandoned creature. My grandma, my rock and the foundation of the family, welcomed and consoled me before taking me back to school. There we met my mom and my homeroom teacher who by that time looked for me everywhere in deep anxiety. The reunion finished my misery with the happy relief and realization that, at least that one time, I employed my own solution to avoid an older bully's threat.

Physical education invariably makes the top of the favorite classes list for my American grown kids and their friends. I wanted to escape it at all costs. One obvious reason was my lack of athletic brilliance or, for that matter, any potential. The other, more significant reason was that PE teachers had a habit of yelling at those of us who were not good at their subject. To be more precise, all the teachers were guilty of such a propensity. Many a lazy and disinterested kid got a verbal slap for failing to answer a question when the teacher called on him (the gender stereotypes usually prescribed the lazy and rebellious behavior to boys), or for fooling around, or trying to attract a classmate's attention. In most subjects, I was a quick-witted, advanced and diligent student never neglecting homework or attracting the teachers' ire. However, my awkwardness, lack of coordination and terror of guided physical activities combined to create my vulnerability and inhibited me from any degree of success in PE classes.

The fact that the teacher was male, stern and seemingly immune to human weaknesses made matters worse. Aleksei Afanasyevich rarely smiled, spoke in a tense voice, and pronounced words in a funny and stilted way, emphasizing and drawing out his "o"s—he was from the Volga region and spoke with an accent not common to our ear. "Otsenka—Odin!" (Grade equals one!)[1] he would say to the disrespectful or negligent boys not following his instructions and raise his index finger to underscore the deplorable fact in case anyone was in doubt. Later I realized that he was simply too engaged in his subject and too focused on making us fit and successful athletes. He organized a PE club which took place after the end of our second-shift classes, around 7 p.m., where we could sharpen our skills. I doubt he got reimbursed for this extracurricular activity. He pushed us to run faster and jump further not realizing that it was not a feasible goal for all.

Our PE lessons did not include dodgeball, basketball, knockout or any other games that make the subject so enjoyable for American kids. Instead, we were expected to approach the subject with the seriousness required of future Soviet athletes. We were supposed to pass the required minimum of jumps, cross kilometers, push-ups and crunches. A select few could cope, the rest suffered silently. Those who demonstrated extraordinary results and resilience were recommended to go to special "sports schools." Often these were boarding schools or regular schools, where kids, undergoing endless intense training, severe schedules and many sacrifices, were cultivated into future champions and Olympic participants. My mom was good at figure-skating and was selected for lessons at the sports school where she went after her regular classes to skate for four to five hours a day, sometimes in snowy, windy weather with temperatures of -10 degrees Fahrenheit.

In regular schools, they did not expect much, but still challenged us to climb rope, compete in track and the long jump, and master basic gymnastic skills like front- and back-rolls and balancing ourselves on bars. Those balancing acts terrified me most with vivid images of awkward falling—a few of us fell or were close to falling. Despite the fact that I was tall, thin, and more or less flexible, there was absolutely no PE activity in which I excelled except for sledding or biking, which did not make the required PE activities list. My arms grew increasingly weak as I pulled myself up the rope. I kept stepping on the line when long jumping. I felt vague pains in my side when running which made me consider the possibility of appendicitis or liver damage. I thought of breaking my neck when forced to do front rolls—I practiced them at home with grandpa's help but never lost the fear, although I slightly improved my rolling skills. I felt dizzy and panicky as I climbed the bars—before even trying to balance myself.

The exercise that crowned my fears employed a gym tool called "a goat" (the official English name might be "a horse," but we had a different tool called "horse"). Professional gymnasts use it as a prop for jumping, and I have never seen it in American school gyms. If you did not support yourself properly on its two handles when trying to jump over it, you had a high chance of hurting yourself. However, supporting myself properly when also trying to run and accelerate before jumping was almost impossible (at least, for me) without adequate practice and training. The effort that went into acceleration would leave me no time, coordination or strength for getting a good grip on the handles, lifting myself high into the air and accomplishing a successful jump over the long body of the hateful goat.

Students took turns jumping, or trying to jump, with the rest of the class watching. I would wait for my turn with increased anxiety, which did not help my concentration, and finish the torture with pain and resolve that I would not return to the school gym. Fortunately, my mom, who always did all she could to shield my childhood from outer world tempests, agreed that I endured enough physical training in strenuous circumstances and procured a doctor's note to excuse me from PE. Thus, she saved me from suffering and disgrace for a considerable part of my school career. I often did some classroom duties to help the teacher to compensate for my physical inactivity, but I did not mind—especially since there would be another girl or two with a similar note who shared my plight.

In winter, Alexei Afanasyevich would take us skiing around the park adjacent to the school. With frosty weather and firmly packed snow, skiing provided an energizing and entertaining relief from school routine. The fun became less intense when the snow started to melt and convert into gray and mushy slush, which stuck to our skis and made us feel like prisoners with our feet chained to heavy weights. We struggled and pretended to ski with streamlets bubbling happily along our path. The contrast between the spring-like weather and winter sport made our aspect particularly pathetic to passers-by and sank our mood deeper. After returning to class, we reclined at our desks with real or alleged pain in some part of our bodies and took turns confessing it to the teacher with a Dostoevskian pride in our suffering. I cannot remember how much I truly suffered, but I am almost certain that we did not hesitate to take advantage of this misadventure to turn ourselves into victims, solicit the teacher's compassion and waste a good part of the next lesson.

Since my unlucky experience with PE, I did not seriously consider vigorous physical activity for a long time—until finally realizing its value for health in my late twenties. My relations with American fitness instructors were much smoother, and since then I have mastered and enjoyed yoga, step, Zumba, kickboxing, core strengthening and more. I go to the gym at least twice a week, and my mom is amazed at how athletic and coordinated I have become since the factor of obligation was removed from the sphere of physical activity. Nonetheless, I still shudder at the recollection of the goat and the bars although I think of Alexei Afanasyevich with a lot more fondness than I felt in my school days. I know he was sincere and earnest in his struggle to make us healthy and athletic.

My next fear encompassed all the school personnel in general and teachers in particular. Inspiration of fear must have been an integral part of educational departments' curriculum, and many Soviet instructors were extremely good at it. The school program itself was designed with the purpose of instilling discipline and fear. A minimal aberration from the prescribed rules could involve public shame and punishment, such as scolding the victim on the school radio announcements or picking him out from the group of his schoolmates and analyzing his crime in front of everyone. "Hey, you, in the green pants!" heralds the thunderous voice of our principal through the depths of my memory, portending trouble to some unfortunate rascal. Being extremely shy and doing my best not to stand out from the crowd due to either blunder or accomplishment, I hated the thought of finding myself in those green pants—even if trouble was far away from my mind.

Even the janitors inspired fear. I remember a troupe of gray-haired "babushkas" in blue uniform robes and red and white kerchiefs over their hair, violently rubbing the floors with rags of an undefinable color twisted around a mop stick. They dipped those rags in buckets of murky-looking water and splashed it around, rubbing the same spot over and over again. If we carelessly stepped on the spot they had just cleaned in this manner, it spurred their fury. Some of them were actually sweet, but tiny and gaunt Tetya Dusya overshadowed their images in my memory with her menacing and frowning look of a warrior ready for battle. If her eyes fell on a child who, as she reckoned, was breaking the order in some way or interfering in her cleaning process, she would raise her mop like a spear and lance it at the culprit with preciseness unexpected of an old lady. I tried to avoid her at all costs, taking a different route if I saw her, unless it was in a restroom where the encounter could not be prevented for there was only one for the whole school.

I was also terrified of medical procedures, such as random screenings, obligatory flu shots or occasional tuberculosis tests. Medicine was injected into the back of the arm for TB testing, and we spent a few days in nervous expectation of the results, observing the injection spot for possible inflammation. In the case of the positive reaction, we had more to fear—a repetitive test or an indication for other in-depth screenings. My friend Lena, an instinctive connoisseur of child psychology (or, perhaps, only mine), sensed and exploited my weakness. From time to time, she would casually inform me that doctors would be visiting school the following day with a mission of particularly painful shots or a checkup. My gullible nature trusted her because her mom was a teacher who, I was sure, provided her with reliable information. I would fidget all night trying to summon courage for the upcoming trial only to discover, the following day, that Lena's predictions were nothing but rumors, or, more likely, a fruit of her fantasy which rejoiced in witnessing my torments.

My early school days were tainted by this atmosphere of fear. Positive reinforcement was not abundant. Students of pedagogical institutes—our future teachers—probably did not focus on the concept of praise and considered it hurtful for the moral upbringing of Soviet youth. In a curiously similar way to Christian educational values, Soviet propaganda upheld humility among the most important virtues of the young generation. Praise could spoil youngsters by making them prone to self-aggrandizing and excessive pride. My susceptible nature absorbed these moral lessons with gratifying speed—I never liked hearing my parents and grandparents talk to friends or acquaintances about my excellent grades, successful performance at musical school or victories at school academic Olympics. I preferred to blend in and synch myself with "the collective"—the key term in the Soviet bureaucratic jargon that emphasized the importance of not "sticking out."

The importance of modesty also revealed itself in clothing and grooming styles. Girls never wore unbraided, long hair to school—otherwise they would send a message of (potentially) loose behavior. A big bow from white or black nylon ribbon (black for every day, white for festive occasions) crowned the artistic creation of one or two braids sometimes curled and crisscrossed in a pretzel-like shape. Jewelry, makeup and painted nails were out of the question. Boys had similar haircuts of the state-determined length, which our teachers periodically checked and sent a warning to the parents if it exceeded the allowed standards. Our nails were also checked for length and potential dirt in early grades to teach us the importance of hygiene. White cuffs and collars on the school uniform needed to be switched every few days.

The state continued to enforce modesty and propriety standards for school graduates. Pants—a frivolous piece of clothing—did not become common for women in the workplace until the late eighties, and I can hardly imagine any of my schoolteachers wearing pants, even nowadays. A choir teacher in the music school once dared to wear pants and paid for this audacity—brought up in conservatism, we dedicated our attention to discussing her look during the entire class. Women did not leave the house in track suits unless it was for a clear athletic-related purpose. Even grocery store visits required careful hair styling and a proper outfit complete with formal shoes. Careful attention to one's appearance, particularly for women, is so deeply rooted in our culture that foreign visitors immediately note how well-dressed women are on city streets at any time of day or night. Our women stand out in international airports and American shopping malls for their glamorous attire, sometimes a bit exaggerated for the occasion. Once in Ukraine I saw a lady going to the beach in high heels.

Modesty standards, however, were severely undermined during perestroika when old habits became the target of mass criticism, and young people started to gain access to Western media. The most daring and rebellious youth challenged the old Soviet conservatism with colorful punk hair styles, exaggerated Gothic makeup, black leather jackets punctuated by safety pins and other metal decorations. Police no longer hunted these rebellious-looking youth but eyed them suspiciously for their threat to public tastes and the social danger they represented with such nonconformist looks. Most young people tested new grounds with more care—boys gradually lengthening their hair and girls shortening their skirts and lifting their hair in "aerodynamic" hairdos typical of the 1980s. Sometimes they even added a number of piercings in their ears—a previously unheard-of brashness. During a visit to Moscow in 1989, I was amazed at the sight of a young woman with her hair painted pink—I had never seen this hair color before. Older people grieved these transformations as a harbinger of moral collapse of the modern youth, losing respect for all authority and all social norms. Youth reveled in this challenge to the old conservatism and in the freedom to blend in with the West, at least in appearance.

While I hardly remember our teachers praising us, severe episodes of scolding easily surface in my memory, perhaps thanks to the colorful metaphors and similes they employed. "Do not donkey around!" Yelena Aleksandrovna, the mastodon math teacher, would rebuke an unfortunate joker. Her resolve to cut short an attempt of comical relief amidst the school drudgery actually had the opposite effect; the imagery she employed was just too expressive for us to stay serious. "If you don't learn math, you will go straight to the collective farm and spend your life twirling cows' tails!" Or "You can donkey around at home with your parents when you find a comfy spot on top of the polished armoire and dangle your feet from there!" We never learned why that specific position proved best for donkeying around, but efforts to visualize the scene brought memorable diversion to our math routine. Yelena Aleksandrovna could teach us math in a way that enabled me to help my own seventh-grader with equations almost thirty years later. Aleksandrovna could also compete in the contest for the most temperamental and eloquent math teacher of all times.

Schoolteachers, and particularly administrators like the principal and vice principal (called "the official in charge of the scholarly work"), frequently acted as dictators, or, at least, appeared to do so to us. Lessons did not incorporate an element of discussion (at least in my school), and few students would dare to ask a question if something was unclear, let alone challenge the material presented. Once in her university course on foreign literature, my mom tried to interject something she had just read during the lecture of an inveterate professor reading from his notes yellowed by time. He angrily denied the validity of her comment and gave her a grade of "four" for the semester, the only non-excellent grade she earned.

In our school, the first hour started with a radio program where the principal reprimanded students for poor behavior or for defying the school protocol. The list of transgressions included the failure to secure a timely haircut, missing a part of the required wardrobe (missing a Pioneer tie was the most serious deviation), not tying a tie properly, wearing earrings or makeup or perming one's hair. In her speeches, the principal did not spare derogatory terms, nor worried about preserving anybody's privacy, just like Nikita Khrushchev swore and insulted writers and artists at the 1963 Communist party reunion for trying new forms of expression. Likewise, teachers would publicly scold students for poor work, poor behavior, coming to school with dirty nails or dirty ears, forgetting a textbook, forgetting to attach freshly-ironed cuffs to the jacket (which was usually their parents' fault) and other crimes. Twice a year, homeroom teachers would hold parents' meetings where they would discuss planning parties and other events, distribute cleaning or repair duties during the break (parents were responsible for repairing and remodeling the classroom), and scold parents of poor students for their offspring's failures. Such disregard for privacy sustained the system of universal sharing of public knowledge about everything and everyone. We could not hold secrets from the state or from each other, and it was particularly obvious in small towns where everybody knew who was going out with whom, who just got pregnant, and who broke up with someone.

I do recall the extraordinarily elated reaction of our elementary school teacher Nina Fyodorovna at the correct response blurted out by one of the poorest students in class. She was so genuinely happy for him that she called him "umnichka" (little clever boy) and even kissed him on both cheeks. She was about to pour more affection on him on another occasion when he eagerly volunteered an answer not only raising his hand, but almost jumping from his seat during a so-called "open lesson" when top regional administrators visited class to control the quality of teaching. To her dismay, he could not produce many meaningful sounds once she called on him. "Why did you volunteer with so much ardor?" she yelled at him later. "I was so happy to see that you had learned the lesson and were ready to participate! I thought, 'My Lapochka [*my baby*] is ready—I should give him a chance to stand out and shine.' And you used this chance to disgrace me in front of all those administrators!" "Nina Fyodorovna, you told us to be active and participate as much as we can," was the naïve answer of the boy whose Soviet upbringing had taught him the importance of putting up a good show.

Volunteering an answer was a risk that provided an opportunity to earn teacher's favor, paving the way to the good or excellent grade and to future benevolence on teacher's part. It was also a daring step, for it invited murky consequences—universal attention, judgment, perhaps disapproval, mockery and resulting humiliation. I rarely volunteered because it meant summoning all of my strength to conquer my shyness. Instead, I dealt with the constant fear of being called on in class, which increased proportionally to the length of time since my previous public response. This fear invaded me the night before and prevented any possibility of enjoying school. The immutable first component of every lesson consisted of questioning students to check their readiness and homework preparation, and the answer made up their participation grade. The academic year was divided into two-month quarters, at the end of which students would receive a quarter grade—it equaled the average of the participation, homework and periodic tests grades. The teachers usually did not call on the same student twice in a row, and we relaxed for a while after answering in class. Some perfidious teachers, nevertheless, violated this unwritten rule, enjoying the (usually unprepared) student's reaction.

When called to respond to a question, the student had to give an extensive, clear and well-formulated response while the rest of the class rejoiced at not being the one under attack. The sympathetic audience often whispered helpful suggestions or shoved the open book in the area of the respondent's eyesight. The collective spirit strongly rooted in our mentality was inherited from the early Slavs living in communities called "mir" where they shared everything. This spirit was later strengthened by Communist propaganda reinforcing the value of collective effort. Helping a comrade in trouble produce the right answer was therefore the only possible moral choice, and anybody withholding help could be branded an egoist and possibly boycotted or teased by the class community. The reasons for failing to learn the lesson did not matter—whether it was a temporary loss of linguistic ability from a sudden attack of nerves, the fear of public speaking, or downright laziness—anybody could and eventually would be in the victim's place. "Treat thy neighbor as thyself and help him when he did not learn his homework so you shalt expect the same treatment in return"—this was our principle.

The collective spirit also instilled in me the fear of being different—I hated looking different, dressing different and standing out from the others even (or especially) if it implied appearing smarter. Besides all my other fears, I was in desperate horror of being branded a nerd and did everything in my power to hide my knowledge in striving towards mediocrity. If I knew the right answer when no one else did, I obstinately kept silent. I was highly disciplined with my homework which I completed immediately after coming home, but hated raising my hand to volunteer an answer and waited for destiny's choice. I had a good voice and an ear for music, but felt extremely self-conscious singing solo for most of my life. I especially abhorred playing the piano in public (unless it was in obligatory recitals) and dreaded the moment when my parents implored me to play in front of guests during family celebrations.

I generously shared my homework with everyone who asked me to let them copy it in the sincere desire to not appear greedy and to help friends in need. Some people who struggled with schoolwork or with laziness actually called me on the phone before it was due, asking me to dictate the answers to them, which I did. Some of those students volunteered the answers in class the following day and got excellent marks for their zest, and I did not resent it. I lacked ambition, which somehow did not hurt my progress, as teachers always recognized my behind-the-scenes efforts. By the final year of high school, however, I became intensely interested in foreign languages and focused all my efforts towards the university entrance exam which I successfully passed.

This was my second greatest achievement since graduating high school with the golden medal of excellence (the highest possible award). The thought of the future, quite hazy in the economically unstable young Ukraine, nevertheless filled me with joy, excitement and pride at my new title of "student." I had always heard that university is the best time of one's life, and I was ready to embrace it.

Exams

In spite of my excellent performance in school, exams were another source of fear. Whenever in the course of my studies in the United States I felt anxious before an upcoming test, my thoughts went back to my Soviet schooldays, and this worked like a tranquillizer. Both in high school and at the university, we dreaded the approach of the "exam session" as it was called, as if it were an imminent execution. My mom first started suffering from insomnia because of anxiety before her fifth-grade botany exam. Just as in the United States, the school year culminated in finals, invariably cumulative, and, in most cases, stressfully oral, not written. The result could influence one's final grade for the subject and even the student's ability to enter the university. There were no re-takes. If you got all As at the final high school graduation exams (called "state exams" for their significance), you would be entitled to the highest graduation honor—the golden medal.[1]

The golden medal recipients could take only one university entrance exam out of three generally required, if they succeeded in the challenging task of obtaining an excellent grade. If that were not the case, they would continue their crucifixion in the area of the Ukrainian language and the history of Ukraine (then a very murky subject as we had been taught the very recently revised history for only a year or so, and it contradicted the old version we had learned for the previous nine years). After the last exam, students found out if they accumulated the requisite number of points for admittance or if they faced an indeterminable year of trying to figure out their future.

I was terrified of the latter scenario even more than the actual exams. Since I hated the thought of needing to find a job without an education, I used every minute of spare time in my final year of school to study for the exam in the area of my chosen major—English. I doggedly reviewed grammar structures, completed endless exercises and practiced speaking, writing and listening comprehension with my mom—my primary teacher. Then I practiced more speaking with myself since, as I was self-conscious, it was alone that I felt most comfortable in the treacherous realm of communicating in a foreign language. I also took two-hour private lessons with another English professor twice a week. She lived in a remote area of Kharkiv—it took a thirty-minute train ride, a forty-minute tram ride, variable waiting time and a thirty-minute walk to get to my evening class. My grandpa met me on the way home to accompany me on the late train ride back. I did my homework and reviewed more English texts on the way. Occasionally, I met friends on the train that broke my gloomy routine with indefatigable Ukrainian humor and cheerfulness.

In my final years of school and at the university, the beautiful month of June was spoiled by cramming and recharging our batteries for the next torture session of exams. In preparation, we reviewed the entire year's worth of material in minute detail and rehearsed extensive answers to fifty or seventy questions, such as "What were the goals and the results of the second five-year economic plan?"; "What were the new forms of socialist economic competition throughout the duration of the second five-year plan?"; "What was the historical significance of the establishment of the proletariat dictatorship in Russia?"; and "How did V.I. Lenin evaluate the attempted 1905 revolution in Russia?" We also answered more meaningful questions like "Explain the reasons behind and the development of World War I" or "Talk about the defeat of German troops by Moscow during World War II."

Towards my high school graduation in 1992 when the Soviet days were over, our history exam questions became more reasonable. My generation was lucky to miss by a very narrow margin the detailed history of the Komsomol or the principles of Scientific Communism assessed by my slightly older comrades who graduated high school in 1990. They had to commit to memory the year of every congress of the Communist Party and even developed a special system to make the process more bearable. They added the number eleven to every congress, starting from the seventh: 7+11=18, hence the year of the seventh congress was 1918, and so on.

During earlier grades our institution was dominated by Communist doctrine, and we had to take into consideration Lenin's opinion on almost every subject, including biology or, in particular, literature—what he thought of Natasha Rostova, Raskolnikov or Bazarov. Political philosophers and social revolutionaries Karl Marx and Friedrich Engels were other unquestionable authorities. An anecdote satirized their role in our academic and public life in general: A medical student taking the final exam of his last year of studies was asked to characterize two skeletons in front of him. He kept silent. "What have you studied in all these years?" the professor finally inquired. "No way! Are they really Marx and Engels?" ventured the marveled student.

Math and science were a different matter: They were mostly free of Marxist-Leninist ideology and required serious thinking rather than cramming to solve logarithms, algorithms, volume of cones and parallelepipeds.

Math and composition exams were taken in writing, which brought some relief since we didn't have to worry about public humiliation. Oral exams, however, were taken in the presence of not only the examining teachers' panel, but also several fellow students preparing for their own trial in the same room. This embarrassment factor could crush shy, anxious or under-prepared victims, most of whom were barely conscious after the night-long review and serious nerve damage.

On the fateful day, we pulled one of the myriad "tickets" peppering the examination table with two or three questions written on it. We had ten to fifteen minutes to prepare the best response we could or improvise something of the jumbled-up facts in our exhausted brains before pouring out our expertise on the subject. Some lucky devils whose tongues were particularly "well attached" and whose nerves stayed under control could find their way out of tricky situations by improvising eloquently meaningless speeches and earn a grade of "5" before the examiner realized the inadequacy of the response. Others panicked and froze. It was a trial not only for our knowledge, but for our resourcefulness and self-confidence in stressful circumstances.

The school exam experience was more tolerable than the university exam process because after spending ten years with our fellow students, we knew them so well that we got tired of embarrassing each other or feeling embarrassed. If we made it to the realm of higher education, we had to prove to each other and to the professors that we truly belonged at this altar of knowledge, and our presence was not accidental. We met some of our professors or at least saw them from a close distance for the first time in the whole semester: They did not hold office hours, nor did we exhibit a particular desire to see them before an exam. Courses not related to one's major area of study were lectures, sometimes with a hundred or more students enrolled, and few professors checked attendance or called on us. Thus, we could happily spend precious time, especially during the rare spells of good fall weather, in a more valuable way—sipping coffee at a nearby café or singing in the park with a guitar. Student folklore glorified the irregular but mostly nonchalant nature of student life in a jocular song: "From one exam session to the next, students live merrily. Good thing, the sessions happen only twice a year." Retribution arrived during the final exams when the professor did not recognize our faces or perhaps did not like students' empty expressions. She could crush us with her authority, arrogance or erudition, and if we were not completely confident, we could do nothing to withstand her undeniable dictatorship and, often, mockery of our academic inadequacy.

Joys of Labor at the Soviet Schools

"We are going to kolkhoz!"[1] This call to action on the collective farm was frequently heard in our classrooms in the fall and was typically greeted with screams of exhilaration and applause. Collective farm trips involved semi-strenuous, non-paid toil at the schoolchildren's expense, but they also hailed a break from schoolwork and outdoor fun with friends. Schools and universities volunteered students' (and sometimes teachers') labor when state-sponsored resources were running short for coping with the harvest. Starting in third grade we would miss an average of ten to fourteen school days in the fall gathering carrots, giant zucchinis resembling fat greenish piglets we could barely lift, and radishes, which were easy to lift but made our hands itch with their bushy, rugged tails. These minor troubles did not overshadow our enjoyment at the prospect of hanging out with friends and getting home dirty and tired but rewarded with small shares of goods we helped gather.

On the designated morning, rain or shine, we assembled at the school entrance in work clothes and rain boots—buckets for harvesting, lunch packs, thermoses with hot tea or coffee in hand, and anticipation of adventure on our faces. Sometimes more than one grade level would be crammed together in a bus creating an intimate although not very comfortable ambiance. We didn't mind sitting, falling and stepping on one another during a short ride to the fields although the bus seemed ready to explode from being packed to the ceiling with schoolchildren eager to apply themselves to farm work. I lost my mom's raincoat on one of those comfy rides, and she still remembers it with great tenderness and sorrow for it was sturdy but thin, easily folded in such a way as not to occupy too much space in a bag. Soviet-made outerwear could not exactly be described as attractive, but was usually well made and lasted for years. Besides, poorly supplied stores and an efficient underground distribution network of the supplied clothes among store workers and their relatives made it challenging to find new stuff. We valued what we had and regretted the loss of an item as if it were a dear friend.

Occasionally, the bus would not show up and after wasting an hour in excited expectation and improvised games like "break the chain" in the schoolyard, we walked for seven kilometers to get to the fields. We were not in a hurry—we savored each moment. Boys would scuffle on the way and jump over a fence or two to help Yuzhny citizens with harvesting pears or apples from their orchards and devour them immediately afterwards. Girls laughed at the spectacle and gossiped about the boys along the way. Once we approached the coveted destination, the narrow street under the cupola of tall trees gave up its spongy and dusty asphalt for a bumpy dirt trail waving through the expansiveness of yellow fields on one side and a still pond hiding in reeds on the other. In the summer, boys bathed in it after work, shedding their outer clothing—nobody cared about swimwear. Working in the fields sprawled on rolling hills, we could see the town at our feet and the view, always etched in my mind, added an esthetic pleasure to harvesting.

We pulled the stubborn vegetables to fill our buckets and took them to the teacher who evaluated the yield and provided constructive criticism or, in rare cases, praise, regarding the quality or quantity of the products. Carrots would slide easily from the moist, soft soil after the rain but the soil would also easily stick to our hands, boots and clothes, ensuring busy afternoons for our moms and grandmas who had to deal with the consequences. It didn't matter—the aroma of fresh produce in the crisp air intoxicated us, and the spirit of socialist competition seized us. The teachers divided us into groups usually corresponding to our Pioneer "link" units which competed with each other to harvest the most crates or kilos. Teachers kept track of our results, and the highest-scoring units and winning classes would be awarded with a laudatory announcement on the school radio the following day.

Buckets added up to crates, and the contents of crates combined to form tall, appetizing piles. We could only hope that collective farm workers would pick up these piles later to deliver them to state-owned stores and not leave them to rot on the ground, as was often the case at the Soviet-run enterprises. Such state-impelled negligence and mismanagement induced massive hunger in Ukraine in the thirties when mountains of harvested grain rotted in OGPU (state-police)-guarded dumps or went to special cafeterias for party officials while the last grains were expropriated from the peasants who collected them. They were driven to such extreme starvation as to eat cats, dogs, grass and their own boots while the brutal state police kept searching for their supposedly hidden crops. Sometimes the rain would disrupt our marathon—trifling drizzles or even steadier showers would not deter us, but torrential downpours frequent in the fall did. We would huddle under our raincoats and wait for an intermission, but if it did not come, we made an early exit home—walking, as there was no hope for the bus to come ahead of schedule.

University students were also sent to work on state or collective farms in the early fall or late summer, sometimes before the beginning of the academic year and sometimes after. My mom found out about this on the first day of her university studies, September 1, while her enthusiasm about beginning her academic career was at its apex. It turned out her enthusiasm had to wait a bit as it was announced that the students would not return to their scholarly work until October 17. The farm was far from the city, and they stayed there continuously for almost two months, sleeping and eating at farmers' houses. My mom and her companion, a girl on the third year of studies already quite seasoned in farm work and field life conditions, were assigned to stay at an elderly couple's house which lacked water and other modern conveniences. They tasted all the pleasures of simple country life—washing their faces in the cool water of a nearby creek while fighting off the hosts' geese, and going to the outdoor bathroom right in the bushes, luckily available in abundance.

Our own enthusiasm for farming diminished drastically in summer when kolkhoz visits did not take the place of school, but made up the compulsory "supplementary work" sentence that all schoolchildren starting from the third grade had to serve after the end of the academic year. These would take a good part of June and shorten our vacations. Such practices were intended to build the character and work ethic of Soviet citizens who, in their more mature age, would compete for their industry in so-called five-year plans to speed up the building of Communism in the country. The first plan was introduced in 1928 to reconstruct industry after the exhausting civil war. It pressured factory workers to accelerate their rhythm to almost inhuman rates with slogans like "Let's fulfill the five-year plan in four years!" and then "Let's fulfill the five-year plan in three years!" They turned people into exhausted machines and punished "losers" not able to keep up with such an unhealthy pace, with reprimands in the best case, and arrests and executions in the worst. Socialist competitions reached levels of absurdity when the above-mentioned slogans would turn up on such unlikely institutions as morgues—my mom saw one with her own eyes.

Competitions and rewards could no longer inspire schoolchildren ready for the summer break. Everybody did his or her best to get out of outdoor service by trying to obtain fake doctor's notes or by any other possible means, which in most cases did not help—the "skippers" would not be allowed to pass to the next grade without serving their labor term. The only possible alternative (from which I often benefited) was to serve the sentence cleaning up the home classroom, painting windowsills or dusting the shelves. The advantage consisted in less supervision (as teachers usually accompanied the kolkhoz team) and the opportunity to finish work and escape early without waiting for the bus or working under the baking June sun. A team of cautiously enthusiastic parents sometimes joined us in classroom cleanup or repair work—they would be left with more challenging or dangerous tasks, such as whitewashing the ceilings or painting the walls.

During the school year, schoolkids also had to contribute to classroom cleaning: We took turns to be "on duty" which meant we came to school earlier to water the flowers, clean the blackboard, get a fresh supply of chalk, report absent pupils to the teacher and wash the floors after school. Most of all I hated handling the rag: It seemed to be older than me and was of an indeterminable color, texture and smell. We had to rinse it in the bucket and squeeze the excess water out of it. This water quickly became so muddied from all the dust and dirt collected from the floor that it acquired the consistency of thick, yucky mush. If we emptied the bucket frequently, it delayed the process and didn't help anyway as the new water immediately turned into the same mush. We opted for grinding our teeth and spreading the dirt around the floor with the muddied water as quickly as we could in order to trade the classroom prison for freedom. However, if the teacher determined the next morning that the duty was not properly performed, we risked serving a longer "duty" sentence which could be extended to several days or two weeks.

All the class teams also took turns to serve duty in the whole school—this consisted of placing schoolkids in strategic places in the building at the beginning of the day to check the appearance of the arriving students. Victims who did not display all the uniform pieces—apron, freshly washed and ironed collar, all the necessary buttons and, most important, the Pioneer tie and pin—could be sent home and reported to the school Pioneer committee as violators of Communist protocol. Since our old school building hardly had enough space to house the student body, people on duty also ensured that students came in through one particular entrance and used the other to exit only. When invested with such a responsibility, even the worst behaved students acquired an inflated air of self-importance and, just as happened with all the Soviet bureaucrats acquiring a bit of power, treated everybody else with arrogance and superiority. They often acted quite roughly, pushing people away in an effort to guarantee the appropriate entrance procedure.

As if all this complementary toil was not enough, the socialist work ethic in our schools was enhanced thanks to the special class called, unambiguously, "Labor." It was introduced in the fifties, and my mom's generation was among the first to benefit from this experiment of organized labor education. In such classes, you could learn lots of useful skills if classes were well organized and if a school was well equipped with sowing machines, cooking stoves, milling machines, or other handy tools. Students often received diplomas of some trade skill upon graduation. For many years in our grade, the class fell, appropriately, on Monday. I have fond recollections of learning to fry eggs, make coffee and even sew a kitchen apron in my younger days. My mom, who had also started with an apron (an all-time Soviet "labor" must), reached much more serious heights by sewing a nightgown and a bathing suit for herself.

However, the day came when girls had to share their proletarian labor on par with boys in adherence to the politics of gender equality promoted by our progressive state. We were herded to the dark, low, dilapidated and unheated workshop resembling a war bunker to sharpen hooks for clothes hangers on deafeningly noisy and clumsy machines. They looked suspiciously capable of chopping off our fingers. We stood there for two hours in our winter coats pressing the hook to the threatening rotating wheel for just the necessary number of seconds on each side to reach an adequate degree of sharpness. The processes repeated on the next, the next and yet another one until the droning machine seemed to drill right through my brain, bursting the remaining drops of my concentration and patience.

The new labor teacher (our draconian math teacher Yelena Aleksandrovna's husband) in Stalin-like manner showed us the basic sharpening and safety steps and walked rhythmically along the rows to supervise our tortures. "My eye is as sharp as a diamond," he would say to remind us of his strict quality control and threaten possible punishment in cases of poorly executed duties. I think the punishment might have consisted in increasing the number of hooks and the length of our sentence. The droning mumble of hooking machines and monotonous, mind-numbing movements slowed by the awkwardness of our heavy coats convinced me for the rest of my life that I needed to perform well in all of my subjects and escape the horror of menial work.

In the upper grades, two hours of labor no longer sufficed and we had to dedicate our entire Wednesday to help build the socialist society. Again, we rejoiced at the welcome break from schoolwork timed perfectly in the middle of the week. Part of the group went to work on the faïence factory stacking and packing plates. I belonged to the group working in the school cafeteria and washing plates—by that time, the school acquired a huge dishwasher that almost took the space of an entire room. All I remember from my washing apprenticeship is the overwhelming smell of a kitchen mass-producing soup and cutlets enhanced to a dizzying effect by the steam of the wash room. When some ten years later I returned to the school cafeteria, which a friend rented for her wedding celebration, the memories of my school work days and of the unforgettable smell invaded me with a strange mixture of sweet nostalgia and relief.

Boys occasionally repaired furniture or built some mysterious projects, but the only trace of their activities stays in my memory thanks to a photo

Boys in labor class in our final year of school, 1991. Seryozha/Borya is in the middle front row.

in which they are holding a hammer, a saw and a drill. In the spring and fall, they would also dig the soil for planting, and in winter they shoveled the snow to clear passageways to school entrances. They did not complain. No one complained about shoveling, painting, raking leaves, digging, washing, sharpening hooks or harvesting. My mom finally complained when labor teachers under the guidance of the school administration decided to use our efforts for embellishing the territory surrounding the school in a very unhygienic way. We collected dirty scraps and rubbish strewn around the park, naturally without any gloves or special uniforms. This abuse transcended the limits of my mom's tolerance due to the potential danger it posed to our health. Her diplomatic skills with this delicate matter must have brought welcome results for we did not have to do it again.

Generally, however, complaining did not do much good. In the Soviet Union, the state was always right and the people—free recipients of its generosity in educational and medical care—gratefully conceded to minor inconveniences and paying tribute for the benefaction. It seemed fair, after all, to contribute a bit of labor in exchange for the comprehensive and overall excellent quality education (with the exception of social sciences heavily influenced by Marxist ideology). Whenever my American friends express disbelief and disapproval at the exploitation we endured through all these forced activities, I do not bow to the speculation that we were abused by the socialist system. Perhaps a little bit—but it helped build our work principles and contributed to fun recollections of childhood. That is, except for collecting trash or sharpening the hooks in the dungeon workshop.

More About School

In my young days, no one drove their kids to school. Not many people owned cars. Those who did would not consider spoiling their children with this unnecessary luxury unless they were sick. Our public transportation system was well developed and safe, and the street infrastructure was perfectly adapted for walking. Everybody knew a twenty- or thirty-minute walk in any weather could only be good for the kids. Those who lived in nearby villages took a bus, or, if buses stopped running because of snow, walked up the steep hill, crossing the railroad, for thirty minutes or more. Heavy snowstorms lengthened the walk but also made it more fun, especially on the way home. When the burden of intellectual labor no longer clouded the moods of young scholars, they could stage a snow fight, slide down the hill using their schoolbags as sleds, or build a snowman.

On the other hand, getting ready for school in winter was no fun. We woke up and walked out in complete darkness—the daylight would not come until after eight a.m. Rain, sleet, puddles and snow obviously complicated our morning walk. For protection against the nasty weather, we wore heavy boots and layers of tights, warm leggings, socks, sweaters, coats and hats. No responsible parents let a child go outside without a hat, a pair or two of mittens and warm tights under the leggings or pants. There was no thought of taking off a hat until the warm weather returned towards May. We also carried a pair of shoes to change into once we entered the school building. The rainwater froze once, and the town became one huge skating rink. In Dallas, where I now live, they cancel classes at the smallest hint of snow or ice. Soviet authorities would not give in to such weakness. We had to grow up strong and resilient, not swaying from challenges, and we made it to our destination without tardiness—half-crawling, half-rolling and holding on to everything, including trees, fences and each other.

In the first grade, we had four forty-five-minute classes, with a five-minute break in between and a twenty-minute recess in the middle of the day. Boys played soccer or hockey, and girls walked around in circles hand in hand or stood in groups keeping a cool look and their eyes on the boys. In upper grades, the boys and some girls switched from sports to smoking behind the school wall. The teachers did not supervise the playground as they do in American schools—they were probably scared of the kids. The premises resembled a jungle or a battlefield during the respite from classes. Yet everybody made it back to the next lesson more or less safely and punctually after the fierce ringing of the school bell announced the end of recess.

In the first two or three years of school, they brought us hot milk with buns for a snack in the middle of our second-period class—the treat cost ten kopecks a week. All the kids, except for me who did not react well to any food not cooked, fried or boiled by my Grandma, rushed from their seats towards the tray. I winced at the thick skin of the milk, the sight of which made me gag, and thought about my grandma's tea or cocoa. Whatever she prepared seemed to be the height of culinary art, and I refused to try any product of the state-owned cuisine, especially if it looked as unhealthy, unsavory and unsanitary as was sometimes the case in the state cafeterias.

In winter, the heating system at our old school did not reach into all of the classrooms, especially those in the corners of the building, and we dressed in many layers to stay warm. Once our whole class was punished for some students' naughtiness, and we were sent into the coldest classroom with hardly any signs of heating at all. We sat through lessons in fur coats and tried our best to write in mittens until our parents complained to the administration. The teachers were happy to agree to the end of our several-day-long sentence which they served with us.

When I was in the middle of the seventh grade, a new school building was completed—a spacious, three-storied marvel with a huge gym, performance room and well-equipped classrooms. Well-lit hallways now separated youngsters from mature high-schoolers brimming with the tremendous weight of their life experience. Teachers poured all their effort and creativity into lovingly decorating their rooms to convert them into mini-museums. Biology teachers created a true replica of the natural world with marinated baby frogs, dried-up leaves and beetles, a huge tortoise shell, some animal horns, mollusks, pinecones, models of snakes, bones and—the most fascinating exhibit of all—the real human embryo. The museum of human anatomy provided the school with this gem, but I don't remember the teacher ever actually making use of it in the classroom. I recently brought it up in the conversation with a friend who grew up in Moscow, and she happily confirmed that a similar fetus (a twin brother?) inhabited the cabinet of her biology classroom, intriguing teenagers about the miracles of life.

Our homeroom teacher Lubov Aleksandrovna, who specialized in Ukrainian language and literature, transformed our classroom into a Ukrainian hut with the help of embroidered towels, an ancient coal iron, an old washboard, a spindle, a pair of big iron forks used by Ukrainian women to take hot ceramic pots out of the oven, ceramic pots themselves, imitation sunflowers and a lovely country landscape painted on the wall with the figure of the greatest Ukrainian poet Taras Shevchenko in the middle. An icon framed by the Ukrainian towel and spears of wheat blessed us from the bookshelf in the front part of the classroom.

It was delightful to sit in such a cozy atmosphere, even during gatherings of an administrative, organizational or political nature. The home-like surroundings mitigated Lyubov Aleksandrovna's reprimands on account of our lack of initiative and poor progress and enhanced praises for our occasional achievements. Those walls witnessed the collection of money for class improvement projects or Pioneer membership fees and heard our political news presentations. Tall windows taking up one of the walls let in plenty of light and helped us absorb Vitamin D, as we contemplated the lesson-free life outside and spotted lucky acquaintances passing by.

I invariably chose the seat by the window and gradually migrated towards the very last row where I felt more productive combining my extracurricular activities with learning. In my teenage years, I developed a

The back wall in my Ukrainian classroom. The painting is of the great Ukrainian poet Taras Shevchenko.

more nonchalant and defiant attitude, compensating for my previous submissiveness. For one, I caught up on chatting with my friend Lara. The rest of the afternoon, which we also often spent together, did not suffice. This prompted Lubov Aleksandrovna to award us with certificates "for active conversations during class time" at our graduation party. The back row also allowed for easier bite-sneaking in case physical hunger prevailed over my thirst for learning. Finally, if the lesson started to induce boredom and fatigue, these seats provided an advantageous position for catching a refreshing game of cards with Lara and two guy friends sitting ahead of us—Valera and Seryozha. I can't recollect where we positioned the cards—on the seats or on top of the desks or hiding them behind the books. It was very entertaining—especially since the risk of discovery and punishment spiced up the activity.

At the sound of the end-of-the-lesson bell, kids rushed outside in a hurricane as if they had been denied freedom for the past ten years, with their collective force crushing everything in its way. The last bell heralded only temporary freedom, for invariably substantial homework awaited us upon

Physics class in the final year of school, 1991. I am in the second row by the teacher (white shirt, upper middle) and only my head is visible. My friend Larisa (also wearing a white shirt) is beside me. We are laughing and talking to each other, not paying much attention to our teacher—Larisa's mother!

Checking out textbooks on September 1, 1991, our final year of school. I am in the back row by the window. My friend Lena is on the left. The title of the textbook was *History of the USSR*. The union had only four months to live before it was dissolved on December 25, 1991.

our arrival at home. We would have envied American schoolkids—my fourth-grader does not bring back any homework; he says he finishes it in school. Soviet fourth-graders brought home several math problems, several exercises in Russian and/or Ukrainian with verb conjugations or noun declensions, text analysis or a poem to memorize for a literature class, a history text to read and prepare for oral reproduction, and geography or nature studies lesson to memorize. We also carried around backpacks with thick textbooks, apparently non-existent in modern American schools. The Soviet educational system, while caring about not overburdening the finances of the students' families, also cared about recycling everything. We did not buy textbooks—we checked them out at the beginning of the school year and returned them at the end, thus passing them on to the next class of scholars. In case of damage or loss, we paid fines.

The Soviet educational system embraced all children regardless of their socio-economic background and did everything to erase any economic differences that might exist. Our uniforms—brown dresses and black aprons for girls, dark blue or brown pants and jackets for boys—prevented us from standing out from the crowd. The cuffs, collars and aprons allowed for the only display of individuality that could lead a seasoned Soviet resident to assess the owner's approximate economic status. Our moms or grandmas sewed the collars and cuffs to the dresses and changed them every few days, attaching the fresh ones anew. Plain white cotton was the most common material for our collars and cuffs, but some people could afford more expensive and difficult to obtain lace. My grandma sewed lace adornments for me herself—they were second best to the industrially made ones. Lace aprons were very rare and available mostly to people with access to the commercial sector who had a chance for firsthand purchases of the best goods. My friend's aunt lived in Lithuania, famous for better-quality textiles, and brought me a nylon black apron with flouncy wings, which became the object of my pride for many years.

All the schools in the entire country also had the identical curriculum designed and approved by the Ministry of Education. This meant that you could move from Kyiv to Vladivostok in the middle of the school year and find the same schedule of classes, the same textbooks, continue studying the same chapter in the textbook and, perhaps, continue with the same home-

September 1, 1991—the first day of my final year of school. I am wearing a special occasion "parade" uniform (white apron).

work. With the breakdown of the Soviet Union close in sight, an attempt was made to reform the school system and approximate it to the Western model lengthening it to eleven years. However, since the curriculum was only provided for ten years, we simply skipped one (non-existent) level and pretended we were in the eleventh grade. I can see how such a transition can seem absurdly unnecessary to the Western reader, but our life was full of such absurdities that became the topic of popular jokes we called anecdotes and shared on the streets, in public transportation and at home.

One such joke is based on a saying by Nikita Khrushchev, or, at least, commonly attributed to him, that one of our legs already stepped into Communism. The anecdote developed it into a conversation with an old Bolshevik who inquired in response, "And for how much longer shall we stay in such an awkward semi-squat?" Another anecdote satirized corruption pervading all spheres of our life and taken for granted by everyone: "The winner of Miss Kazakhstan was announced to be the forty-four-year-old nephew of the Head of the Municipal Government." Some anecdotes were rather dangerous and could only be confided to trusted friends behind closed doors: On Easter, Brezhnev was greeted with the typical Orthodox greeting "Christ is risen!" (the typical answer to this is "Indeed he is risen") to which Brezhnev replied, "Thank you, I have already been informed." People gradually became bolder recounting these jokes as their heroes—our former idols—passed from honor to ridicule. Such was the case with Lenin whose motto "Study! Study! And once again, study!" was displayed on the walls of educational institutions to encourage us to follow in his footsteps. The immortal phrase became a focus of another anecdote: Lenin told his wife that he would be busy with his lover, and he told his lover that he would be busy with his wife. In the meantime, he escaped to the attic so that he could study, study, and, once again, study.

Soviet children all over the country also had identical holidays and celebrations. Classes all over the country started on September 1 (the day of knowledge) with a festive outdoor ceremony complete with speeches, concerts, rhymes recited by students who thanked teachers for their patience and resilience, and, of course, "the sound of the first bell" symbolically announcing the beginning of classes. The kids then presented their teachers with giant bouquets of chrysanthemums, mums and georginas—their smell in classrooms heralded the beginning of fall and many months of hard work in store.

Parents, grandparents and many residents of the town, even if they had no kids in school, came to watch. We wore our "special occasion" uniforms (called "parade uniforms" in our school jargon) of white aprons, instead of black, and white shirts with navy blue pants for boys. A festive look for girls of all ages also prescribed big white bows in hair tied in ponytails or braided and curled in two rings called "krendels" (a loose equivalent of "pretzels").

September 1, 1982—my first day of school. I am third from the left.

Accompanying my kids on the first day of American school where they go to their desks without any festivities is deeply disappointing as I recall the cheer and pomp of the inauguration of my school class. The festivities used to dispel the sadness of the ended summer and awareness of the long winter to come.

The day would proceed with a lesson of peace when we were reminded of the happy place in which we were growing up, and the role the Soviet Union played in preserving peace throughout the planet. Local veterans of the Great Patriotic War (as World War II is known in the Soviet Union) were often invited to speak about their experiences. Once they invited my grandpa. I was very nervous before his speech, the way kids feel when they worry their parents or grandparents will say something embarrassing in front of their peers. But when my grandpa started speaking, I immediately felt pride for what he had gone through and how he described these experiences to captivate a nine-year-old audience. In the beginning, silently, he got out a small piece of rye bread and showed it to everyone. "See this piece of bread?" he said. "Will it be enough if you are hungry? Just imagine that during the war this piece was all you had to eat for the entire day. You had to make the most out of it."

More About School

"Field kasha" picnic, 1983. Our teacher Nina Fyodorovna is in the middle. The girls are sitting in a separate circle from the boys.

 The beginning-of-school picnic also cheered us up after the lessons on September 1 or a day before. Popular kids' options of hamburgers, chips or hotdogs had not yet made their way to our diets, and we prepared a traditional wholesome meal of "kasha" under the guidance of our parents and teachers. "Field kasha" (or "kulesh," as people sometimes call it) lacks an exact English translation. A traditional fare for soldiers or backpackers, it resembles a think millet soup made in a big iron pot over a fire, with pieces of stewed pork fat and meat, seasoned with egg and butter. It is used metonymically in expressions like "to go to kasha" to imply a picnic with cooking, drinking (for adults), eating, playing sports and relaxing. Some friends of mine, whose class groups were particularly close-knit, carry on the regular kasha gatherings for decades after graduation, bringing their own kids to share in the fun.

 The next big holiday was November 7, the anniversary of the Great October Socialist Revolution of 1917—the most controversial event not only in the former Soviet Union, but in all the modern world history. The strange inconsistency of the name and the date of the holiday stems from the fact that prior to 1917, Russia used the old Julian calendar which was then switched to the Western-style Gregorian calendar for every purpose except for the religious calendar (which is why the Orthodox Christmas comes two weeks after the Catholic/Protestant equivalent). How many stories, songs and movies dedicated to the revolution we saw and heard in our childhood! We imagined fighting in the ranks of the Red Army against the "Whites" (anti–Bolsheviks) and climbing on barricades with a red flag. For my entrance exam to the musical school, I chose to sing one of the most popular children's revolutionary songs, "Cruiser Aurora," named in honor of the navy vessel, which shot the fateful cannon to announce the beginning of the new socialist-dominated era. "What do you see, Cruiser Aurora, when the morning rises over the Neva river?" I also remember my grandpa singing one of the other traditional revolutionary songs for me as a lullaby: "Beware Red Army, the black baron prepares for us the tsarist throne again."

The Whites, the tsarist army, were the enemies of the revolution deemed unequivocally bad by our textbooks. The Russian intelligentsia of the early 20th century who sided with the Whites out of caution and fear of the new party of peasants and proletarians eager to crush everything in their way would be driven to exile or pronounced enemies of the people. Anybody with aristocratic or clergy ancestry, and even belonging to well-to-do peasant families, would also be included in the category of enemies of the people. Textbooks painted the world of the revolution with red and white stripes in a very precise, straightforward way, not permitting any shades of pink or anything else in between. The Greens, the anarchists, the socialists of any other faction except the Bolsheviks (the radical proponents of the revolution as the only efficient way of battling the old regime) were rebuked in our history textbooks as enemies of the great cause.

In high school, when the Soviet regime mostly collapsed and previously hidden facts started to emerge, we tried to fill the gaps with the help of new history textbooks, which now included a more realistic history of Ukraine. The earlier textbooks ignored and dismissed it as the history of nationalist movements fighting against the Soviet army eager to side with the Nazis. We slowly worked to reveal the true history of the bloody and cruel times dominated by dictatorship and fear and tried to discern the real villains and victims. I have slowly and very gradually come to the realization that everyone had his grain of truth which he tried to defend with all his strength in the chaos of the breaking world order, amidst the civil war, destruction of churches and old values. I have come to comprehend that there are multiple truths and multiple histories. In middle school we studied Soviet history through a censored prism, in which everything was easy and clear. This grew fuzzy and complicated towards our time in high school, as everything we had previously digested was now reversed and confused. New truths, previously obscured, came out. The previously known traitors now became heroes, and all-time heroes became ridiculed.

We didn't know who to believe and instinctively held on to the old truths or at least some of them—they were safer, clearer. They were also surprisingly tenacious, and the new leaders of many independent states, including

Ukraine, grew out of the same Communist party ranks camouflaging themselves under the new pseudo-democratic guise. The same, or slightly changed propaganda, lived on in eastern Ukraine among the predominantly Russian-speaking population where I grew up. It influenced public opinion and shaped a popular view that all the fighters for the independence of Ukraine were villains, eager to destroy "moscals"—the popular folksy nickname for Russians or Russian descendants. This propaganda contrasted eastern and western Ukrainians having us, easterners, believe that all the Ukrainians from the west disliked us for speaking Russian or Russian-accented Ukrainian. After visiting Lviv (the cultural center of western Ukraine) in 1996 and a few times afterwards, I realized the falsehood of those myths and the new truth: The people living in the west of our country are friendly, hospitable, open-minded and cheerful in the same, or, perhaps, stronger way than us. Our accents and some of our traditions differ, but we are the same people who love the same country and desire for it the best future.

The Russian propaganda of the new post–Soviet imperial type also laid the groundwork for the recent invasion of Russia into Ukraine under the pretext of protecting the Russian-speaking population. The fact that nobody took into consideration that this population never asked for protection was ignored by the Russian state media, molding a favorable public opinion about the invasion within Russia. Instead of achieving the alleged goal of protecting Russian speakers, these events revealed and enhanced patriotic feelings in many of those who demonstrated that language does not serve as the dividing line between Ukrainians. On the streets of Kharkiv, you can now see people proudly wearing Ukrainian embroidered shirts, not a common sight just a few years ago. We improved our knowledge of the Ukrainian language and revived old Ukrainian folk traditions, like the feast of Ivana Kupala—the summer solstice celebration coinciding with the John the Baptist Christian holiday. On that day, concerts and dance shows of Ukrainian music are held in parks and old estates around the countryside, girls throw flower wreaths with burning candles into rivers or ponds, men catch them in hopes of later catching the girl's love, and everyone dances around tall fires. Another tradition guides couples to jump over the fire to test their love.

Back in the eighties, however, propaganda also made many of us kids happy participants in the demonstrations and political meetings in honor of the Great October Socialist Revolution. We were proud to see the exhibitions of power of our motherland. We did not always know of the bloody abuses and tortures inflicted by that power on its own citizens, as well as on citizens of other socialist countries who dared to express dissent. Our parents, who knew more than us, did not dare to speak, out of fear for us and our future. Since our school was in the suburbs far from the Kharkiv city center, schoolchildren were not required to participate in any political demonstrations. We watched them on TV on the morning of November 7. A social animal who loved crowds and gatherings, I deplored being excluded. I dreamed of taking the place of one of the children on TV who watched marching soldiers and tanks on the shoulders of their dads, waving a small red flag. I had to remain content with school events honoring the revolution where we listened to patriotic speeches and recited patriotic verses and sang revolutionary songs like "The International" or "Cruiser Aurora" while applauding our marching troops.

Not all the school events were infused with propaganda. We organized intellectual games with two teams competing against each other and answered tricky questions based on erudition or knowledge of cultural, literary, historical or geographical facts. We participated in various interscholastic academic Olympics held in different towns around the region. I was the best in Russian and English language events, often winning first place, but I also represented the school in regional math competitions. Once I related my solution to an Olympic problem to my mathematician godfather at a family party on the same day of the competition. He immediately and resolutely rejected my solution. Then he started discussing it with other mathematician friends present at the table. After several minutes of analysis, silence and baffled looks ensued. Another minute later, my godfather declared, in an incredulous tone, "I believe she is right after all!"

I was happy to go to the academic Olympics if they took the place of regular classes. I was not so happy if I made it to the next round, normally reserved for the weekends. Dragging myself out of bed on a snowy or rainy February morning to take an electric train and travel a couple of hours to a remote town to solve math problems or write a composition on a challenging topic was hardly anybody's idea of fun. My intense sense of responsibility and conscientiousness never allowed me to skip or feign sickness, however. Worst of all, even if I won top places, my only reward was an honorary mention in the school radio program. I felt it was an enormous injustice for my great sacrifice to be crowned with such a poor trophy. On top of that, during one of those Olympic events, somebody stole my wallet and sack lunch out of my bag. Refusing to believe in people's dishonesty and perfidy, I kept trying to convince my parents that someone merely took them by mistake and would return them if he had a chance.

The happiest event of the whole year, surpassing by far all patriotic, civil and intellectual celebrations, was the end of school year. The assembly of "the last bell" attracted all of our closely-knit Yuzhny community since most residents either graduated or had someone in their family graduate from our school. We stood in a half circle in front of the school wearing our festive uniforms and listened to the principal summarizing our yearly work in pretty much the same terms year after year. Nobody cared—we were too excited by the spring breeze and the approaching three-month vacation. To be sure, it was closer to two months as the first week was reserved for field trips to regional museums, a local bakery, a clothes factory, a milk-processing factory and a ceramics factory. We got tired of the factories after the third day. The rest of June was taken by "laboring off" (otrabotki)—a special term referring to free students' work benefiting local collective farms or school building improvements. On the usually sunny day of May 25, however, the thought of physical labor was still far from our minds and concerns. We were too full of energy and strength accumulated during the academic year, and we would eagerly apply it to hoeing the fields or corralling a bull, as long as it was anything other than mental toil in the confinement of the school walls.

After the principal's monotonous rambling, the vice principal called the deserving students from each class to receive the certificates of academic excellence in front of the whole school. It was our second of fame—the whole town was watching and applauding us. I keep a stack of the identical certificates with Lenin's approving smile as a memory of those brief moments of glory. Then we listened to the USSR national anthem with our right hands raised in salute to our red Pioneer pilot hats. The solemn melody honoring our great and powerful Soviet Union, "created by the will of the people" and united by "Great Russia," always filled me with emotion and pride for being the product of our almighty motherland.

After the "last bell" ceremony in third grade, 1985. I am the tallest student in the middle of the back row, and only half my face is visible behind the other students.

Receiving honorary certificates in first and third grades, 1983 and 1985, respectively.

The ceremony concluded emotionally with a pair of graduates-to-be carrying a small first-grader on their shoulders as a symbol of the transfer of educational wisdom to a new generation. The child was ringing a school bell to herald the end of the year and the graduates' school career. The stereo played the classic school-leaving melody "When We Leave Our Schoolyard,"

Graduates carry a first-grader ringing the "last bell" symbolizing the end of secondary school, 1985.

bringing tears to our parents' eyes. We students, on the other hand, did not feel quite as sad.

Homeroom teachers supervised the same groups of students from the fourth to the tenth grade and often became attached to the point of feeling like they were saying goodbye to their own kids. They remembered the students from "their classes" for years to come (for better or for worse), and they were (and still are) always invited to school reunions. I still feel at home visiting my school, where most teachers remember and welcome me—in a much warmer way than when I was a student. My old worries and fears seem quite insignificant during such visits, and I sentimentally cling to the good and funny memories from my past.

The whole town also assembled to watch the high school graduation party in June—a sort of a fashion show which competed with final exams for the primary spot in the girls' minds for more than a year. You couldn't blame them—people came to watch, analyze and discuss graduation gowns. Since state clothing shops offered hideous specimens that only jokingly could be referred to as dresses, nobody bothered to look there. Instead, we acquired the attire from so-called "speculants" or ordered them custom-made at tailor shops. A "speculant" was a private buyer with a knack for business who obtained rarely available, stylish attire through some unofficial connection to the supplier or from a trip abroad and then sold these goods at a nice profit to clothes-hungry acquaintances. A significant disadvantage buying from them was that you did not know beforehand what they could offer for sale, nor how much it would cost.

If we opted for a tailor-made dress, our parents started hunting for the appropriate fabric a year or longer before the event since good-quality fabric was similarly difficult to find. My grandparents kept some silver brocade in their attic coffers for years for such a special occasion. For a couple of years preceding the graduation I would climb in there to touch and admire it, my heart beating faster as I envisioned my future star appearance. To make a dress, we visited a tailor my mom knew well in Kharkiv, and she did a magnificent job of sewing precisely the modern princess dress I imagined—short, flared bottom, tight-fitting top and puffy bell shoulders. Hairstyling and make-up jobs were mostly taken care of at home by collective family efforts, but shoes presented another challenge. Again, Soviet shops and Soviet-made footwear were out of the question, and speculators were our only hope for decent options. Speculant visiting sessions were a delight for us style-hungry Soviet consumers: They unpacked stacks of tempting models we could try on for hours on end, savoring for as long as possible a look we could not necessarily afford. My graduation was an occasion for splurging: Mom bought me Italian-made, white classic sixty-ruble shoes.

Receiving my high school graduation certificate and the golden medal at the graduation ceremony, 1993. School principal Liliya Aleksandrovna, in dark glasses, is standing.

As I come to watch the modern school graduation parties, I observe in amazement the evolution in the level of tolerance of the school administration, which now allows low-cut or short dresses unimaginable in my times. I can only fathom the explosion of sarcasm and roar if our draconian principal Liliya Aleksandrovna saw any graduating girl present herself in such an outrageous attire or flout the risqué dance moves they now employ for graduation performances.

The official part of the graduation party also took place in front of the school and, when the new school was built, in its spacious inner courtyard. Administrative officials happy to not have to bear the sight of troublemaking students any longer slightly modified their speeches for the occasion to make them less monotonous and more upbeat. Graduating homeroom teachers also made a point to design a special entertainment program which differed each year but always included an element of dances, jocular songs dedicated to the school, funny awards and dress up. I dressed up as a gypsy and predicted the fortunes of our teachers.

The official proceedings and concert were followed by a feast in the school cafeteria, which our parents had diligently prepared, and a dance that lasted well into the night and was open to the town residents. Some of these would instigate fights which, as our old saying goes, were an integral component of a true celebration. After one such fight, they moved graduation parties out of the school, and students' parents are now responsible for renting nearby cafes to host parties. This move, sadly, put a stop to the unique Yuzhny tradition of walking to the pond after the dance and watching the dawn together. Many guys would jump in and go for a swim in spite of the early-morning June chill which made our breath turn to steam. That first dawn after graduation, the end of the grueling exams and the freshness of morning aromas felt so young, so hopeful, so exhilarating.

Our graduation party heralded the end of the first serious stage in my life, just as it did for all the other graduates in the Soviet Union and everywhere else. For my generation, it was more than the end of compulsory schooling—our graduation coincided with the end of the Soviet era which had completed its cycle just six months before. Although Americans usually think of the breakup as an exciting period that promised freedom and new opportunities, it felt nothing like that. Our ruined economy, more severe deficits than we had ever known and lack of job security and future prospects gave us shivers when thinking about what was to come next.

Living on Land

Not many Americans have heard about the Colorado beetle. Most Ukrainians, however, are closely acquainted with this colorful pest, especially if they had to compete with it for the potato harvest in the hungry and tumultuous post–Soviet nineties. With bright yellow wings and contrasting black stripes, they could be seen on Yuzhny streets in summer advancing in steady and focused columns towards the edge of town where the fields stretched to the horizon on the waves of picturesque rolling hills. These monsters sensed the irresistible pull of potatoes—their bread and butter—planted by our residents in the hope of survival through the long winter, and they prepared for a feast. Along with their maggots, they clung to the leaves of potato bushes creating flashy patterns, and if not disturbed, quickly reduced them to bare stalks, after which the potatoes could not fully develop in the ground. After gorging, they would drill themselves into the soil for a rest that could last as long as two years and in the meantime produce some voracious babies eager for a life of similar plundering.

When the Soviet economy broke down and no longer could subsidize agricultural production, food staples like potatoes, meat and sugar became scarce and difficult to afford for the population that stopped receiving regular salary payments. In an effort to mitigate the dire economic crisis and to compensate for the lack of food in the stores, the government divided the land previously owned by collective farms and distributed the plots to the citizens. These plots would become our life boats, to which we would desperately cling as if to an oasis of survival in a desert, and, ironically, entertainment in those hopeless and drab times. Planting beets, carrots, string beans, tomatoes, cucumbers, and, most important, potatoes, and then giving them plenty of care throughout spring and summer could provide sufficient and even lavish subsistence for the winter—unless the vicious Colorado beetle destroyed the plants.

The echoes of the Slavic agricultural past made it easy for people to return to the earth traditionally pictured in Russian and Ukrainian folklore as a nurturing mother—"dear Mother Earth." Many people in the Soviet Union used to own some sort of "dacha"—a summer house which could range from a luxurious two-storied mansion on the Black Sea for government workers to a half-ruined hut with barely enough space to sleep for regular citizens. A typical dacha of the Russian pre-revolutionary aristocracy emerged from the pages of Chekhov's works as a pretty wooden house with an attic, an open verandah and a latticed fence drowning in lilac bushes and fruit orchards. Some Soviet workers happened to be lucky owners of similar summer residences, but for most this was a dream model, a reason for aspiration and daily toil. Most city dwellers, however, had a patch of land and at least a modest shelter for cover in the countryside which gave them the means to escape the dusty city once the temperature rose above freezing so they could reconnect with Mother Earth. There they would temporarily become gardeners and farmers experimenting with planting, seeding and cultivating tree hybrids through what we called "tree vaccination" so as to receive better-quality fruit.

The brutal nineties transformed this hobby into a necessity. Scientists, engineers, professors and singers stopped receiving regular salaries as their institutions broke down or lost state support, and they became part-time farmers while also carrying on their regular jobs. They basically donated their free labor to the state machine—as voracious as the Colorado beetles but far less efficient. After work, professionals rushed to their terrain to mull over the soil, hoe, plant everything they possibly could, pull weeds, water, rake the soil into small heaps around the shoots to help preserve moisture, and, of course, battle with nefarious beetles. Residents of small towns like Yuzhny did not need agricultural training: We lived near the land and practiced these skills yearly in our backyards. Their limited space and abundant shade, however, sufficed for yielding just a few buckets of tender new potatoes, but not enough for feeding the family for an entire year. The news of an additional plot of land for a nominal-payment lease brought us hope for relief.

Older people still preserved the memories of caring for similar plots during the hungry post-war years when the devastation and ruined economy forced them to provide for themselves. The economy was now in ruins once again, but fortunately, devastation had not reached disastrous post-war proportions. Agricultural plots thus ushered in an unexpected opportunity for entertainment and socialization beyond the material support. We pulled ourselves away from newly commercialized TV screens to get reunited with family, neighbors, friends and casual acquaintances. We shared the joys of working the earth and rediscovered a sense of community. In the evenings after work, school or university courses, the whole town gathered in the fields, the young working side by side with the old, and the kids chipping in with light tasks like picking vegetables or watering.

We laughingly compared our experience to the serfdom which the Bolsheviks decried so severely and which they ironically brought back upon us more than a hundred years after it officially ended. The difference was that we worked for no one other than ourselves. The only exploiter was our formerly great state which could not afford to pay people for their official jobs while they continued to work anyway out of a sense of duty. Nevertheless, by some strange paradox, I did not dread the prospect of spending my evenings in the field coming back from the university, but actually looked forward to working in the fresh air with a beautiful view and the company of close friends or desirable acquaintances. In fact, I headed to the field on the memorable day when I received the news I had won a highly-competitive full scholarship to study in the United States. I worked as my heart danced, rejoicing at this hard-to-believe opportunity.

In those days, I also became convinced of the wisdom of the old Soviet slogan frequently posted in school hallways or official buildings: "Labor makes the person nobler." After working outside, I would go home pleasantly fatigued and in a good mood from all the exercise and socialization. Maintaining a positive attitude, however, required much more effort as the season progressed and along with it the spreading of weeds and of the infamous exotically-named beetles. My American husband, who first visited Ukraine in 1996 when we still continued laboring the plots, conjectured that the fields full of people meant everybody was indulging in the popular hobby of land cultivation. Once we explained to him the true reason for their efforts and the obstacle to our success, he grumbled that the American name of the pest probably originated from the Cold War hatred nurtured among the Soviet people towards the United States. I refused to believe this theory and kept casually researching scientific sources until finally coming across the name "Colorado beetle" with a corresponding picture in some American encyclopedia. From this followed option A: Americans had long ago exterminated the same pest, or option B: they dispatched the hateful bug to our parts in the hope of undermining the Soviet agriculture.

No means of warring against the Colorado beetle was successful in the long term. We avoided strong chemical agents since we grew potatoes for our own consumption, but tried every other way: spraying leaves with a home-made solution of soap and onion shells, using small brooms to shake off the bugs into buckets and, finally, manually picking up the tenacious devils from the plants and collecting them in glass jars. Thinking back, I wonder why we used glass and not metal jars so often—perhaps some sort of sadomasochism gave us strange pleasure in scrutinizing the imprisonment of the swarming striped masses. After filling jars, many people took them to the road separating the plots, emptied them out and executed the nasty enemies by stomping on them. I hated the crunching sound, the bumpy sensation under my feet and the pungent smell left by the bugs. To avoid it, my grandpa invented another method: pouring oil in the jar so they eventually drowned. We still could not trust this technique to be entirely effective and burned the bugs to conclude the gruesome procedure.

If this description seems nasty, collecting baby bugs—the most voracious sort—was even more repulsive. At this stage, bright red maggots lacked a hard shell and felt particularly slippery to the touch. Some of them were extremely small and demanded good practice for a proper grip. Squishing them resulted in a yucky, slimy mess. These measures were most efficient, however, since the bugs had not yet reached sexual maturity and could not reproduce. Some elderly people got so attached to the practice that they used it in lieu of regular morning exercise. One of our plot neighbors, whose back hurt from slouching over this meticulous occupation, would simply lie down among the bushes in a comfortable pose which allowed close contact with the baby bugs.

Ads for chemical solutions supposedly efficient against this enemy started to appear—although no one knew exactly how to use them as they would come either without instructions or with instructions in little familiar languages. People started spraying vile smelling liquids that seemed to work more against themselves than their targets. The cunning pests activated their miraculously efficient immune systems and got adjusted to the new agent in a matter of days. A joke circulated in those days about a guy who, like all of us, was searching for the perfect anti-bug remedy. Having heard a new recipe from a friend, he asked if it would really work. "Well, maybe it would not exactly kill them," answered the friend, "but their health will be definitely shaken."

As if the Colorado beetles were not enough, another pest, perhaps not as relentless, but even more dangerous in its surprising and sneaky nightly attacks, spread through the fields in August. When potatoes started to mature, field robbers—parasites with no inclination to work but plenty of desire to live off the fruits of their fellow residents' labor—would raid the fields and leave them empty of all the harvest towards the morning. This implied a real tragedy for the people who had invested potatoes to be planted and a huge amount of time, effort and care in the future crops they suddenly lost. To combat this new enemy, plot owners organized themselves into an association and made a schedule of guard duty when several men would spend a night watching the fields. Women would also participate but their duty did not start until dawn. From what I heard, the guards enjoyed these "watch parties" which also provided an occasion for socializing and drinking a shot or two of vodka accompanied by *salo*, a pickle and perhaps something more serious. They might have even had too much fun as potatoes still occasionally disappeared from people's plots during the guards' watch.

We did not suffer from the lack of rain in summer, but long spells of heat from time to time dried the soil so much that we also risked losing the harvest for this reason as well. Since we could only dream of a more or less normal watering system reaching the fields, we had to make up for it by our own physical effort bringing barrels of water to the plots. I am not talking about the lucky car or motorcycle owners—they had it easy. Our plot—ironically reserved for the veterans of the Great Patriotic War—lay in a distant field separated from the road by a thorny and bushy ditch. Thus, my family and many others literally cultivated those potatoes and tomatoes with their sweat—pulling the cart with a water barrel along several blocks of relatively smooth street, pushing the cart down the ditch, pulling it up all the while holding the barrel to prevent it falling and spilling, and finally rolling it some more on the dirt road to make it to the plot. The watering process itself seemed a pleasurable diversion after all of those drills.

Once, the rain deviously waited for the precise moment when my mom and grandpa had finished thoroughly watering the crops and covered up the plants with paper and burdock (a common Ukrainian weed with particularly large leaves) so the sun would not burn them. The weather forecast had not promised any change in the hot and dry spell. The dirt road quickly turned into a boggy mess, and their heavy cart got stuck with little hope for letting itself loose. My poor folks spent three hours in a heavy thunderstorm trying to free the cart wheels and clean them of mud before the wheels would stick back there again and again. They eventually made it back after such Sisyphus's labor—soaking wet, covered in mud and unable to move. This was the price we paid for procuring food staples that had been easy to afford during the Soviet times. Suddenly, they became equal to gold in value and in difficulty of obtaining them.

Finally, a day in August came when potatoes were ready to be harvested. I remember the excitement of the anticipation of getting up at dawn, grabbing a quick breakfast of cottage cheese and coffee, picking up my aunt Galya, my spirited godfather and his son Roman who would join us to help, and working in teams until about noon. I worked with Roman, my mom with my godfather Volodya, and my aunt Galya with my stepdad. Men dug out spadesful of potatoes and we picked them up, cleaned the dirt from them and put them in buckets. My godfather, who had a cheerful yet commanding nature, would yell out directions and urge us to hurry up. My musician stepdad, who had no natural inclination for agricultural work, would regularly dig in the wrong places and damage the potatoes. Then, throwing out the dirt from the fresh dig, he would cover up previously removed potatoes. My aunt would get mad, scold him and complain about being paired with such an inadequate worker. Then we would all break into song, until the next command or complaint cut short the entertainment. To infuse the procedure with even more fun, we competed between the teams. My aunt/stepdad's team would invariably lose, which brought even more of my aunt's ire upon my poor stepdad.

Towards noon, with all of the potatoes in the buckets, we would load them in my godfather's car and head back home where my grandma was preparing a feast to reward us for our toil. We would spend the afternoon celebrating and rewinding the morning's events to share the details with my grandparents and relive the fun. The year my beloved grandma passed away, my mom took her place in the kitchen, putting all of her might into trying to fill the void Grandma left behind. Mom made vareniki—potato, stewed cabbage and fruit dumplings—from scratch, preparing and rolling the dough, cutting it into circles, filling the dumplings up and shaping them into pretty shells (I have never been able to master the art myself). She also made borsch and served it all with great elegance, adding multiple appetizers and plentiful supplies of vodka and wine. Creating abundant meals of diverse dishes, especially when company was expected, was an art form the Ukrainians inherited from their ancestors and have never lost—even in times of need, when the value of the food on the table exceeded an average weekly salary.

Home-made products—preserves, sauces, pickles and jellies—came in very handy for garnishing the table. Ukrainians and Russians, especially those living in the countryside, have always excelled in preparing preserved foods to stock up for winter. Peasant women started the tradition out of necessity long before the refrigeration process. Russian and Ukrainian classics, such as Turgenev, Saltykov-Shedrin, Honcharov, Gogol and others, deliciously describe summer kitchens full of steaming, boiling, stewing and canning women workers. Communism converted nearly everyone into peasants and most women became well versed in the process of pickling and preserving fruits and vegetables, partially out of need and partly out of love for the process of creating home-made food. Even nowadays, modern technology and well-equipped store shelves cannot dissuade people to stop summer canning marathons.

In late June, people would crowd in their backyards rich with berry bushes to collect strawberries, raspberries, black and red currants and gooseberries. These berries are hardly known in the central and southern parts of the United States—I occasionally find them in whole food markets, where a pint costs six or seven dollars. Black currants, extremely rich in antioxidants and Vitamin C, taste pretty sour, but the jelly, with the addition of plenty of sugar, make a delicious spread to use with bread and pancakes (bliny), as a pie filling, or even by itself, with tea. Many other fruits ripening in our backyards offered excellent material for jelly, and Ukrainian women let nothing go to waste, thus occupying themselves for the rest of the summer. When the last currants and gooseberries, if any are left, fall from the bushes, apricots signal a new stage of preserve-making. Peaches (less common in our parts), plums, apples and pears follow towards the end of the summer and continue into the fall since various types ripen at different times. Fall mushrooms conclude the preservation season started by cherries in early June. In between come cucumbers and tomatoes which people pickle in huge quantities to stock up for eating as sides, as accompaniments to vodka or ingredients for the ever-popular salad "Olivier." And more ingenious, creative and indefatigable cooks find more original ingredients to surprise their guests in winter—rose petals, pine cones, dandelion flowers, walnuts complete with a green shell and such. Some people pickle watermelons—although I do not understand the pleasure of eating them sour. I remember when I was a child, the sight of watermelon in winter tremendously excited my appetite. The taste, however, quickly disappointed me as it only remotely reminded me of watermelon in texture, but not in anything else.

It seems that people would purposefully complicate the pickling/preservation process to make sure they did not spend their summers in idleness. For example, they would take out pits from cherries—this process alone can absorb an entire day. In the case of apricots, I heard, it is compulsory as pits give the jelly a bitter taste and may actually be poisonous. As if taking out the pits was not enough, one recipe dictates opening up the apricot pits and taking out the white sweetish hearts in order to return them to the jelly. Although the process sounds like voluntary prison labor, I have to admit jelly tastes wonderful with the white hearts counterbalancing its tanginess. Gooseberries—green, fuzzy, crunchy and extremely sour—would probably win the crown of the most complicated fruit in the jelly preparation process. In order to clean its insides from the mucousy mass of seeds, we would snip off the tails, squeeze a paperclip through the holes left by the tails, carefully rub the insides with the paperclip and take out the seeds. One try would not suffice at first—the gooseberry entrails were very slippery and stuck to the fingers or would not come out all at once.

Meticulous practice helped develop the art of seed removal to perfection by the end of the day when you couldn't look at the fruit any more and doubted whether you wanted that jelly after all. But that was not all. Another important preliminary step for ensuring the future jelly's special aroma required boiling cherry tree leaves slightly, pouring the resulting liquid over the gooseberries and letting it cool down overnight. Since the huge basin would not fit in the largest of the refrigerators, my grandpa would take it to the dark and damp cellar—the most ancient Ukrainian refrigerator, which we used for storing all the preserves as well as the harvested potatoes and other vegetables.

The following day, grandpa would bring it back to light so that the actual jelly making could begin. Just as the preparation was time-consuming, this process was also long, tedious and strength-consuming. The most proper procedure prescribed boiling the berries in sugary water three times to ensure the firmest texture of the fruit. My grandma stood guard by the stove making sure the mixture would not burn or "run away" from the basin, stirring it all the while. She had to catch the right moment of the liquid breaking into a boil when she would remove the basin from the stove and cool it down before repeating the whole the process a while later. She would know the jelly was ready when a drop of it would not run down too quickly from the tip of a spoon, but rather stay nearly still in one thick blob. Then came the canning: Special lids covered the glass jars, previously sterilized by a long steaming process, which would then be dispatched to the cellar until the joyous moment of consumption was to arrive.

I almost forgot about juices and compotes, which held an important place in the hierarchy of homemade preserves. Most of the above-mentioned fruits also provided wonderful material for these essential products loved and craved by all. Not many types of juice were sold in the Soviet Union in winter. Although the situation is completely different now and grocery store shelves are filled with all kinds of exotic juices, people continue producing their own by habit, passion or need. Fruit compotes, particular to Ukrainian and Russian cuisine, are normally not manufactured industrially and hence have a natural reason for their preparation. Unlike juices which require the fruit to be squeezed, compotes use the fruits whole, boiled with sugar. The same pitting and peeling procedures apply. In hot and cold weather alike, compotes are warmly welcomed at Ukrainian tables, and three-liter jars disappear from a table with astonishing speed, thus justifying the preparation of huge quantities in the summer.

Additionally, many vegetable mixtures and "squash caviar"—grated and stewed squash paste—make their way into the preservation product line. "Konservazia," the Russian word for the "preservation process," has become a code for a sacred ritual when all the festivities stop and the daily activities become subjugated solely to the god of pickling. Evoking the signal word brings understanding looks to friends' faces if they happen to suggest an outing or a cookout—nothing can disrupt the ceremony. I often wonder, however, if all the labor and time investment is worth the pleasure of indulging these treats, a lot of which can now be easily purchased. I think people simply cannot abandon the tradition tying them to generations of their ancestors. Besides, the hard-working nature of Ukrainians does not allow them to relax. The non-written rule dictates that my people cannot spend a day without working, and if found relaxing with a book under the shade of the tree (as I often do), they are stamped as a good-for-nothing lazy bum forever.

My own parents (with my strong encouragement) stopped producing preserves a few years ago. "You are getting older," I argued, "and can spend your time in a much more productive and enjoyable way." My mom, a lifelong activist fighter against kitchen slavery, easily agreed. "Besides," I continued, "with us living in the United States, you simply cannot eat all that food." Well—my stepdad, an avid and non-discriminating devourer of compotes and any other delicacies coming his way—probably could. It would not be good for his elevated blood pressure, though. The high concentration of salt and vinegar in pickles does not help his health and that of many other Ukrainians who suffer from heart-related concerns. But just as in the case of *salo*, which, as Ukrainians believe, contains a good kind of cholesterol, people ignore the apparently harmful qualities of pickles.

The all-consuming preservation fever can be contagious and even people valuing their freedom become its victims. Last summer in Ukraine, I felt guilty watching my neighbors engrossed in the process and letting the fruit we could not consume go to waste. With my mom at work, I engaged my stepdad to help me prepare my favorite apricot compote. I mixed up the recipes, however, and instead of keeping the fruit intact, boiled it several times until it reduced to a gloopy, viscous soup. Besides, cutting corners, I decided to avoid pitting the apricots and threw away the pits later with the dregs that we filtered. It seemed more efficient until I tried the finished product and realized—too late—that the old wisdom recommending previous pitting was not a waste of time. We hoped that filtering the fluid would make the color more transparent, and it did, but it did not help much and the juice/compote remained quite muddy. After multiple filtering efforts and endless additions of sugar in an attempt to reduce the bitterness, we gave up, having canned only three jars of the concoction. The preservation business proved to be too challenging after all.

Since then, I suppress any feelings of remorse about my lazy moments in the midst of pickling fever and dedicate them to my children's or my own continuing education. I lie with a book in the shade of our overgrown garden no longer filled with berry bushes as we no longer tend to them. I am content—unless the Colorado beetles attempt to reconquer our land.

Extracurricular Activities

The Soviet cult of childhood as the most favorable stage for molding one's proper socialist character presupposed not only political education of young minds, but also well-rounded cultivation in the spheres of arts, music, dance and physical culture. In the 1930s, Pioneer palaces took the place of former nobility mansions in each city to promote kids' creativity in singing, dancing, art, gymnastics, engineering and other classes, all offered for free or for a nominal cost. Later, music, sports and art schools opened up, with most offering lessons after regular school classes, and others, designed with a comprehensive curriculum of regular subjects and an in-depth study of music or arts, accepted only truly gifted children. My stepdad, who knew from age six that he wanted to be a brass instrument player, went to one of those. He started to learn at the Pioneer palace and was quickly selected for the specialized study of brass instruments at a highly specialized music school—there were only five of this type in Ukraine. He referred to it as a "concentration camp" for the iron discipline that reigned there and high demands imposed on students not only in music but also in general academic disciplines. He has bittersweet memories of this institution, since it enabled him to enter the world-renowned Moscow Conservatory upon graduation.

I never burned with desire to waste my childhood in an attempt to become the next Mozart. My mom, however, harbored some hopes for my artistic future and signed me up for the music school in Yuzhny. I wanted to go to art school and draw, paint, cut, glue and sculpt. The family council decided that exposure to music and learning to play an instrument would shape me more productively, and I could draw, paint and glue on my own. They were right, of course—I used the same reasoning with my own kids thirty years later. Plus, we already had a piano occupying a place of honor next to the TV set in our living room. I was an obedient girl and did not protest. Thus, my fate was determined for the next seven years. The completion of homework, which I always did immediately upon return from school to get it out of the way, did not bring me freedom as I was heading to music classes or practicing the piano afterwards.

Tchaikovsky's niece, Rymma Aleksandrovna Kupov'yanova, who lived in Yuzhny and had no heirs, presented her family mansion, two pianos and an accordion to the community in 1963 to be converted into a music school. She moved to a tiny house, where servants probably used to stay, in the backyard of the school. "I am giving everything that I have to those who own the future," she said. "Let there always be music in my house." In 1968, she also sponsored the addition of the small theater to the old building where recitals and exams were held. Grateful teachers and students took care of Rymma Aleksandrovna, cooking and cleaning, for the rest of her 97 years. She died in 1989.

The Soviet system provided a solid and comprehensive music education, which ensured that my after-school schedule was full for the whole week. I had my main subject—piano—twice a week for 45 minutes; sol fa (music literacy) twice a week after the piano class; and choir once or twice a week. A couple of years later, music theory, accompaniment, and composition were added to my curriculum. All of this instruction cost my family a nominal fee of 14 or 15 rubles per month. Although I had a good voice and an ear for music, I cannot say I displayed exceptional abilities, at least not in my initial years of study. I was frequently rebuked by my piano teacher who also tapped my fingers to reinforce the point. Sol fa was more entertaining since we studied as a group and had a chance to socialize between learning the chords and writing music dictations—the notes of the melodies the teacher played for us. My accompaniment teacher—the school principal—was a fiery and temperamental lady who could break into song or screams in the middle of the class, depending on her mood. Once, she encouraged me to yell at the top of my voice in the classroom to help me lose my inhibitions. I never did.

My stepdad in concert attire, 1982.

Most of all, I dreaded the chorus class—the teacher rarely smiled, often yelled and generally treated us with cold and harsh resentfulness. She kept choosing the most obscure songs which none of us had ever heard, with absurd lyrics, like "Fat Aunt Piggy had a baby piglet and bought him four hundred diapers" or "They made the revolution without me, and they fought against the Whites without me." The song ended with the desperate call "Please don't do anything else without me!" The line inspired my mom's sarcastic remark about "them" (the Soviets) having put the country in such a mess that the songwriter had to implore them not to undertake anything else.

I really enjoyed the composition class which was added to my curriculum in the fifth or sixth year of study. A young and enthusiastic Inna Petrovna taught me to compose anything that came to mind and helped me improve the melody and break it down into the parts played by different instruments. Thus was born a cycle of pieces in the style of Russian and Ukrainian folk music which later, quite unexpectedly, won me the third and the fourth places in the All-Ukrainian competitions of young composers. My photo appeared in the local newspaper, and feeling inspired, for the first time I considered the possibility of continuing my music education professionally. The fancy of a musical career did not last, but I performed the pieces in various concerts—we created an ensemble with a few other students, one of whom sang, another played the violin, and the third played a tambourine. I still maintain a warm friendship with Inna Petrovna, who later moved to New York and sadly discontinued her music career.

When I was in the sixth grade, two music teachers organized a spring break trip to the town of Klin, Tchaikovsky's birthplace, situated not too far from Moscow. The cost was very economical since we stayed at the local school which put together some beds in schoolrooms for us, and a group of six or seven students, myself included, happily took advantage of the opportunity. My mom went as well—she didn't consider that I was mature enough to go on my own, and the teachers valued her help with finding the way around Moscow. She visited the capital often for work and knew it well. The first day we saw everything there was in Klin—mainly the house of the great composer and the surrounding park—and dedicated the rest of the trip to sightseeing in Moscow. A trip to Moscow took, a bit inconveniently, three hours by a slow local train. It didn't squelch the enthusiasm of young travelers like us, and we happily ventured out of Klin every morning to walk the entire day around Moscow and return to our school hotel in the evening. It made for quite exhausting days by any standard but we were happy. Life in a big and bustling city excited us with its opportunities. We visited museums, ate in cafes, drank Fanta, which I tasted for the first time there, and hung out at the pedestrian street Arbat.

One adventure spiced up the culture-drenched routine. One day, we were admiring art in the Pushkin museum when the alarm rang. Chaos followed and we soon found out that a painting had just been stolen in a room next to the one we were in. Our detective story-thirsty minds started to conjure the images of the robbers and devise strategies for tracking down the culprits. It turned out that a girl from our group had been in the same room with the robbers and felt confident she saw them before the crime. She was questioned as a witness while we continued to investigate the mystery on our own. The administration closed the museum doors and would not let anyone out. As it was nearing nine o'clock, we feared the possibility of spending the night in the museum or, at best, at a train station. Fortunately, they let us go and we managed to catch the last train to Klin. We looked around us all the way home and imagined we saw the criminals chasing us to take revenge for Oksana's eye-witness account. Recently in Yuzhny, I ran into one of the guys from the group, and we reminisced about the accident. He was now a policeman and he said that the incident had inspired him in his career choice for, according to him, he was instrumental in helping the militia solve the case. I searched in my head, not able to find any recollection of his role, but congratulated him anyway.

I spent eight years in music school. When I graduated at the end of my eighth year, I felt relief. Now I could have my afternoons to myself, once my homework was done.

Death of a Leader

People knew something was wrong when *Swan Lake* and other classical music masterpieces were all you could catch on all three state TV channels, with no cable or satellite to provide any variety. Ubiquitous all-day broadcasting of classical tunes became a tradition from 1982 to 1984 as three elderly Soviet leaders would pass away one after another in approximately the same season—from early to late winter. The election of youthful Mikhail Gorbachev by the Supreme Council of the Communist Party in 1985 put an end it, but by that time people started to associate the romantic tunes with the foreboding of drastic change in the government.

Three decades earlier, the news of Joseph Stalin's death from a cerebral hemorrhage drove people into frenzy. Mom, who was a child at the time, recalls seeing people sob on the streets. Accustomed to seeing the leader's image on TV and in newspapers, offices, classrooms and flower beds on the streets, people mourned the loss of the father of all the nations and peoples of the Soviet Union who had sent millions to torture or death. Many rushed to his funeral and hundreds were killed trying to pay their respects at his casket as the bulging crowd smashed them against buildings, traffic light posts or trucks on the streets. Those who had the misfortune of falling could not rise again as the human wave crushed them; people didn't even realize they were stepping on human flesh. Still, people were convinced that some conspirators caused this human mincer. With Stalin's death, many felt desperation, believing no one else could take care of them and lead them towards a bright and peaceful future. Many were convinced that no one could protect the country against the threat of the Cold War enemy invasion any longer and that the Third World War was now inevitable.

Such was the power of the mass hysteria inspired by the evil genius of this individual who terrified the country for many decades. He cultivated universal terror and a universal belief that he was the strongest, the wisest and the kindest. Many people believed that massive arrests were the fault of the secret militia and that Stalin was not aware of the abuses. They tried to

My mom's class with Stalin's likeness in the background. Mom is in the second row to the right of the teacher who is smiling.

write letters asking him to investigate the wrongs, and when they did not receive a reply, they believed he never received them. Stalin held the country under his fist, and if he said that two plus two was three, people were ready to enthusiastically embrace the new math. When members of the Communist party congresses applauded him, the ovation could last for ten minutes, for no one dared to be the first to stop applauding.

A few months after Stalin's death, Mom and her parents happened to be in Moscow. An essential part of any tour of the capital included a visit to Lenin's mausoleum—the first question friends would ask upon your return necessarily centered on these impressions. The old inhabitant Lenin now lay in the company of his successor, whom he actually did not trust. The line to this Soviet mecca, which I remember from my own visits, wound around Red Square and threaded into the Alexandrovsky Garden, behind the square. Since both leaders attracted double curiosity and adoration, there was in the air a feeling of danger that not everyone would be able to enter the crypt. Those at the back of the lines, particularly alarmed, suddenly started to push against the rest of the line, jumbling up the order and instigating panic. The efficient Soviet police, enriched by the bitter experience of the March funeral, reacted immediately and restored the line and the people's hopes of seeing the greatest individuals in Soviet history. My family were, in fact, able to get in and snatch a look at the leaders before the harsh commands of the armed guards drove them on. During my own visit in 1997, I remember the barking yell of a guard warning me not to open my purse when he perceived a slight motion of my hand in the vicinity of the sacred tomb. By then, the line became much shorter and consisted mostly of foreign tourists attracted to such an unusual curiosity. I never came back to the macabre place, although such a sight has fascinated my political scientist husband.

Since the aftermath of Stalin's death was not as terrifying as people had thought and many freedoms even became possible, Tchaikovsky's melodies heard from the screen in the late fall of 1982, when Leonid Brezhnev died, brought us mixed emotions. Fear was no longer part of them and neither was sadness, although a friend of mine recently confessed to me that she actually cried. Whether she was really grief-stricken or merely obeyed the force of tradition, she no longer remembered. I did not notice anybody else arrive at that emotional extreme. We felt some sympathy for the deceased and his family, although no one took him to be truly alive during the last years of his rule. His slurred and jumbled speech made him sound as if his mouth was constantly full of kasha. The face with extremely bushy eyebrows hardly moved and resembled a mask more than a human expression—that is how my mom, who saw him briefly in front of the Kremlin hospital in May of 1982, remembers him. We felt some wonder at what would happen, but for us kids, the strongest of all emotions was the excitement of breaking away from the routine and skipping school work the day of the funeral.

Unfortunately, we could not stay home the entire day. Everybody—starting from the first and going to the tenth grade—had to gather in the school gymnasium for paying final dues to the abstract symbol who mattered much less to us than the shop assistants at the local grocery store. Standing solemnly and not allowed to move so as not to show disrespect, we watched the funeral ceremony on a small TV with a black-and-white image not clear enough for all of us to catch the important details. Only after a couple of hours when the ordeal was over could we indulge in the pleasures of outdoor freedom. We were too engrossed in our busy worlds of games—which were many in the absence of the Internet and electronic gadgets—to worry about the fate of a politician who scared us with his bushy eyebrows and mummified expression. We were too shielded by our families' love to seriously worry about the future of the government or our own future.

The long period of Brezhnev's rule was later characterized by Gorbachev as "stagnation" for the absence of any political and economic upheavals and general stability. To be certain, the disastrous Afghan war threw a shadow over this stability, but our media skillfully camouflaged its ugly effects. They would nevertheless reveal themselves occasionally in the mental struggles of soldiers who, like the brother of my "kuma" Olga, returned traumatized from the obligatory military service in Afghanistan or in the "black tulips," as zinc coffins of fallen soldiers sent back home were known. In spite of these "minor" backstage challenges, the country continued to accumulate new cities and towns, cities new buildings, military industry new weapons, space exploration new heights, and sports and cultural sphere new prizes. Living standards improved—many could now afford buying new furniture or a car, that is, if they had enough patience and time to wait for their turn in "line," which, similarly to the line for an apartment, could stretch for years.

At the same time, censorship also maintained its grip on writers, thinkers and musicians. Industries stopped their development, and nobody expected anything out of the ordinary from the future. It was during this period that the nuclear physicist and Nobel peace prize winner Andrey Sakharov was arrested and exiled to the city of Gorky (now Nizhny Novgorod) for his active human rights work. It was during this period that the winner of the Nobel prize in literature, Alexander Solzhenitsyn, was expelled from the Soviet Union for his writing denouncing the crimes of the regime. It was also during this period that Joseph Brodsky, long persecuted for his "parasitism" (absence of an official job) and anti–Soviet poetry, was forced into exile, even though he declared that did not want to leave his motherland. Living in the United States, he won multiple prizes in literature. In 1987 he won the Nobel Prize for literature.

The long-time head of the KGB, Yuri Andropov, was instrumental in these persecution operations against dissidents, and this professional success led him to the position of the next general secretary of the Communist party. He imprinted himself in our memories through an active fight against corruption and parasitism. Militia battalions were sent to movie theaters, parks, hair salons and barber shops to hunt for parasites skipping work. My godfather, Uncle Volodya, a mathematics professor at the Kharkiv Automobile and Highway Institute, during his winter break accompanied me and his son Roma to the New Year's kids show at the Kharkiv Palace of Sports and fidgeted nervously during the whole event, fearing an official roundup.

Brezhnev's stability had extended to political offices, which meant that if you got a hold of a chair in the government, you stayed there forever. It was a refreshing change after the shudder of Stalin's terror, when any wrong move could lead to a political execution, or Khrushchev's tumult, when a slight change in his mood could induce a change. Brezhnev initiated the period of the oldest living government cabinet with the average age above 70. After Andropov followed Brezhnev into the other world in a little more than a year's time, 72-year-old Konstantin Chernenko, hardly remembered by anyone at all, took the throne. After his death a few months later, we were a bit tired of state funerals, even though they did afford an occasion for an unplanned day off. It was nice to see a fit and a cheerful leader take the stage for a change.

Gorbachev was a fresh breath air in the highest post in the country not only due to his unadvanced age (at 54 he was a youngster in Soviet politics) but also due to a number of unusual reforms he undertook, such as the prohibition of alcohol and destruction of invaluable old vineyards in the country. He attempted to fight the biggest ill of our people, but immediately earned himself countless enemies, for Soviets could not possibly enjoy an alcohol-free celebration, let alone a dry wedding. The endless resourcefulness and adaptability guided them to assemble moonshine apparatuses which they ran behind tightly closed kitchen doors (since then the closed kitchen door has become associated in my mind with this mysterious bubbling and dripping procedure). The incorrigible alcoholics rushed to find a cheap substitute for spirits in the form of eau-de-cologne and paint thinners. The director of the renowned Crimean winery Magarach, biologist Pavel Golodryga, committed suicide in 1986 because he could not bear witnessing the brutal destruction of the vineyards cultivated and cherished throughout centuries. The prohibition campaign, promoting weddings flowing with juice and soda on TV in reality worsened the alcohol problem and the health of the population.

People also resented Gorbachev's flashy wife Raisa Maksimovna as a show-off who accompanied him on all the official trips and delegations. We were used to invisible wives of politicians who never thrust themselves into the public eye. The unusually confident manner of Raisa Maksimovna parading herself in front of everyone in designer clothes and expensive fur coats while the majority of the population had to cultivate their own food appeared a brazen offense for the Soviets. The contrived and condescending way in which she spoke to people in informal meetings did not win her any friends either.

The Chernobyl disaster added to the negative aura surrounding the new leader. While Westerners admired Gorbachev for his charm and progressiveness, Soviets ridiculed and criticized him with a new fervor afforded by glasnost (newly proclaimed openness in speech). They ridiculed the birth mark on his forehead, saying it resembled the shape of the Soviet Union (people in the United States saw Europe); his country accent; his wife; his absurd reforms which only worsened conditions for most people; and his funny manner of speech, or, rather, his babble. He could talk for hours, spicing up his speech with some vague foreign words, such as "pluralism," "mentality," "consensus" and "referendum." Their sounds were too cumbersome for our unaccustomed tongues and ears, but for some reason, Gorbachev ignored their more digestible Russian equivalents. No matter how long he carried on his discourse, it was next to impossible to summarize it—the meaning of it escaped the listeners. Once he was invited to give an inauguration speech addressing world youth at the San Remo film festival in Italy, and he exceeded the five-minute limit by about fifty minutes, changing the topic of the speech to philosophic reflections on human values and the importance of music to the friendship among the peoples of the world. Some of his linguistic gaffes became hallmarks of Soviet oral humor: "Let me say what I said"; "I am leaving you feeling impregnated" (he really meant "enriched"); "I will respond to you in a Gorbachev way. You know that it will be more complicated than a simple answer"; and other pearls.

A caricature using the motif of the Russian folk tale "Turnip" appeared in the *Trud* ("Labor") paper to satirize the vain efforts of the perestroika (literally, "restructuring") campaign. Instead of the traditional version of the illustration where the grandpa is pulling up the turnip followed by the grandma, the granddaughter, a dog, a cat and a mouse, all pulling at one another's backs to help ease the turnip out of the ground, the drawing featured the opposite order of a mouse pulling at the turnip, with a cat, a dog, the granddaughter, the grandma and the grandpa following. The caption said: "We restructured ourselves."

Meeting Gorbachev after his talk at Kansas State University in 2005.

Death of a Leader

I am grateful to Gorbachev for opening the door to the West and starting a peaceful dialogue, which granted me an opportunity of a lifetime: study in the United States on a scholarship by ACTR/ACCELS (the American Council of Teachers of Russian and the American Council for Collaboration in Education and Language Study). Gorbachev and Ronald Reagan signed the agreement to seal this academic and cultural exchange program in the mid-eighties to expand peaceful contact between the citizens of our countries. I later thanked him for his courage and peace-promoting efforts in person when he came to speak at Kansas State University in 2006. His speech was as verbose and jumbled as ever, but his personality struck me as down-to-Earth and charming. He appeared as a kind, happy grandpa, happy to see his grandkids spread around the world. His daughter Irina was equally approachable and charming. We exchanged a few jokes and I felt like I had known her forever.

The next time TV broadcasting stopped in favor of *Swan Lake* was not until August 1991. This time, preoccupation and wonder became more pronounced as my peers and I were older, perhaps smarter, and knew that the death of the still-vigorous and healthy Gorbachev was unlikely. The previously unheard-of foreign words "coup d'état" and "military junta" crept—or, rather, jumped suddenly—into our vocabulary when we found out that several hardline party members, unhappy with Gorbachev' policy and the plunge of the country into immorality and economic chaos, arrested him. Since *Swan Lake* swallowed up any news broadcast, we could understand little of what was going on and felt confused and scared. When uncertain TV announcers finally brought the news of Gorbachev's sudden illness and the formation of a state committee for the state of emergency, we felt even more confused and preoccupied.

I was by then more politically informed, felt more patriotic consciousness and believed myself to be progressively minded. The news, which disrupted my planning of a sunny vacation day with friends, made me realize the shakiness of our democracy. For the first time in my life, I felt worried about the possible return of dictatorship to my country—at that time still the USSR. The disorganized putschists quickly lost control of their actions, and the country, under the new guidance of the strong-willed but whimsical Boris Yeltsin, dissolved in the next few months. An uncertain future was our new reality, and the long-awaited freedom hardly brought us happiness.

Healthcare

"Healthy mind in the healthy body!" proclaimed a popular socialist slogan emphasizing the importance of staying fit, and the theory was put into rigorous practice. Ubiquitous one-station radio sets installed in every apartment started their daily broadcast with a program of morning exercises accompanied by lively music: "Hands up, hands to the sides, hands down! Hands on your hips, lean to the right, lean to the left! Jump!" "Morning gymnastics" also inaugurated the day's activities for kids at daycare and at schools. In the fall before the onset of the nasty weather, we congregated in front of the school building twenty minutes before the beginning of classes, in lines formed according to our grade, and followed the order of the PE teacher. We bent down, we jumped up, we made circles with our waists. Those who dared to misbehave or not follow the instructions had to come up front and perform the exercises next to the teacher, much to their peers' amusement. We performed the routines in our regular school uniforms—that is, the girls wore their uniform dresses. Fortunately, only conservative rudimentary gymnastic moves were involved—teachers did not experiment with strenuous Zumba-like or kickboxing elements that would not exist for years. Before proceeding to classes, we checked our names in the rosters to avoid being reprimanded for tardiness or absenteeism.

The words of another popular proclamation—"Soviet Healthcare is the Best in the World!"—were often cited and paraphrased ironically once the proletariat dictatorship days were over. Nevertheless, they held a solid grain of truth. What other country sent doctors on home visits to the sick, even for a simple cold? What other country offered a couple of weeks of paid sick leave, not only to the patients, but also to mothers of a sick child? What other country provided a year-long paid maternity leave which was later extended to three and six years if the circumstances required it? What other country provided working people with so-called "putevka" ("voucher" is the best possible translation although no true equivalent for the concept exists) to so-called sanatoriums and vacation homes where ordinary workers could stay for up to a month, eat three meals a day, plus mid-day snacks, and get medical treatment for a fraction of the real cost or at no cost whatsoever? Finally, what other country provided all this, and other services of highly qualified doctors and nurses, at absolutely no cost?

A high proportion of those services focused on kids, maternity and prenatal care. Expectant mothers started preparing for this important stage in their lives by going on leave a month before their due date or even earlier if health conditions required it. They went to the hospital a few days before their due date, and stayed a week or so after the baby was born, to ensure that it was completely safe to go home. They didn't pay a single ruble for their stay. A nurse visited the mother and the baby regularly afterwards to check on the healing and development process. She would massage the baby and teach the mother to perform special baby gymnastics to lay the foundation for his or her best physical future. My mom was appalled when we took my newborn daughter for a well visit to a clinic in Kansas where she was surrounded by coughing and sneezing patients. She was even more terrified to find out that most American mothers resumed their working routine at a maximum of six weeks after the birth, abandoning their helpless offspring in daycare centers. Back in her days, mothers would not even consider taking a newborn to a friend's house, much less leaving her with a babysitter or taking her on shopping trips. Superstitions also prevented some people from showing their baby to acquaintances and even friends for a couple of months after the birth, for fear of her receiving the malicious effects of "the evil eye" and falling ill.

Such restrictive traditions and utmost concern for the baby's well-being put some limitations on mothers' lives for the first year after the birth of a child. At the same time, the state and grandparents' support eliminated a lot of the stress faced by American mothers. My mom always says that the first year of my life allowed her to collect the memories that she treasures among the happiest in her life, even though she was about to get a divorce. My grandma took care of cooking for the family, and Mom dedicated her time to feeding me, playing, talking, singing and walking with me. Children in the Soviet Union were cherished and cultivated like plants in a greenhouse, and when a child was born, all the family's (parents' and grandparents') attention and efforts became channeled into his care and education. Perhaps such intense attention accounted for at least one reason why very few families had more than two kids.

I never went to daycare because my grandma didn't work and took care of me when mom's maternity leave was over. Therefore, not being exposed to many viruses, my immune system had not built up well when I started school, and I started catching every bug that bumped into me. Sometimes I was sick for two weeks or a month at a time, confined to bed until all the

It was essential to take children and babies outside in any weather to provide them with fresh air. To protect me from harsh winter temperatures, my parents wrapped me in several layers of clothing and padded the stroller with a mattress, a pillow, several bed sheets and a blanket, as seen in this picture from 1975.

signs of a runny nose were gone. Our kind family doctor, Anna Mikhailovna, with her warm, encouraging, Ukrainian-accented voice, the best possible kind a doctor could have, checked on my progress, coming by a couple of times a week before giving her approval for my release. She also granted sick leave for my mom who brightened my days with her cheerful presence, play time and even homework and news from school, which she visited when I could not go outdoors. I enjoyed the first days (unless the fever was too high or another discomfort too bad for fun) because they gave me a chance to rest, read and be with family. Then I would start to feel anxious. My friends came by on their way from school, also bringing me homework assignments and news. They sat around my bed in a circle and chatted happily about what happened that day—I felt glad to see them, but sad about the life I was missing. When I was finally allowed to step outside, I felt dizzy and shaky with the sudden excess of oxygen and brightness around me.

For the whole year, Soviet citizens waited for summer when we could go on a lengthy vacation to strengthen our immune systems and "healthen up." Educational and scientific institutions and factories usually subsidized a vacation center or a sanatorium providing material support, and in exchange, they could send their employees with a reduced-cost "voucher" to spend a month in those places, usually in summer, but occasionally in the fall or even in winter. Vouchers did not always come about easily, especially in the popular summer and early fall periods. Human resources departments distributed them with approval from above but oftentimes found a way to award their family members, friends or important connections ("necessary people," according to the common folklore) first. My grandpa's trade union paid for a considerable portion of his vacation voucher, but those vouchers would not be distributed until late spring, or, sometimes, the very last days before his vacation and thus we often did not know our destination until the last minute. This caused my grandpa considerable stress in trying to procure train tickets, which sold out with extreme speed in summer. A remote acquaintance in Yuzhny working at a railroad ticket office was our only hope, and she usually saved us, in exchange receiving the gratification of a few rubles above the cost of the tickets.

Before perestroika and the Soviet advancement into economic ruin, these vouchers allowed us to go to vacation centers (literally called, in Russian, "houses of rest") in the Caucasus and Crimea on the Black Sea, the Dniester River in Moldova, and Liman Lake in the Kharkiv region—my least favorite destination for its lack of exoticism. Five smokestacks from the nearby electric station added the only exotic touch to the Liman scenery, with smoke rising high above the lake as we were swimming. Sometimes we rented private apartments in beach towns of Yalta and Sochi. I loved the flexibility they afforded, not obliging us to appear for breakfast, lunch and dinner at the particular time and the ready, often unpleasant fare we had not chosen. We reserved our spot on the beach early—or, actually, my grandpa, who woke up before all others, did. He went to the beach around seven in the morning, rented loungers and made a tent with some sheets for UV protection. Coming after eight was useless—the bodies were packed on the hot pebbles, mattresses and cots so tight that hardly a leaf could fit between any two of them. It was a cozy companionship of vacationers—we made friends with our neighbors as often we kept the same spot day after day, shared snacks and jokes and often maintained our friendship for years.

I became good friends with a girl from Moldova named Karina when I was around nine, and we exchanged letters for four years until her family emigrated to Germany. She introduced me to the word I was not familiar with: "Jewish." She confided in me that she was Jewish and asked me to keep it a secret. I didn't know how to react as I could not understand what the problem

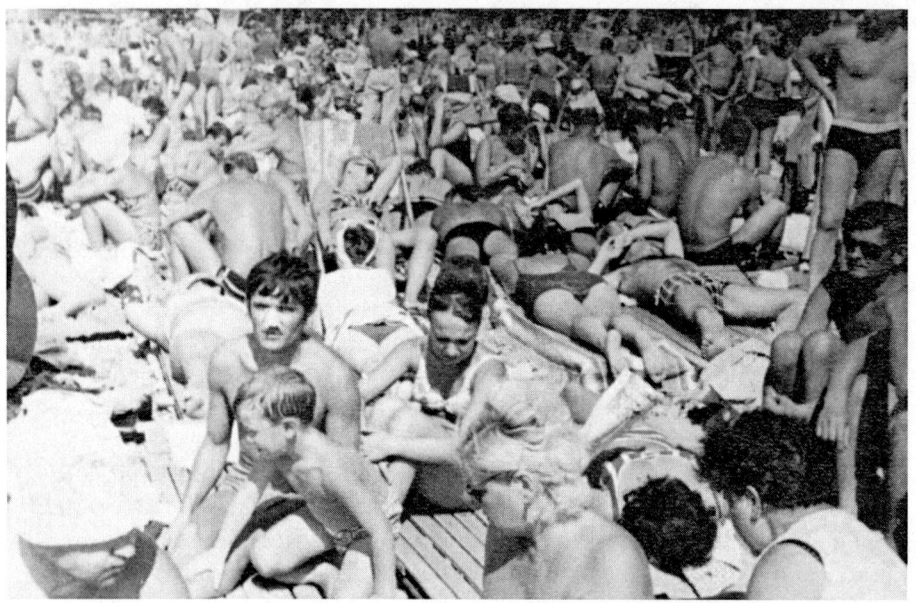

At a beach in Sochi, on the Black Sea. Sochi, where the 2014 Winter Olympics were held, was the most popular resort town in the Soviet Union. Mom told me she used to meet colleagues and acquaintances on its beaches all the time during vacation.

with this term was, nor what it really meant—membership in a clandestine society? Party affiliation? Nationality? Not many Jewish families lived in Yuzhny, and many must have also been hiding this fact, afraid of the official or unofficial persecutions, abuses and insults plaguing their people for centuries. I looked forward to Karina's exciting letters which were full of wit and engagingly described her theater and museum visits, her music achievements, and parties with friends. I was sad when her letters stopped after she emigrated, and I wondered how her new host country treated her. I still hope to find her in one of the modern social media sites and tell her what a wonderful experience it was knowing her.

The vacation centers where we spent our summers were the Soviet equivalent of all-inclusive resorts, offering a bit more austere living conditions than their Western counterparts. Showers and bathrooms were often communal, sometimes located in a separate building a hundred or so meters away from the cabin where we stayed. Three meals a day, in addition to a late afternoon snack of kefir and cookies, varied widely in their quality from place to place. Vacations at Liman in the Kharkiv region are memorable for the least appetizing meals and the amount of fat in what supposedly were meat dishes. "Why is there so much fat?" my grandpa once inquired of a kitchen employee.

During a walk at the Sochi port with the ship *Admiral Nakhimov* in the background, 1982. The ship later sunk in a wreck.

"There is no meat without fat," was the answer. "But likewise, there is no fat without meat," Grandpa observed, logically. He soon discovered the whereabouts of missing meat: stopping by the kitchen to request a sack lunch, he found the employees savoring a highly nutritious dish of meat severed from clients' meals.

At a vacation center on Lake Liman, in the Kharkiv region, 1981. Smokestacks from the local electric station are in the background.

Brought up on my grandma's healthy cuisine, I remember with shudders the kasha caked to a stone-like condition, along with fatty cutlets and dry veggies. I spent meal time with my back turned to the table. Grandma, not able to get a respite from household duties on her long-awaited rest, later cooked me meals I could digest on a small stove we brought along with us. In spite of their drawbacks, vacation centers offered nightly entertainment consisting of movies, concerts and dancing. During the daytime, they organized festivals on the beach and games for the kids. We sorely missed these places when most state enterprises ran out of money to support vacationing employees, and we could not afford a month-long all-inclusive rest. The last place we went as family was Liman in 1988 or 1989, and then I missed even this place.

In many countries I have visited since that time, I have yet not found an equivalent to our "sanatoriums"—a type of a medical resort or an all-inclusive Soviet spa including medical checkups, physical therapy and different procedures. I heard that Germany has something similar. Going to water spas or "going to the waters," as Russian aristocrats used to say, was already popular in the 19th century among the rich for curing tuberculosis or simply for general health improvement. The heroes of the great Russian writer Mikhail Lermontov spent entire summers at the spas drinking mineral water, taking baths and being idle, as the aristocracy used to do, finally bringing upon themselves the ire of the working class. Shortly afterwards, Soviet authorities turned these water spas into a paradise for the working class and intellectuals alike, where people could enjoy benefits never before imaginable for the proletariat anywhere in the world.

While after the demise of the Soviet Union many sanatoriums closed following privatization or the closing of their state benefactors, many others miraculously survived and continued functioning with diminished support from the state or in a new, privatized condition. We visited one of those surviving dinosaurs last summer. The Myrhorod resort, founded in the city of the same name, is well known as the birthplace of the Ukrainian-Russian writer Nikolay Gogol. It celebrated its one-hundred-year anniversary in 2017, the year before our visit. The first time my friends and Robert and I had passed through the place in 2012, its well-kept buildings, mosaics of Ukrainian folk scenes, neat, well-groomed alleys lined by cypress trees, graceful flower-and-grass structures of cathedrals, monuments of Gogol's characters and his own portrait made of flowers attracted us with their welcoming local flavor. The place was teeming with happy vacationers, and the view of the lively beach over the pretty river put the final cherry on top of this bright image. I knew it used to attract people from all over the Soviet Union with its mineral waters and natural beauty and was pleasantly surprised to see the place up and running, unlike the vacation centers in Yuzhny, which were by now almost completely in ruins. We vowed we would come back there with our kids and my parents, and finally, six years later, in 2018, we decided to realize this ambition.

When we arrived, I quickly realized that not only the best Soviet traditions survived at this place. The check-in process provided a surreal picture

With Mom in the pine forest by the Liman vacation center, 1981.

of Soviet times with an infusion of capitalism. At the main resort we were informed by phone that there were no vacancies, but the lady I spoke to kindly referred me to another number. Although nobody answered for a while, I finally got hold of a receptionist who gave me a quick price reference (which I immediately forgot due to the complexity of price levels). Then she invited me to check out the rooms in person. We found them impressively clean and spacious, with basic but sturdy furniture and austere, freshly-painted beige walls. When we got back to the reception area to verify, again, the complicated price scale and the options, the lady was busy checking in other visitors and asked us to wait for "only" half an hour. I did not manage to convince her that a quick price check would help us spend those thirty minutes in a more productive way, comparing the prices to those of other accommodations in town. Instead, I had to attend to my husband struggling with a fit of post–Soviet traumatic stress. He became very familiar with Soviet customer service nightmares when we got married in Kharkiv in 1996. That summer, we had to overcome multiple bureaucratic hurdles that seemed to come from the pages of Orwell's novels in order to obtain the official permission to get married and for me to emigrate to the United States. Unforeseen challenges with price inquiry brought flashbacks of those tough times.

It wasn't that bad—the lady at the resort was incomparably nicer than Soviet officials, although hardly any faster. After completing a thorough documentation for the people ahead of us, which must have included information on their education, work experience and a detailed background check, she finally turned to us and started a similar process. It appeared to be slightly shorter—she was obviously intimidated by our foreign passports and spelling complications this circumstance entailed. However, another complication soon surfaced: As we arrived in late afternoon and food had to be ordered ahead of time, she informed us there might not be enough food in the cafeteria to serve our six-member family. Communicating with the cafeteria to make sure they could serve us at least some "sosiskas" (hot dogs) took another fifteen minutes and a blood pressure surge for my husband.

An hour and a half after we arrived, the receptionist was finally done checking us in. We were so happy to settle in and start the vacation that we did not immediately notice that our rooms also offered some sweet absurdities left over from the Soviet times. It took me many years of living abroad and my husband's grumbling to recognize the nonsensical nature of some of our devices and constructional peculiarities with a fresh, unaccustomed eye. The rooms boasted modern appliances, including flat-screen TVs and refrigerators, all of them apparently unplugged. Looking for plugs offered an opportunity for puzzle-solving, which we were not ready to handle after almost two hours in the lobby. Robert finally found the plug for the air conditioning unit hiding behind one of the beds on the opposite wall. Fortunately, an extension cord, also discovered behind the bed, afforded a successful connection. We did not manage to solve the plug riddle in the other room without help from the room attendant who, for a while, was no less puzzled. Both the TV and the refrigerator were plugged into a short extension cord leading nowhere at all. After a careful search, we discovered an available plug behind a huge, not-easily-movable wardrobe. The only other plug was located on the opposite wall where the cord could not reach no matter how hard we tried. The room attendant finally brought us a new regular-length cord—and did not even hint at the necessity of tipping.

After the initial mishaps, the vacation went surprisingly smoothly: The resort surprised us with varied and well-balanced meals and a variety of therapies we could request from a sympathetic doctor. The cost for the stay, including three meals a day, massages from a six-foot, two-hundred-pound woman who particularly enjoyed making my husband grunt in pain, aromatic and bubble baths, physiotherapy for my parents and other treatments we did not consider, was only slightly higher than the cost of a nearby hotel with no such options. It amounted to about $55 U.S. per day. For meals, we could choose from three meat or fish dishes (served even for breakfast), kasha (milk cereal), cheesecakes or pancakes, salads with all the meals, soups for lunch and regular and herbal teas. The only dessert option for dinner included fruit since it was a health resort where we were not supposed to indulge in bodily caprices. We sinned a little by supplementing our healthy diet with pastries, salami and wines from a local supermarket to brighten our evenings.

Another, and perhaps the most important benefit attracting people to resorts like Myrhorod, is the mineral water from springs around which the place was built. The information sheet inside the water-drinking pavilion (or "buvet") promised that drinking one type of water in the correct amount and at the proper temperature would help heal a wide list of ailments, from gastrointestinal problems to purifying radioactive elements and preventing oncological diseases. Drinking a different type (a doctor had to choose the most appropriate type and amount for every patient) "improves bile formation and secretion, and helps to rarefy slime and discharge it from the stomach." The sign also warned that contact with air "quickly ruins the organic matter," for which reason the water had to be consumed in the water room only.

A triangular building full of sunlight flooding through three glass walls and stained-glass pictures of the local sites and countryside contained rows of water taps with the type of condition indicated next to each one. It was the main hang-out of the resort: People flooded the building along with sunlight before and after meals, sipping this miraculous fluid from plastic cups or specially-designed ceramic mugs with drinking spouts, expressions of concentrated bliss on their faces. We also assumed appropriate expressions and joined the sanatorium crowd in hopes of miracles for our own bodies, but not having consulted a doctor, we got lost in the myriad of possibilities. When we did see the doctor, she prescribed 150 ml of lukewarm mineral water forty-five minutes before meals for my husband, kids and myself, and 200 ml of a different type of water one hour after a meal for my parents. This regimen, in addition to the massages, baths and physiotherapy, filled a rainy afternoon to exhaustion and fostered a welcome nap to everyone except the kids, for whom the bubble bath seemed to give a fresh charge of energy. We tried to sleep as they bounced around the room waiting for our revival.

Being quite energetic myself, I do not prefer relaxing vacations, and hardly ever spend more than three hours on the beach. I hate lonely beaches with few people in sight, no entertainment or happy crowds. In Myrhorod, I didn't mind visiting an open-air movie theater or areas for dancing ubiquitous at my childhood vacation centers. Curiously, these simple entertainment options disappeared with the breakdown of the USSR as if the proper technology for them was no longer available. Perhaps the demand for these outdated venues diminished as cell phones and other gadgets ousted them. There was a "cultural center" on the grounds, and we bought tickets to one of the concerts by a winner of the Ukrainian equivalent of *The Voice* singing competition. A potpourri of songs from the eighties, both local and Western, raised the spirits of the audience who filled about a third of the theater. People aged three to ninety sang and danced along to pop classics as only devotees or amusement-thirsty vacationers could do.

Notwithstanding the lack of active fun, I was content to pause my hectic lifestyle and submit to the calm, healing regimen of the sanatorium for the sake of experiment and my family, who needed a break from busy schedules and constant rain. I found that I quite enjoyed the results although my unaccustomed back hurt from the vigorous massage, and I grew hungry very fast after consuming healthy sanatorium cuisine. I realized that I am too capable of enjoying an adrenaline-free rest not packed with activities. Also, my heart smiled at the home-like atmosphere and sincere friendliness of the staff not so common in our official public life. A Western customer who is used to sweet waiters and cheerful police officers would probably take them for granted, but any Ukrainian knows that such concepts as "cheerfulness" and "an official" can be combined only in an oxymoronic way. We cannot conceive of a police officer without a menacing and frowning expression indicating that its owner never abandons his troublemaker-searching duties. We know well that an official in a public service position cannot and should not smile as it would detract from his importance. We know well that customer service is a gift we should value and appreciate and never take for granted to give homage to the abuses older generations and ourselves underwent at the hands of the customer service officials. That is why smiling, helpful and jesting personnel—administrators, doctors, janitors, guards and cafeteria assistants who smilingly wished us a good day—worked, according to a Russian expression, "like balm on our souls."

When the sun went down, vacationing families, young and elderly couples and groups of teenagers poured outside, roamed around the alleys and conglomerated around the main entertainment center—a fountain which dazzled people with a show of lights and music at nine every night. We joined the crowd, roamed around and engaged in people- and fountain-watching just like everyone else. I felt my pace sync with that of my fellow vacationers, my pleasurable indolence reflected in their eyes, and I imagined myself transported to a vacation center from thirty years ago, where people were similarly united by the same healthy regimen, the same place of eating and sunbathing, and the same pleasure of summer idleness. Such vacation centers were a symbol of our synched existence in the big family of the Soviet republics, and they painted it with a happy face.

Bureaucracy

"Woman, what do you want?" Such a conversation starter was the warmest welcome one could expect to receive when visiting a Soviet or post-Soviet public office. We did not consider it rude. We were used to mistreatment, abuse and insults. Humiliation of visitors was ingrained in the blood of Russian officials long before the Soviet times, which only solidified and validated old habits. A minimal amount of power and awareness that someone else depends on your favor validated people's self-concept and helped fight off any inferiority complex a bureaucrat might have.

Nikolai Gogol, the great 19th-century Ukrainian-Russian writer (born in Myrhorod), paints a sarcastic portrait of a high official in his story "The Overcoat." It is a Very Important Person—who does nothing all day, but puts on airs and pretends to be extremely busy as soon as a petitioner arrives. He keeps a poor guy waiting just to inflate his self-importance in front of an old friend visiting him for a chat. Then he finally receives the petitioner, speaking to him in a menacing tone he purposely rehearsed in front of the mirror: "Don't you know the proper procedure? [...] You should have first of all submitted a petition to the chancellery; it would have gone from there to the head of the proper division, then it would have been transferred to the secretary, and the secretary in due time would have brought it to my attention."[1]

The same procedure, perfected throughout years of bureaucratic practice, still applies to our officials. Gogol's character, exposing the ills of the Russian officialdom, also provided a prototype which shaped not only generations of Soviet bureaucrats, but also many present-day leaders nourished on pseudo-democratic ideas. The ills and twists of administrative tunnels became part of Soviet lore. We were pushed around from one location in the city to the next in order to gather multiple documents, "essential" for processing the petition but needed mostly for supplementing the income of the officials. In the early days of perestroika, the tradition dictated thanking them for their hard efforts with a something like a bar of chocolate. As perestroika advanced, these tariffs increased to a bottle of good wine or cognac, and finally to cash payments which had to be derived through a challenging mathematical procedure or verified with trustworthy sources of insider friends or acquaintances. A relative working in the institution or a related department could help solve a challenging matter, but the luck of having one placed in the right position did not often present itself to regular mortals.

    I got lucky the first time. Aunt Lena (the one who later, at our wedding, predicted our firstborn would be a girl) saved me from the unsurmountable difficulty of obtaining a foreign passport through the regular channels thanks to her valuable connections at OVIR (Office of Visas and Registrations). Soviet citizens, and later citizens of former Soviet states, had two passports—one "internal" for matters like registering one's place of residence, and the other "external" for rare opportunities of foreign travel. When I got the exhilarating news of being accepted to the exchange study program in the United States, my first sobering thought was of acquiring a foreign passport. None of my relatives or friends had one, and we harbored only an obscure idea of the trial this would entail. The official processing time, we found out, was three months, which would make me two and a half months late for the start of the American academic year. No expedited mechanism was listed in the official OVIR materials. When my mom and I came to the office bright and early in the morning, we saw a line so long it would keep us waiting until my assigned travel date. We were recently reminded of that menacing line at the discount store Five-N-Below where we stopped on the day before Christmas. The difference was that the OVIR line moved at the rate of one person per hour, with frequent "technical breaks" and a generous lunch break dragging out our torment. Aunt Lena, whose friends arranged the passport in what must have been a Soviet Olympic record-breaking one-week time, spared us the nightmare of being stuck in that dark, surreal corridor for an eternity.

    Nevertheless, no Soviet citizen could avoid the bureaucratic machine, and it caught up with me when the time came to leave the country to reside abroad. Naturally, Soviet citizens were not free to leave the motherland whenever they wished, and the mere thought of emigrating abroad was deemed sacrilegious—only ungrateful traitors voluntarily decided to abandon their native land. Visiting foreign countries, especially those from the enemy West, was also discouraged, but it was practically impossible anyway during Soviet times, unless, of course, you obtained permission from the authorities and somebody paid for your ticket and stay—a possibility akin to a dream. Such permission was granted for official government delegations, athletes, scientific expeditions, journalists on foreign assignment and, occasionally, for tourists sufficiently well off to be able to buy a "voucher" for leisure travel abroad. In my childhood, I only knew of one person, a dentist, who traveled to western Europe and Japan for leisure.

After the breakup of the magnificent empire, the stigma associated with immigration started to fade but the administrative hurdles did not disappear. I had to be "unassigned" from my place of residence, surrendering my internal passport and receiving a seal of approval in my external one. The handwritten approval was placed on top of the seal, which was issued by the USSR even though Ukraine was already an independent state. In order to be "unassigned," I had to visit the housing management presiding over our apartment and present multiple documents justifying the reason for leaving this place of residence, returning several times for one or the other page was missing or photocopies were not properly done.

I also had to obtain a new foreign passport when I was preparing to emigrate since I changed my last name after my marriage. The intricacies of this sinuous process are blurred into one prolonged nightmare in my memory, except for one episode which emerges from its depths. Just before the passport went into processing, my mom suggested I check the spelling of my name in their computer. After some persuading, they let me see the last name spelled "Rodrigez." Glad that I found the mistake in time, I asked them to change it to the correct "Rodriguez," against which they presented a solid argument: "The computer knows better how to spell it." It took me some courage and a bar or two of chocolate to convince them that I wouldn't be able to explain to every American official seeing my last name in the passport spelled differently from my husband's that our Ukrainian computer knew better how to write it.

When I got the stamp of approval for being "unassigned" from my place of residence and surrendered my domestic passport, I also had to collect a document from my biological father, divorced from my mother since I was two, stating that he had nothing against my emigration. Considering my relationship with him ended at my parents' divorce, this visit implied a certain level of tension and discomfort. However, nothing could compare to the stress one experienced facing a formidable employee of OVIR, who seemed to be entirely immune to any human feelings except for the desire to torture her official visitors. Every time I came back with a new paper hoping the process was nearing its completion, I trembled at the sight of the omnipotent lady in the militia uniform scrutinizing every letter and comma on my new homework. Every time, I expected her to reject it for some minor fault of a photograph placed at the wrong angle or signature missing a twist. She justified my expectations—I returned again and again, with "the proper state of fear and trembling," just like Gogol's hero.

Customer service and public service officials never let slide any occasion to demonstrate their superiority to the plebeian crowd. Even a janitor on duty could berate you for not vacating the room in a timely fashion to allow her do her job. Aunt Dusya, school janitor and a threat to anyone who dared to walk on the floor she recently cleaned, was one of the first employees whose intimidating image impacted me for the rest of my life. Such images surged into my memory every time I stepped into a public office. Our school principal solidified my fear. We lost our voices when we needed an X-ray, a doctor's consultation, or, God forbid, official permission to marry a foreign resident. We came ready to be shaken up and thrown out because the people in charge always found a way to demonstrate their superiority and use it to deny the request or service for any reason they pleased.

Mom's first bureaucratic nightmare accompanied the good news of her receiving a free apartment from the state, or, to be more specific, from Kharkiv State University where she worked. During the time she waited for the apartment, she got married and had a baby, and thus was qualified for a two-bedroom apartment, instead of the one-room flat that was available for her. This annoying circumstance was further complicated by the fact that another candidate, without real connections to the university, but with more powerful connections to some top gun, was tempted by the only available two-room option. Thus, Mom started her several-months-long paper-collecting and multiple-office-visiting odyssey with no end in sight. Some chief poked his finger at one of the numerous forms asking, with the irritation typical of administrative bosses, why one of the lines was left empty. The line was requesting information about employment and the address of the petitioner's children or child, who, at that point, had not even turned one year old. Mom would have probably lost the battle with the establishment or continued it up to the present day if not for the help of the sympathetic university rector who finally authorized an accelerated granting of the two-room apartment.

I also have to give credit to my husband who was thrown into this mess of post–Soviet bureaucracy and economic headaches, shocking after living in American orderliness and efficiency. For the most part, with minor occasional setbacks, he kept his cool. His experiences visiting Argentina in the 70s somewhat prepared him for life in a country facing political, socioeconomic, and bureaucratic problems. He tasted the finitudes of our administrative system immediately upon arriving: As a foreigner he needed to register his stay with the proper authorities, for foreigners had no business roaming around our country as if it was their own. He briskly headed to the Kyiv OVIR office hoping to get this boring business out of the way first, until he saw the line to the office twisting around the block. As we stayed in Kyiv for only a day, we were obliged to postpone the pleasure of dealing with officials until our arrival to Kharkiv, where matters were not much better. Robert started displaying signs of serious anxiety when it appeared that he would have to spend most of his seven-day stay in Ukraine interacting with OVIR officials and people in lines, still without the hope of ever reaching a successful resolution. As usual, my mom found a happy alternative by getting her friend at the Intourist hotel to issue a voucher as if he was staying in the hotel, which automatically granted the registration stamp.

Other obstacles followed when I had to request special permission to marry a foreigner from the Foreign Affairs Ministry in Kyiv. When we first attempted to visit this intimidating place, the receptionist told us they were not accepting any more clients, although the schedule posted on the door indicated another hour of the work day remained. The bulk of negotiations with high officials again fell on my mom's shoulders as she was the most experienced and diplomatic person in the family for navigating bureaucratic mazes. We kept coming back daily, as if to work, with a new document required from us the previous day, and exiting with the burden of a new assignment. One of them required my husband to appear before the U.S. embassy personnel and signing a sworn statement that he was not already married to someone else.

In Ukraine, you get a particular passport stamp once you get married, which serves as official proof of your civil status. Since no such rule exists for American citizens, a sworn statement was the next most reliable document Foreign Affairs Ministry was willing to accept. Finally, we were told the permit would be ready in a week, which exceeded the possible limit of our stay in the capital and the planned date of our marriage ceremony. The process was significantly hastened by a monetary donation, which made the document appear, magically, on the same day. The date of the ceremony could not be confirmed until the permission was secured, about five days before the wedding. Good thing our guests were flexible. Unfortunately, this lack of certainty and difficulty of travel to Ukraine at the time due to visas, permissions and registrations made it impossible for any of Robert's family and friends to attend the wedding.

Not only did state organs require navigating a bureaucratic maze for the trying process of marrying a foreigner, but the Russian Orthodox Church also had to give its blessing for a union of an Orthodox to a Catholic. My mom secured a special appointment for my groom-to-be and I with the metropolitan (the rough equivalent of a bishop) of the Kharkiv region, and we presented ourselves, trembling, for another stage of interviews. This visit turned out to be unlike any other official proceeding any of us had ever had—before or since. The atmosphere in the metropolitan's office was quite intimidating—perhaps because the room lacked windows, but mostly because the host barely acknowledged our presence as he entered. We had been invited to sit in his office and wait for his arrival. When he entered with a wave of his hand, the metropolitan sat down and started reviewing our written request in utter silence. As our nerves increased with his alarming quiet, he slowly removed his regal cap. Then, maintaining his silence, he got out a comb and starting combing his hair, followed by combing his waist-long gray beard. Our alarm switched to mirth as we silently watched this imperturbable grooming routine, and we squeezed each other's hands tightly under the table, trying hard not to laugh. After another minute or so of quiet grooming, the honored sir finally broke his silence, directing a question to my mom. Recognizing Robert's Hispanic surname, he inquired of his origin, and here a divine surprise awaited us. Quite unexpectedly, he turned his attention to us and spoke in pure Spanish, and, even more astonishingly, with a clear Argentinean accent! It turned out that he had spent twelve years in Argentina serving as a head of the Russian Orthodox Church of Latin America in Buenos Aires. At that moment, Robert knew that our marriage in the Orthodox Church would be granted, as the connection was finally established. The metropolitan carried with him fond memories of Robert's country of heritage, and after a most pleasant chat, he blessed our marriage by assigning the church and date our marriage would take place. He then presented us a couple of Orthodox icons, which have hung in our bedroom ever since as a permanent reminder of this happy encounter.

At the wedding palace before the start of the ceremony, Robert was subjected to extortions of various registration fees at the most unexpected moments (the last payoff took place just before the start of the ceremony). They resembled blackmail more than official procedures and were most likely due to the groom's foreign origin—a foreigner could clearly afford donating some extra cash. An official was the king or queen of his or her office (no matter how insignificant it was) and squeezed the most pleasure and practical usefulness out of his or her position, such as a bribe or, if such was not possible, humiliation and refusal. If he or she decided to grant you his or her regal signature, stamp or service, you felt immediately that you were forever in his or her debt.

It goes without saying that I felt great liberation when I received permission to exit the country—not because I was eager to leave, but because I was anxious to leave behind the nightmare of dealing with our pen pushers. Little did I know that it was not so easy to shed the Soviet heritage which persecuted me even as a resident of the United States. When I returned for a visit two years later, waiting excitedly to see my native land, the guys at passport control grounded me to the Ukrainian soil quicker than I had anticipated with the question "Where is your stamp of registration with the Ukrainian consulate? Didn't you know you had to obtain one upon your arrival to the new country of residence?" After some nerve-wracking moments, they finally let me enter on the condition that I would return to my favorite OVIR to acquire a temporary stamp registering my stay in my own country, until securing the consulate stamp back in the United States.

Visiting Ukraine has become a lot easier for tourists in the past two decades since no visa or OVIR registrations are required any longer. However, a few vestiges of the Soviet past still live in the public sphere, mostly in the form of the poor treatment of petitioners, implanted in the bureaucratic DNA. The officials simply cannot deny themselves the pleasure of insulting or humiliating us by pointing out our mental inadequacy or slowness resolving an issue. During my latest visit to Ukraine in 2018, I needed an X-ray of a tooth and inquired if the facility had a bathroom. The receptionist handed me a key, but I attempted to open the wrong door. Instead of directing me to the right place in a polite way, the lady asked derisively, "Ma'am, where do you think you are you heading?" Such instances are becoming less frequent as even this sphere, most impenetrable to expressions of humanity, is slowly improving under the influence of people's increasing exposure to the Western habits. As travel to Western countries becomes more common, so grows the comprehension of positive and friendly human communication, even if it takes place in a public office.

On the other hand, I came to realize that bureaucracy also exists in the West. When I was trying to fill out a form for posting a package in Italy, a friendly but stern worker remarked that I could not use a red pen for this purpose, as it was not "legal." In the United States, bureaucratic pitfalls reveal themselves most clearly to potential residents filling out an application for a permanent resident card or "Green Card." They have to indicate all the addresses where they have resided since the age of eighteen, secure a certificate from the police about any criminal history from all those places of residence, and indicate detailed information about their parents and their work history as well as exact dates of travel to foreign countries over the past ten years. If a document attached to the online file happens to be positioned horizontally instead of vertically (which could be easily remedied with one mouse click), the whole file has to be resubmitted. I also heard a few horror stories of people whose documents and files were occasionally misplaced or lost back when they were submitted in paper form. The lines at the INS office which I visited in regard to my Green Card and citizenship application could be comparable, if not equal, to OVIR. Immigrant and non-immigrant entry forms to the country ask visitors if they have ever engaged in genocide, human and drug trafficking, prostitution and other similar activities.

I also discovered that American officials working in Ukraine were susceptible to post–Soviet influence themselves, or perhaps they simply did not consider it worthwhile to treat Ukrainians with the same respect and dignity they reserve for their own citizens. The first time my mom applied for a guest visa to visit us in the United States, petitioners could not request an appointment in advance. Instead, they had to reserve a spot in a line stretching around a block, at five or six in the morning, if they hoped to enter the building on the same day. People spent hours in the rain and snow, typical for late November, with no bathrooms close by. To dilute their boredom, they could fill out visa applications while waiting, managing acrobatic acts in the process. They wrote without any hard surface, holding an umbrella and trying to shield the precious papers from precipitation.

When five hours later Mom reached the end of the line, a grim-faced official asked her a couple of questions about her other children (she had none except for me) and about her income. The whole interview took no more than five minutes. As the Ukrainian professorial income was determined to be too meager for visiting the United States, the visa petition was rejected, with no right to reapply for a year. When Robert visited the same consulate a few months later (because he had the privilege of American citizenship, he didn't have to wait in line) and tried to appeal, another stern official informed him that there was too much danger in granting guest visas to too many Ukrainians. In his view, they would all gladly exchange their motherland for staying forever in the States. "You have to realize," he said, "Ukraine is like Ghana," thus insulting both Ukraine and Ghana, and sealing our image of American consulate workers as heartless and nasty bureaucrats no better than our own. Since my mom was denied the opportunity to visit the United States, we headed to the Argentinean consulate instead. There she received a visa on the spot, and we planned a joint South American vacation.

Nevertheless, the American bureaucracy has a long way to go before reaching the perfection of the Soviet and post–Soviet standards. The following "Song of the Bureaucrat" by the greatest Soviet filmmaker Eldar Ryazanov, performed by Sergey and Tatiana Nikitin, summarizes the perdurable nature of our officials a lot better than I ever could:

> We do not plough, or sow, or build[2]
> We take pride in our state machine
> We are important paper people
> We have always been, we are and we will be.
>
> Our task is extremely challenging:
> We have to guess the desire of the boss.
> Guess, agree, do not argue
> And not spoil our careers.
>
> In order to push the paper,
> We need flexibility and boldness.
> Granting our signature or agreement
> Is like walking on a ledge.

Turn to Democracy

When people learn that I come from the former USSR, they ask me about the exciting early days of democracy preceding and following the breakdown of the repressive empire. The truth is I shudder when my thoughts return to those chaotic and dismal times when the first breath of freedom often blew away people's consciousness, the first steps towards capitalism led the state to the rise of kleptocracy, and store shelves became emptier than ever. Pensioners found themselves with hardly any means of survival as rapid devaluation destroyed their savings and reduced state pensions below the minimum living standards. In the meantime, state finances allotted for social benefits paid for the luxurious residences and exotic vacations of new democrats. Patients in need of surgery were admitted to the hospital only with their own bandages, bedclothes and medicines or not admitted at all. Staunch Communist party leaders repented their political mistakes and precipitously became liberal democrats energetically deriding the old party policy and Soviet excesses. Newly-coined economical experts began liberal reforms that drove the majority of the population to the limits of poverty and gave state resources to the powerful few in the administration who already had access to the state wealth.

"No limit" (беспредел) was the term we often used to describe the spirit of the epoch of the nineties. No limit on new freedom; no limit on inflation and deficits; no limit on immorality and lawlessness. In fact, the only sense of change I remember was the awareness of universal dismay, economic collapse affecting all spheres of life, and desperation at the sudden lack of opportunities. The family photo archive runs dry here—I have few photos from the nineties because more serious survival concerns prevented us from worrying about such trivial matters as taking pictures. Also, it became quite expensive to develop the old Soviet film, which, like everything else, also became scarce.

Freedom brought little joy to suddenly impoverished people who spent their time hunting for daily essentials and worrying about the shaky future.

Freedom unharnessed corruption and loosened professional standards and public safety. Police officers, like everyone else, had to procure means to care for their families—often with the help of small or large bribes. Car owners minimized driving distances to the bare minimum or avoided driving altogether for fear of being stopped with an invented infraction and with a real purpose of extortion. They also struggled to pay for car repairs and gas. My godfather Dyadya Volodya could not afford to take his aging Zhiguli to be repaired and its bottom rusted away. At the time his family hosted an exchange student from France, and they had to warn him about putting his feet in a safe spot before riding in the car to avoid finding them dangling through the hole in the bottom.

The post-Soviet version of accelerated privatization also known as "grabbatization" ("прихватизация") allowed agile young capitalists, as well as old Communist party lords, to grab the state land and property at a minimal cost through loopholes in the emerging legal system. As a result, thousands of workers and intellectuals suddenly found themselves with no employment or holding on to jobs that provided a place of work but no financial remuneration until the indefinitely postponed better days. Factories not having the money to pay their workers instead awarded them the fruits of their labor—ceramic plates, tin buckets, spoons, knives, shovels or brooms. Employees had to master a new occupation of salesperson and find a way to sell these tools or survive without a salary. A sale could be relatively easy or extremely challenging based on the practical application of the tool. Automobile plant workers enjoyed the most comfortable living since their goods—whether in a complete, finished form or as separate parts—were always met with big demand. Broom or bucket factory employees had to challenge their brain—or friends—if they wanted to squeeze any profit out of their unfortunate bounty.

People equipped with practical instincts joined newly found stockbroking or other companies of an ambiguous nature or engaged as salesmen at local outside markets. If people did not have a knack for business, they stretched their creativity to find any use for excess tools—giving them away as birthday gifts or exchanging them for other semi-useless tools their friends similarly were awarded from their factories in lieu of salary. In the meantime, people kept hoping the state economy would get back on track and provide enterprises with sufficient means to pay their workers salaries. In most cases, their hopes did not materialize—many factories closed down completely or got sold off to oligarchs who changed their profile altogether. A ceramic factory near Yuzhny that produced plates and vases that were distributed all over the Soviet Union and sent to other socialist countries tried to stay afloat thanks to the enthusiasm of its local employees, but eventually met its tragic end. In its prime days, the factory had received orders for special gifts, such as a vase for the anniversary of the victory in Great Patriotic War, made especially for Stalin. The first copy of it, rejected because of a tiny, nearly invisible scratch, is now displayed at the Kharkiv History Museum.

The fate of intellectual workers was the worst, for their intangible labor could not be converted into any adequate material goods. They also proved to be the worst kind of businesspeople and therefore the least adapted for survival in the new capitalist climate. My mom, belonging to this social stratum, summoned her spirit and struggled to keep the family afloat, offering private English lessons to people from ages four to about fifty-four. On the days Mom did not teach at the university, these people came to our home in groups of three to five starting from three in the afternoon, right after the end of school lessons or their work day, until nine or ten in the evening. Lessons took place in our living room, the central space in the house, and the rest of us had to minimize our movements throughout the area. Mom knew how to make the lessons fun, and the demand for her services grew along with her professional reputation in our town. Soon she had only Sunday free from teaching, and that is when she did household duties and prepared for the following week's lessons.

Many of Mom's students provided valuable services in return, such as dentistry, access to fashionable attire or footwear, or getting a hold of railway tickets. This barter system often functioned more efficiently than actual cash transactions. Whenever trouble came, Mom referred to her mental list of professional services or helpful people to whom her students had access and help would be on the way. Sometimes these relationships turned into strong, enduring friendships. Two of Mom's students—a couple named Tanya and Sasha—later became our close friends, and Tanya is the godmother of our son.

What did the new, chaotic freedom mean for a teenager nearing a high school graduation? Cancelling long-time plans to tour the ancient cities of Ukraine and Russia with Mom. There were no other trips in mind. The unsatisfied craving for real chocolate, which disappeared completely and emerged in falsified form of sticky yellow soy. Drastic deflation of the years of savings our family kept in the state bank for my eighteenth birthday to buy me a new coat or jewelry now barely sufficed for a box of candy. Dark streets and suddenly increased danger of walking outside at night when your hat or a purse might be snatched away. Fear of falling victim to a horrible crime as previously unfathomable sexual maniacs also got new freedoms under the lax and corrupt post–Soviet militia. And dark houses—the newly independent Ukrainian state did not produce enough electricity and economized it—particularly the least privileged residents who lived in the outskirts.

My friends living in the center of the city suffered programmed power cuts a couple of hours per day, but the time span increased proportionally to the distance of one's residence from the center of the city. While the power outage schedule was observed within the city limits, authorities did not consider such formalities necessary for country bumpkins who could easily adjust to life without extra luxuries. I remember days when the power would go off around noon as I was getting ready to leave for the university (I studied in the second shift) and would still be off when I came back around seven. My grandma had to devise creative ways to preserve food and cook and clean without the light. She had to take everything out of the refrigerator to prevent it from thawing and floating in previously frozen water, and she had to carry the provisions outside if it was cold enough or to the cool cellar if it was hot outside.

Doing my homework by candlelight, I tried to stay calm and summon the strength not to yield to un–Christian vindictive rage against the impersonal mammoth state causing such suffering to its citizens. The promises of the Soviet leaders of bygone years that future generations would live in the bright Communist future frequently came to mind as an ironic prophecy of the dystopic post–Soviet reality. People joked that our sad present was the bright future of our fathers. We learned to survive on the bare minimum, and a day when community services worked without interruptions was a holiday. We got used to candles and kerosene lamps we had thought were long gone with the post-war days. Water carrying pumps or electronic devices often burned out because of outages or extreme changes in electricity.

Feeling our helplessness to bring about any change for the better, we did our utmost to take revenge on the state. We saved our devalued money by not paying for public services whenever possible. We bought electric train tickets to a closer destination, claiming a mistake in case we were caught by ticket control agents. Some people, like my cousin Roma, did not buy them at all—if he saw train inspectors approaching, he would leave the train at the closest station and run backwards to the car they had already inspected. In the subway, he would cover the movement sensors with his hands, passing through the control machine as quickly as he could without paying. "If the state cheats me, afford me a tiny pleasure of cheating it back," he would say with the proud smile of a winner if he managed to save a few kopecks on transportation.

When the energy situation eventually started to improve and the power cuts decreased from ten to four hours a day, then came water shortages. I do not mean lack of hot water for bathing. I mean just any water. In the suburbs, we would go for days and sometimes weeks without any water appearing from our taps. At night, we left buckets under them in the hope that it would bring us a few drops of rusty liquid. We could only hope for the future appearance of the normally clear fluid, for the antique pipes overstressed by constant disruptions in the water supply accumulated so much rust that the water, when it would finally appear, was intensely auburn. When Robert, my husband-to-be, came to Ukraine on his second visit for our wedding in the summer of 1996, Ukraine welcomed him with extremely cheap (by his standards) services, irregular electricity and rust-tinged, irregularly supplied water. Tradition required him to spend the night before the wedding at a different place than his bride, and our good friends living nearby offered him shelter. Although, as usual, hardly any water dripped from the tap, they did their best to ensure the best toilet under the circumstances for their guest, but their efforts could not transcend the limits of our reality. He will never forget the exotic red-water bath on the morning of the wedding.

To integrate Robert completely into our reality after the wedding, we took him on our daily trips to the local well a few blocks away, taking with us a cart and a considerable-sized cistern we had to push up the hill when it was filled. Sighing and panting, he confronted us with what seemed like a logical question: "Do you pay for water in Ukraine? Why?" We gave him the only logical answer we knew: "Out of hope it will come back one day." The water supply, although vastly improved, is still irregular in the Ukrainian countryside, where local administration cuts it off in summer, particularly during the draught, when water usage increases for crops and plants and when people need it most. Outages also result from the outdated equipment, often not changed from the Soviet days. When Robert returned to the United States, the town where his family lived experienced a sudden power outage that lasted only a few minutes. People panicked, and he acknowledged Ukrainians' patience, resilience, ability to adapt and help each other in difficult times.

During his first month staying in Ukraine after our wedding, these very qualities also amazed and amused him. On one occasion, we saw a group of male passengers get out of a public bus that had stalled and push it up the hill until it gathered enough power to go on its own. Twenty years later, I witnessed the same scene on a trolleybus when a bunch of men came out and helped push it instead of abandoning it and catching another one. On another occasion, during our honeymoon in Crimea, we took a tour van to the tatar Khan's Palace in Bakhchisaray. After a couple of blocks, the strong smell of gasoline started to permeate the van, and after a while we saw gas erupting in small geysers right inside the rear part of the van. The driver tried to fix the problem, and our fellow tourists waited patiently. I got ready to wait along with them, but Robert's Western rationalism and lack of tolerance for similar malfunctions pressured me to get out. An anecdote was born during perestroika to mock our people's unlimited endurance of state bullying: A meeting at the central city square was announced, and a mayor declared, as an experiment to see how far people's patience could stretch, that tomorrow they would be hanged en masse. Complete silence followed. Finally, a lonely hand rose, and the governor thought with relief there was at least someone trying to protest. It turned out, however, that the "protester" wanted to inquire whether they were supposed to bring their own ropes.

The medical sphere also suffered a heavy blow during this regime change. A Soviet hospital patient could count on entirely free care, including medical procedures, surgeries and after-surgery care, medicines, and food (although not necessarily appetizing). Sometime around the eighties a so-called "gentleman set" (a bottle of cognac and a box of chocolates) slowly crept its way into the doctors' hands, making it customary to thank them with such goodies after an operation or the birth of a baby. Medical personnel was highly qualified, efficient and attentive, although not necessarily sweet. The weakening of state support following the empire's demise made doctors depend almost exclusively on patients' donations, which, unfortunately, were far from voluntary. You could now be refused a critical surgery if you could not pay not only for the medicines the hospitals no longer carried, but also for the doctor's devalued or non-existent salary. Nurses also required financing in the form of regular installments due at the time of any minor service. We suddenly realized the importance of money that we needed not for purchasing a luxury item or a bit of comfort, but for providing ourselves with minimum protection against the new insecurities unimaginable during the Soviet times when people had a basic right to medicine.

When I learned Spanish, I particularly appreciated the song "La Niagara en bicicleta" by Dominican Juan Luis Guerra. He describes the situation in Dominican hospitals as strongly resembling our own, where the doctors have left, rubbing alcohol was used for drinking, thread for stitching was embroidered into a tablecloth, serum was used to sweeten the coffee and X-rays melted. In the summer following our wedding, my husband badly sprained his ankle playing soccer with some local guys. We took him to one such hospital where, fortunately, they had an X-ray machine and a small piece of rubber for his groin area for protection. He got adequate treatment because a good friend of the family who was a doctor arranged for us to go to the hospital where she used to work.

More than twenty years later, the situation in the hospitals has not improved much and perhaps deteriorated even further, with Moscow always enjoying the best resources and financing. Although the medical insurance system is now firmly establishing itself, the pervasive corruption is slow to leave and poor financing of state hospitals continues. A friend of mine who lives in Texas recently told me that her mom, who had completed all the preparatory procedures for the kidney stone surgery, was sent home a day before the scheduled operation because the hospital did not have anesthesia, and she waited another month before it became available.

Although the nightmares of the nineties are hardly possible to categorize, perhaps worst of all ills—and encompassing them all—was the fear of the future. Previously, the state would "distribute" jobs to university graduates according to merit: More prestigious vacancies went to students with higher grades. Thanks to this system, my mom, during her fourth year of study in the foreign languages department of Kharkiv State University, landed a high-pressure but exciting interpreting job at the State Intourist Agency, accompanying foreign tourists around Kharkiv and other cities of the Soviet Union. It was a rare opportunity, not only for practical employment purposes, but also for hearing real, native English at a time when people could see no movies without dubbing and came across very few foreigners with whom they could practice their foreign language skills. Such a job was my dream, by the early nineties as shattered as the State Intourist Agency itself.

Nobody knew what to do after graduation. Some students just gave up the idea of studying altogether since it seemed to offer no practical advantages. Others graduated just for appearances, for their parents' sake, or "for the paper's sake," as they used to say, and went on to a more profitable profession, which usually meant buying and selling goods. Popular custom and the need for survival drove thousands of young people to the markets of Poland, where they would buy jeans, watches, shoes, underwear, stereos, VCRs and whatever else they could not easily find in the former USSR. They brought back their gems and sold them for profit at our markets to the joy of our youth longing for Western-made goods. Kharkiv hosted one of the largest open-air mega-markets in the whole Soviet Union which, ironically, carried the name of the distinguished physicist and academician N. P. Barabashov. From one of the leading scientific and industrial centers of the whole country, our city became the center of commerce specializing in cheap, low-quality, but abundant goods.

The words "imported" or "brand name" worked like magic, boosting the owner's popularity. Most times, of course, the brand name was fake, for few could truly afford a real deal, and masters of imitation were many. Imported attire, whether belonging to a famous brand or not, attracted glances by its cool look, elegant or sporty designs and bright colors, even if the quality did not meet the expectations of superior Western standards. My stepdad brought me several wardrobe pieces from his music tour to France, and they immediately became the object of my friends' admiration for their unique aspect. Everyone could tell that the tight-fitting white shorts and green-red-blue-yellow jogging suit made of crushed fabric, a particular marvel, came from exotic lands. Few could tell that the admired articles originated in a discount store, the only shopping destination post–Soviet musicians could afford on their salaries, decent by our country's standards but quite deficient for decent shopping in France.

Money began to lose value with the speed of light. Soviet rubles gave way to amorphous and undignified "coupons" that looked like Monopoly money and made us think the new rulers designed and cut them by hand. We carried stacks of them bound by rubber bands in our purses and paid millions for milk and butter—if we could find it. Beggars, previously unseen on Soviet streets where everyone could afford a minimum living standard, carried signs that read "Please do not give anything less than a million." We all became millionaires hardly able to pay for their food. Finding the food was another challenge. If subpar items were generally available in the state stores during Soviet times, they all but disappeared in the nineties. To be more exact, they started disappearing during perestroika in the mid-eighties, gradually foreshadowing the imminent crisis.

Just like in times of war, the state (first, the Soviet state during its final shaky years, then the newly independent Ukrainian state continuing Soviet economic traditions) started issuing special consumer cards. These entitled us, upon fulfilling a necessary waiting-in-line sentence, to a certain amount of rations consisting of the most essential household and edible goods. These cards could only be used in specific stores located in the strictly designated geographical area close to the consumer's residence to which the consumer was "attached." For some incomprehensible reason, the list of the most essential items varied from region to region, and the logic by which the government calculated our most essential needs puzzled all. In one region, a person had the right to purchase one kilo of salt, three bars of soap, two boxes of detergent, two hundred grams of butter, two kilos of meat and a business suit during a certain month. In another region, the essentials list included one kilo of salt, a package of matches, two bottles of vodka, three kilos of pasta and four pairs of socks.

Growing deficits in the nineties prompted authorities to grant the right to more household and electric domestic articles, such as underwear, perfume, refrigerators, carpets and hair dryers. Sometimes authorities found an outlet for their sense of risqué humor or, rather, mockery, issuing cards for the right to purchase half a bra or half a pair of children's underwear. Clarification for the readers not versed in the art of Soviet bureaucratese: The consumer could purchase one bra and one pair of children's underwear once every two months upon presenting two cards at once. As salt, matches, detergent and soap were the items most encouraged by the state coupon system as the items of utmost necessity in situations of war or other emergencies, we accumulated them in miraculous quantities and stocked them up in the attic, to be ready. It was a good investment—we still have no need to buy them. When looking for something in the attic, which has since been converted into a spacious second floor, I continuously bump into crates of detergent and boxes of matches dated from 1968, which are now collector items.

Poorly supplied regions (such a designation usually applied to smaller, distant provincial towns) usually received more cards, although not necessarily more goods. Moscow, as the seat of our government, naturally benefited from the best supply network. The second place likely belonged to the Baltic republics since authorities tried their best to appease their independent sentiments and feed them well to prevent their leaving the precarious union on the brink of collapse. They were also famous for a lower level of professional theft in the commercial sphere. During our visit to Lithuania and Estonia in 1989, my mom and I marveled at the diversity of cheeses unimaginable to our emptiness-impacted minds. Somehow we were allowed to purchase some cheeses without cards and passports, which were required as proof of residency. However, once we were further enticed by a hair dryer, a rare commodity in Ukraine, the absence of necessary documents dashed our hopes for one. Fortunately, a nice Estonian lady who must have already had a hair dryer, and who was shopping with her daughter in the same department, took pity on us and kindly agreed to buy one for us with our money and her passport.

Lots of cards stayed unused in people's households as deficits persisted, in spite of all the centralized efforts to improve the supply system. Naturally, such shortages and a cumbersome system of securing necessities required thriftiness, flexibility and a sense of humor. Many anecdotes mocking the paradoxes of our economic system reflected such qualities of our people. One of them goes as follows:

> When guests arrive, the host asks them: "Will you need soap to wash your hands?"
> "Yes, please."
> "Then you will have to drink tea without sugar."

The committee for distributing consumer cards also made sure to provide us with sufficient mental and deductive challenges in our shopping pursuits. The bureaucrats wouldn't simply patronize us by handing us consumer cards—that would be too boring and too simple a task for a Soviet or post–Soviet citizen trained in the art of serious bureaucratic puzzle-solving. Before reaching the point of buying the product or even checking its availability, people had to complete a multi-step process of obtaining an order for consumer cards, obtaining residence proof for consumer cards, securing an invitation for purchase and, in the case of especially rare goods such as refrigerators, appearing for a roll call confirming one's interest in the purchase on the eve of the day when the product *may* become available. Staying occupied with such tasks, each of which could involve significant wait times considering the amount of paper that had to be controlled and stamped, left us little time to think about freedom we could now enjoy.

Mom recalls the shock of the naïve British conductor for whom she was interpreting when a musician asked him for permission to be absent from dress rehearsal because his turn to purchase a refrigerator finally arrived. Sometimes authorities also tested our intellectual capacity with a riddle-solving challenge afforded by cards with specially designated numbers: card #6 could be used for purchasing six packs of cigarettes in November of 1990; card #7 for purchasing two kilos of sugar in October and November of 1990; card #10 for purchasing 0.5 kilos of sausage in May of 1991; and so on. Customers needed to consult local papers to decipher the numbering system.

If a store did not have the goods for consumer-card holders, the card would either go unused or sometimes could be used for a different but related product. Thus, meat, which was always difficult to obtain in its pure form in stores whose employees appropriated the best cuts for themselves and their relatives, became even less available in the nineties. The card holder entitled to two kilos of meat could receive 0.5 kilos of actual, however bony, meat and receive the remaining weight in sausages and/or salo (bacon, pork fat—a product favored by Ukrainians, although not a substitute for pure meat).

My grandpa, by then retired, would undertake shopping trips to the city resembling a weekly hunt for food. He would visit its markets (where you could buy food without cards, but at a higher price) and distant stores in search of decent-quality meat, sausage and cheese. Since we did not have a car, he would take a train. Since only the most successful businesspeople could afford rudimentary brick-shaped cell phones at the time, we often did not know of grandpa's precise location or next destination. Since transportation took its time and grandpa took his, undertaking the most detailed research, we often got worried close to nightfall and went out on the street in front of our house to survey the horizon for his slightly hunched figure. He would finally appear, beaming with joy, a bulky brown briefcase in one hand and a couple of household bags in the other, packed to the brim with goodies he had secured with his resourcefulness and charm.

Many new entrepreneurs looked for every fresh opportunity for enrichment often with little concern for ethics. Chaos and disorientation provided limitless opportunities for swindling the population not versed in fortuity and pitfalls of the free economy. So-called "thimble dealers" enjoyed a wave of success in the early nineties, sparkling gullible types' ardor for easy profits as they believed everything was possible in their new free country. "Thimble dealers," strategically located in the most crowded spots near subway and train station entrances, caught their attention with a sign or a yell, "Sharp eyesight gets a prize!" Swindlers impressed spectators with nimble movements of their hands, switching little cups or thimbles between them, one eventually hiding a small rolling ball. Prizes of five, ten or twenty rubles (a decent, although not a huge amount) went to the person guessing correctly where the ball was hiding—not a daunting task. Successful gamblers ahead encouraged spectators to play again with their just-won prizes. Nevertheless, when it came time to guess and one seemed to see perfectly well where the ball was, he was invariably wrong, and the dealers invariably pocketed the bet.

The game, although illegal, continued to surge in popularity all around the huge country for a couple of years, likely thanks to a friendly understanding with local policemen, until finally dying out, probably thanks to the natural decline in demand among the swindled population finally enriched by experience. To my great surprise, I later discovered that our thimble dealers lacked the originality that we had always credited them with, for this simple game used to bamboozle people as far back as Ancient Egypt and Greece.

Another scheme was devised by the bank and joint-stock company MMM. It extorted investments from naïve TV viewers enchanted by a goofy chap named Lyonya Golubkov—a run-of-the mill, shabbily-dressed Soviet citizen who, just like them, was tormented by the question of how to best use his fifty thousand rubles rapidly losing value. "Come what may!" Lyonya would finally say, buying MMM shares with all his money. Two weeks later he received the dividends, which allowed him to purchase new boots for his wife. Baffled-looking Lyonya quickly became a household name and convinced millions of people to contribute millions of rubles to the apparently trustworthy and prospering new company which a few years later was convicted of fraud and of issuing illegal securities.

The scam worked because people, lost in the economic maze of the post–Soviet tumult and fearing the uncertain future, were eager to invest their savings, and the first investors received their dividends. Mama Galya, who, like most people, no longer trusted state banks, finally submitted to Lyonya's charm and rumors of early investment success, not heeding any advice to the contrary. Like millions of others, Mama Galya lost her investment, but far worse could happen. Some of those who risked particularly large investments committed suicide.

My immediate family, impervious to schemes and dicey temptations, resisted most with admirable resistance. We were one of the few families in town who refused to pay a steep fee for the new, much-lauded private channel offering the opportunity to view foreign movies, usually older releases including a selection of horror, action and erotic titles—all shocking revelations and temptations for the post–Soviet audience. My family's resistance was rewarded—on the day long awaited by the contributing public, the channel started broadcasting on our TV with as much clarity as it did for our neighbors who dutifully paid for the subscription. Some typical oversight or technical challenge in separating paying households from non-paying ones accounted for the injustice, but no one bothered to return subscription fees to those who paid or to make us pay for the service we had never ordered. After a while, the "private" channel became universally free thanks to the difficulties of enforcing a payment system.

There was one scheme to which we did, temporarily, fall prey, and it didn't concern money. In 1989, a Ukrainian psychiatrist named Anatoliy Kashpirovsky did a series of TV programs; he claimed to have the miraculous ability to tele-treat diseases and disorders ranging from bed-wetting to elevated blood pressure to AIDS as well as to cure the after-effects of Chernobyl radiation and help dissolve scars. Regular broadcasts of his program attracted millions of viewers from around the USSR and supposedly helped most of them to get rid of one or another ailment. Program participants from the live audience testified to being healed, bolstering viewers' faith. Some participants fell into a trance and others started dancing or singing under the influence of the hypnotic effect of Kashpirovky's penetrating gaze and confident voice instructing them to relax, calm down and allow themselves to be healed. Many fell asleep lulled by the pleasant quite background music. I never arrived at that stage of influence and got rather bored of the little action and eventually quit watching. The same must have happened to most other fans, for Kashpirovky faded into oblivion in the following few years with the same speed at which he came to fame.

Another psychic (or "extra-sense," the new term that suddenly became immensely popular) specialist named Allan Chumak did not have any medical training, unlike Kashpirovksy. Instead, he allegedly possessed supernatural capabilities, which, besides curing people, enabled him to "charge" water or medical creams with his TV-screen gaze, endowing them with healing qualities. The magical water supposedly held its curing potential for as long as the owner believed in it. People filled jars of water and put them in front of the TV so they would receive a special charge capable of eliminating respiratory diseases, chronic fatigue, intestinal problems or anything else that the faith healer would declare to be under target. The guy would give a few minutes of introduction, explaining the disorder to be treated. Then he continued the session for fifteen or twenty minutes more in complete silence, slightly moving his hands in a series of circling and stroking movements as if kneading dough and then lifting it to see how far it would stretch. His lips also moved, parting and closing interchangeably, reciting some incantation. It resembled a bizarre exorcising ritual.

Chumak would rotate disorders from one day to the next to attract the most people and ensure his screen durability. He claimed such differentiation was professionally motivated, for indiscriminate mixing of different diseases would undermine the efficiency of his therapy. I am curious if it ever occurred to anyone to research what happened to some hapless patient suffering from a psychotic disorder who decided to watch a program on the day reserved for intestinal disorders or vice versa. Chumak's TV time ran out when the law restricting non-traditional treatment methods was passed, some time before he claimed to have finally discovered a universal therapy covering all possible ailments.

Among all the desperation and chaos of the "limitless" nineties, I hoped for something better to come. The Kharkiv University foreign languages department afforded one of the best opportunities for such hopes—after all, the knowledge of foreign languages opened the doors to the West, at least in theory, and beckoned us with an unfamiliar and exciting new life. Besides these practical reasons, I truly enjoyed learning languages—understanding and uttering strange sounds with my own mouth filled me with pride. The job of interpreter, who bridged communication gaps between people and nations with unique skills not accessible to just anyone, seemed like my dream. Some freelance interpreting jobs mostly accessible to students provided a peek at such opportunities.

The first one came to my friend Zina and I when a professor asked us to accompany a pair of elderly American missionaries to the international airport in Kyiv by train. We got to speak English with native speakers for an entire day and received an incredible fortune on top of that—$10 U.S. each. I still feel the pride of holding my first hard-earned currency which I contributed to my family savings. I am afraid we might have annoyed the poor missionaries with our persistent efforts at keeping them entertained—we taught them the tricky Russian card game "The Fool" late into the night in the warmth of our cozy four-person train compartment from which they could not escape. We made sure they mastered all its techniques. Zina might have unconsciously added to the challenge by using invented English words for card suits: Since we had not learned the actual terms for those in our university courses, she simply used the Russian names, decorating them with her best American accent. In the Kyiv airport, we gawked at the stylish and richly dressed people who had the privilege to travel and as such appeared to us like Olympic gods.

More opportunities for peeking at the exotic lives lived by people abroad came as more missionaries visited Ukraine, needing our cheap translation services. Some of them later welcomed me into their homes when I studied at the University of Kansas. Students and professors slowly started to break through the former Iron Curtain, still a very real obstacle for most of us, by taking advantage of rare translating opportunities for those who offered paid airfare to the West. Some students, with the help of the missionaries who had previously employed them, found study opportunities in the United States, which usually required dedicated participation in their churches in exchange. I felt another opportunity would come for me. I was young, hopeful and ambitious. I loved studying languages and worked hard so I would not be caught off guard when the travel opportunity beckoned.

The News

"You are going to Kansas? But there are tornadoes there!" The reaction was invariable since most Ukrainians associated Kansas with an empty drabness and tornadoes thrusting Dorothy into the swirl of adventure. The Russian version of the book was called *The Wizard of the Emerald City*, and although it did not represent an exact translation of the original, it had fascinated me since childhood. The fact that I was going to study abroad at the University of Kansas seemed symbolic and predestined, and I felt like Dorothy ("Ellie" in the Russian book) flying across the ocean, far away from my previously closed-up and protected world towards the new, unknown and exciting adventure that would change my life.

I had not chosen the location for my study abroad experience. The cost of tuition and room and board were out of the question and appeared astronomic even for the rich in the first years of Ukraine's independence. I won a complete scholarship including tuition and room and board for the 1994–95 academic year from the ACTR/ACCELS organizations (American Council of Teachers of Russian and American Council for Collaboration in Education and Language Study). The exchange program fostered by these organizations was established by Gorbachev and Reagan during early perestroika to reinstate cultural and academic collaboration between our countries interrupted by the Soviet intrusion into Afghanistan. The scholarship selection process had been rigorous: Most of the students of English at Kharkiv State University filled out extensive applications and wrote letters of interest in February and sent them, with little hope, to the ACTR/ACCELS office in Kiev, the capital of Ukraine. I had almost forgotten about my application when the letter came in early May inviting me to the second round of the competition, which consisted of an oral interview and a TOEFL exam (Test of English as a Foreign Language)—both taking place in Kyiv.

Two other students from my university were also selected for an interview but did not make it to the final round. In Kyiv, I met many other students from all over Ukraine vying to get into the program. It was my first introduction to a mixer event where I met and talked to teenagers from diverse ethnic, regional and educational backgrounds. We became friendly companions, but we never forgot that we were also competitors in this stressful and fierce struggle. Of the people I met during this selection round, only one girl and I made it to the finals.

I did not allow myself to get my hopes up. I knew that victory was not likely. There were many qualified candidates, and anyway, the program seemed too good to be true. It was the peak of post–Soviet economic ruin. Few people besides politicians and scientific or cultural figures traveled to the United States, and the huge disparity between Western prices and our salaries did not make the possibility of personal travel likely for many years. Occasionally, I heard miraculous stories of students receiving scholarships or some sponsor's support for study in America, but with the pervasive corruption in the former USSR, such opportunities were always more readily available for the relative of a well-positioned boss. In fact, American representatives of the ACTR/ACCELS administering TOEFL in the final selection round did not allow any eager Ukrainian professors to help choose the final candidates. Perhaps my awareness of this endeavor having a low probability of success inspired me with careless confidence and self-assuredness, which must have helped me make a favorable impression during my final interview.

Early in life, I was not a particularly sociable person. Extremely shy and fearful of everything, I had grown up protected and sheltered by the love of my family—my mom, my stepdad, and my grandparents—who were reluctant to let me go anywhere by myself. I had traveled to many vacation spots in the Soviet Union with my family, but never alone to a Pioneer camp or on school trips to other cities, like many of my peers did during our school years. Thus, the news that I was selected to study in Lawrence, Kansas, as the only finalist from my university came as a shock and stirred up intense concern and fear in my loved ones.

The results of the competition were slow to come. My mom, my grandparents and I took turns calling for hours trying to get through the poor-Soviet-connection intercity telephone lines to reach someone in the Kyiv office. When it seemed that we finally got through, the line was busy or nobody answered. I was ready to abandon the whole endeavor, hardly believing that I would be selected. When I finally got the news from my grandma (I called home from a street phone by the university after one of my final exams; my family kept trying to get through until someone succeeded), the possibility still seemed so unreal that I felt myself immersed in a sort of dreamlike haze. I was wild with exhilaration on the one hand. I was also scared to admit, even to myself, that it was true because of the superstitious fear that it would all turn out to be a mistake or fraud.

The unwritten laws of Ukrainian superstitions encourage people to hide good news from others to prevent jinxing good fortune through too much immodest boasting. I hid mine for as long as possible. When I received the acceptance letter, I kept checking it for signs of a scam. I refused to believe that I was going to study in the United States until I held the airplane ticket in my own hands. It did not arrive until August, and my state of suspended doubt thus stretched over two months. The ACTR/ACCELS office also dallied with my placement in an American university, prolonging my torture of uncertainty intertwined with excitement. I found out I was going to the University of Kansas around mid–August, a few days before my scheduled departure, and I began classes a week late.

My grandparents, likewise, thought the whole thing was a scam and felt terrified to let me go. It was my mom who, believing in the greatness of this opportunity and suppressing her own premonitions and fears, insisted that I go. I will be forever grateful for her endless patience, education, courage, support, and care. I can only imagine what she was going through saying good-bye to me at the Moscow Sheremetyevo airport without complete confidence in my future. When I boarded the plane, some Aeroflot official who had seen us part reproached my mom for letting me go God knows where, while so many girls were scammed into slavery in capitalist countries. I will also always remember my grandmother's tears in the last couple of weeks before my departure overseas. She must have felt that she would never see me again on this earth. She passed away suddenly on January 19, 1995, on my mom's birthday, in the middle of my study-abroad year. I got the news in a letter from my mom, which took almost a month to arrive. She did not dare tell me on the phone, and neither did she dare wait until my return. I will always bear with me the pain of not saying good-bye to my dear grandma, who had been an essential part of my life, and the meaning of whose existence had centered on me, in the absence of other grandchildren, for the last nineteen years of her life.

The image of America formed in my teenager's head had been limited and influenced by stories of Ellie/Dorothy, *Gone with the Wind*, Mark Twain's books, images of aggressive, all-consuming materialism in our press, and Soviet propaganda of nuclear explosions and oppression of African Americans. The stereotypes started to melt slowly during perestroika when Gorbachev fostered the policy of "glasnost" (openness) and encouraged the first "telebridges" (direct broadcasts of question-and-answer shows between American and Soviet audiences). We discovered with surprise that common Americans were not necessarily looking forward to destroying us in nuclear explosions or winning the arms race. We discovered that they were also curious about our lives and perhaps interested in making friends in our country.

The greatest breakthrough in the wall of our ignorance actually came during Andropov's period—he invited an American schoolgirl named Samantha Smith on a peacemaking visit. She had written a letter to him asking if the Soviet Union intended to destroy the United States (the same question, but in reverse order, seriously worried Soviet children). She immediately became our hero thanks to her courage, obvious desire to become a friend of the Soviet Union, and sincere, cheerful smile as she blended with the Soviet children in the Artek Pioneer camp. An alley in Artek was named after her.[1] A Soviet child ambassador, Katya Lycheva, followed in Samantha Smith's steps, touring the United States on a peace mission. We all envied her. We could not yet hope for a similar opportunity. Traveling to America was akin to traveling to the moon. Much-televised radiant faces of a Soviet and American girl parading through cheering crowds of people just recently considered enemies inspired us with a hope of something completely new—a promise of true international openness and understanding. Curiously, none of my American acquaintances remember the sensational effect of these groundbreaking trips, which had a huge impact on my generation of Soviet kids.

Highly motivated, self-confident, well read, well spoken, generally too smart for me to compete with—that is how I envisioned American students. Once the realization of the reality of my trip set in and the initial thrill wore off, I started getting nervous. The years of strict discipline at school and university did not fail to affect my self-confidence, never too strong in the first place. In class, I always thought twice, or more like three, four or five times, before volunteering an answer, even when I was sure it was correct. I would be too embarrassed if I didn't produce something close to perfect. When I finally made it to KU, even though I had expected a high academic level, I was struck by the relaxed and confident attitude of American students asking questions, blurting out answers and comments, even when not prompted. At the same time, I was struck by the realization that their answers were not always perfect and, in some cases, did not seem to make much sense at all. By that time, I knew English well, and the frequency of the word "like" used by teenagers baffled me.

I kept silent in most classes, afraid to attract attention to my accent or accidental vocabulary or grammatical blunders. I realized very soon, however, that the grammar we had been cultivating so thoroughly, the proper usage of the subjunctive mood and modal verbs like "I ought to" or "I shan't" attracted more attention than blunders. In fact, grammatical no-no's like double negatives or failure to use the subjunctive in the phrase "I wish I was" (instead of "were") abounded in Americans' speech, which simply crushed me. Some lexical turns also provided conundrums I desperately struggled to solve without losing face in the first months of my stay. When people asked me, "What's up?" I raised my head, wondering what the sky had to do with beginning of a potential conversation. When people asked me, "How are you doing?" I started to recount my present state of affairs and recent happenings, only to see them flutter by without stopping even a second. When people I barely knew asked me, "What's going on?" I started to ponder how to make my answer most informative and relevant, discovering in the process that they did not really care. The most confusion came from the expression "No kidding" and the adequacy of its usage since it seemed to work in any context and in any intonation. I confused people as well by using stilted words like "hackneyed" or "intertwined," which I had studied in my earnest attempts to enlarge my vocabulary and blend in.

Getting acclimated and gradually losing my shyness in the company of Americans, I discovered that we, the former Soviets, were not too badly informed and educated, in spite of the curtain that closed off most of the world. The curtain probably acted as a stimulant, encouraging us to learn more intensely about the forbidden world, so mysterious and enticing. We knew the capitals of the Soviet republics like Uzbekistan and Georgia, but we also knew the capitals of Brazil, Australia and Kenya. We knew about socialist and revolutionary leaders like Patrice Lumumba, Mao Zedong and Che Guevara, but we also knew about Abraham Lincoln, Charles de Gaulle and Martin Luther King. We knew most American states, cities, mountains and rivers. Nowadays, my Ukrainian friends and relatives learn from the news about all kinds of natural catastrophes, accidents or strikes happening in the United States sometimes faster than we hear about them. They call me, worried, inquiring about our well-being while I have no idea about the disaster to which they are referring.

In turn, upon my arrival in the United States, I frequently found myself responding to questions like "Do you miss the ocean?" (the closest body of water to my hometown in Ukraine is the small Azov Sea); "Did you suffer a lot during the war?" (at that time, the last war fought on Ukrainian territory was the Great Patriotic War, or World War II, which was more than thirty years before my birth), and "Ukraine? Is it next to Peru?" The latest question I heard very recently from someone who had actually visited Ukraine was "Is Ukraine part of the Soviet Union again now?" Very quickly, I got used to the lack of recognition on people's faces at the sound of my country's name, and I felt a pleasant surprise when someone displayed some knowledge of its whereabouts and cultural-historical facts.

I encountered my biggest surprise and a serious boost to my belief in myself in language classes, in which I immediately enrolled, for I did not have the opportunity to study Italian and Spanish formally in Ukraine. I chose Elementary Italian II, which I thought was the most appropriate level after a year of studying it irregularly with a private instructor. I quickly found myself at the head of the class, bored with the teacher's patient explanation of elementary grammar. No attempts at actually speaking the language were made by the students or the teacher, and I moved to Second Year I, which did not particularly challenge me either. Next semester I made a shortcut right into the Advanced Italian Conversation and Grammar, a wonderfully enriching course with only five students and extensive speaking opportunities. A similar scenario developed with French.

Thus, I realized that the Soviet educational system (just like our medical care system and many other spheres) actually boasted many advantages, which we had ignored or undervalued. After the fall of the Soviet Union, we became too absorbed in criticizing its faults, or what we perceived as faults, and unfavorably comparing all spheres of our life to their Western counterparts. Life in the United States helped me see my old life more soberly and appreciate its rewards as well as re-evaluate its flaws. As a student of foreign languages in Ukraine, I took English and French courses for four to six hours a day, six days a week, together with seven groupmates. All of us received plenty of daily individual attention from the professor and plenty of writing, listening, speaking and watching opportunities. The classes were divided into phonetics, grammar, oral practice and listening practice in the lab. Perhaps I should add that our higher education was entirely free of charge and, moreover, students received a monthly stipend, based on their academic results, roughly equaling half of the average Soviet salary.

I fondly remember my first-year professor Tatyana Konstantinovna Merkulova, who taught most of those sections with endless energy, patience, good spirits and creativity in designing fun interactive exercises to keep us engaged. Our French professor, whom I remember by her first name Dina, was a fifth-year student of French. In spite of her lack of experience (or, perhaps, because of it), she went to great lengths to find fun materials to supplement our insipid black-and-white textbook and help us learn with authentic songs, poems, movies and skits. She was a friend as well as a teacher. Thanks to her, in just one year I mastered the challenging French pronunciation and acquired a decent knowledge base of the language. Both of these professors organized foreign language parties at their homes, something unusual at the time, to celebrate Christmas the American/British way or to watch a French movie and make a French dinner.

What Ukrainian universities lacked was a campus system. The university consisted of one building where students of all departments mixed in one huge crowd, and we all went home after classes were over. We did not have activities, clubs, sports, parties or gatherings—at least not on the grounds of the university. To be fair, some students participated in sports and organized some clubs, but these activities did not play a huge role in student life, and I never had any experience with them. Foreign language students learned during the second shift from 1:30 to 6:30 p.m., and on the days when I did not stay at our Kharkiv apartment, I took the fifteen-minute subway and thirty-minute train ride back to Yuzhny. Even the dorms were located in a different city district, so there was no sense of the campus spirit I immediately felt at KU. I fell in love with it—a whole mini-town of red-roofed buildings made of limestone, streets, sidewalks, dorms, stadiums, parks, museums, fountains and cafes—all for students who lived, ate, studied and worked there. Here, I never felt disconnected from my friends or fellow students—it was a true community united by the adoration of a strange bird, a cheerful half-jay and half-hawk. In Ukraine, we never felt or displayed such an almost fanatical level of enthusiasm for our alma mater, nor did we have goofy mascots or anthems or chants dedicated to it. I was amused and enchanted, and I joined the ranks of Jayhawks forever.

Another wonderful discovery I made at KU was the library, where I could see, touch and read books as much as I wanted. At my Ukrainian university, we could only dream of such free access. If you needed a book, the protocol required you to fill out a form, wait for the library personnel to process it and wait some more for them to find the book in the library's collections. The process of finding it could take from fifteen minutes to twenty-four hours, and sometimes you had to return it the following day. Thus, even if you needed to check on some fact or find an appropriate quote for your paper, the check-out and retrieval process could take a lot longer than the actual time it took to consult your reference. Besides, with no electronic resources, we never knew what exactly the library had available on any given topic. For this reason, my memories of visiting the library at Kharkiv State University are very limited—I don't think I went there more than three or four times during the entire time of my studies.

I felt immensely indebted to the KU library for allowing me to ramble the endless mazes of tall shelves with the magic smell of old printed paper and getting lost in a myriad of titles. I discovered a whole Slavic section with books in Russian and Ukrainian that was larger than the entire library in my native town of Yuzhny. The media section of the library magnified my enthrallment—I could not believe that I could lay my hands on the most popular Russian- and Ukrainian-language literary journals and news magazines only a couple of weeks old.

Suddenly thrown into the midst of American college life without my family guiding my every step, I had to learn self-reliance and independence. I found that I enjoyed carrying the responsibility for my own decisions in choosing classes to take, food to eat and routine to plan. I found a job at the student cafeteria—cleaning dishes and tables was not a particularly rewarding experience, but it gave me with some extra income and some real work experience. My boss was tough and demanding—he noticed I tended to clean the table where my friends and my boyfriend were sitting with extra special care, and he asked me not to ignore other tables.

Dinner was the highlight of the weekday (on weekends, it was partying). I was a part of the "United Nations" table, which attracted a collection of happy characters from Ukraine, Belarus, Brazil, China, Colombia, the Dominican Republic, England, Germany, Italy, Panama, Paraguay, and, naturally, the United States. Sometimes we had so many people we had to move several tables together. We discussed the university news, political news, our pasts and our futures, shared jokes, worries and joys, and lingered so long after we were done with our meals that the cafeteria personnel had to turn off the lights to kick us out. In fact, it was at this special place that I met my future husband—I was having breakfast with a friend from the Dominican Republic who was also a good friend of Robert's. As Robert confessed later, he had already noticed me, and he decided it was the perfect opportunity to introduce himself unobtrusively. During that first meal together, he said he had always wanted to learn the history of Ukrainian immigration to Argentina (where his family came from) and asked me to help him understand the book on the topic written in Ukrainian. When he brought the book the next afternoon and asked if he could join me in my dorm room for the history research project, a Ukrainian friend of mine named Victor enthusiastically volunteered his help with translation, thus earning Robert's resentment forever.

I also had to learn about tolerance and co-existence. As an only daughter, I didn't have to share my room with anyone after my childhood. Suddenly, I had a roommate. Not the American roommate I had hoped for to help me improve my English and broaden my knowledge of American culture, but a Korean girl with no less accent than I had myself. We didn't know anything about each other's customs, we both struggled to get along smoothly, and we both irritated each other in the process. She spent countless hours talking to her friends or relatives on the phone. I stayed up late and talked loudly to my own friends who visited me as revenge. It got better after a month. I found a job, activities and friends, and I spent little time in the room. Eventually, she moved to a single room. I realized that I should have been more considerate.

During the first months of my stay, I had a chance to experience the efficiency of American police. One night, trying not to wake my roommate (I had started to learn about mutual respect), I was dialing my family's number in Ukraine without turning on the light. I did fine, except I did not realize that instead of the international access code 011, I mistakenly dialed 911. I realized my mistake after receiving a call from the police just a few seconds later.

"Did you just call the police?" a polite voice inquired. Typical Soviet fear of police flowing with blood in our veins, led me to cautiously say, "No."

"Is everything all right there?" the polite voice persisted.

"Yes."
"Are you sure?"
"Yes."
"All right."

I barely had a chance to recover from my police-induced terror when, a minute later, there was a knock on my door. Seized with panic, I frantically started to collect semi-credible excuses to justify my misdeed, wondering at the same time if I should collect my belongings for longer questioning elsewhere. As I was dealing with this internal struggle, my half-asleep roommate, whom I was trying not to wake, went to answer the door and faced a well-armed policeman inquiring if everything was all right. Saving her from a bigger shock than she had already received, I mustered all my courage and, getting ready for the worst, admitted I was the culprit. To my surprise, the policeman did not arrest me, did not fine me, and did not even scold me—he only asked me to say the truth the next time I made the same mistake. To be sure of our safety, he looked around the room, then departed, wishing me a good night and earning my eternal recognition and admiration. My roommate was not happy, however.

During my year of study in the United States, I became smarter, wiser, more mature and more tolerant. I became aware of great diversity and wonders of the world, but also of its injustices. I met friends from all over the globe, with whom I still keep in touch. A company of Russian-speaking students from Ukraine, Russia and Belarus who came on the same scholarship program became my family. They and my future husband supported and comforted me on the sad day I got the letter with the news of my grandma's passing. One of them, Lena, became my best friend whom I always keep in my thoughts in spite of the distance between us. We try to visit each other every few years. My English, Italian and French skills improved and I started studying Spanish after meeting my future Argentinian-American husband. At least partially, I lost my shyness and gained self-assuredness. Most important, I realized that the people of our countries could not be enemies, for in the end, we are the same—all of us have our joys and sorrows, our strengths and faults. They are just expressed in different ways.

American Afterword

I have lived in the United States for more than twenty years now—more than half of my life. I feel completely integrated in the American way of life, which I admire for the great opportunities it affords and its efficiency and self-reliance. I am grateful for my family—my husband whom I met during my study-abroad year at the University of Kansas (and who loves to visit Ukraine), and my American-born children who speak Russian and Spanish in addition to English. At the same time, I still feel suspended between the two worlds, both of which I consider my homes. I know many immigrants attached to their native land and, sometimes, their children feel something similar.

I hesitate filling out a form which requires an indication of race or ethnicity. White would be the natural choice due to the color of my skin. At the same time, the immigrant experience of someone who does not belong to this country in the same way white Americans do pushes me to disassociate myself from the majority. My other shade of whiteness reveals itself when I open my mouth. I notice how people start conspicuously searching the geographical map in their minds to pinpoint the origin of my accent. "Where are you from?" is an inevitable question, and I face a dilemma. Should I name my current hometown of Rockwall? Lawrence, Kansas—the place where my children were born and where I lived for fifteen years? My home country Ukraine? Or the Soviet Union where I was born?

I have heard many people in similar situations choose the hometown and thus cut short any attempt at further questioning. I lean towards clarity and choose the home country, conscious of the interlocutor's desire to clear the doubts regarding the origin of that accent. Once curiosity is satisfied, questions do not cease: "How do you like it here?" Considering I have lived in the United States for more than twenty years and believe it to be my home, I cannot answer without going into the history of my arrival, initial amazement, subsequent culture shock, disappointments, getting accustomed to the differences, and finally integrating. I would find such a question more natural in reference to Ukraine, where I no longer participate in daily life, except for a summer vacation.

If I specify the considerable length of my sojourn in the United States, people cannot hide their astonishment—or disappointment. "And you still have your accent?" is a poorly-disguised rebuke at my inability to properly imitate the Texas drawl. The accent, unfortunately, does not usually disappear if you arrive to the host country after turning fifteen. I have often wished it did when trying to make a favorable impression during public presentations, job interviews, newly-started conversations with strangers and with the native Texans who are parents of my children's school friends. But I feel at home in the Modern Languages Department of the University of Dallas where many professors speak with accents, and it is an advantage, not a hindrance, in our job. And I have grown to love and appreciate my accent. It gives me a touch of exoticism. It is a part of my "other" American whiteness.

If I don't visit my native country each year, I feel an important part of me is missing and a growing, gnawing nostalgia festers inside of me. I miss my small town of Yuzhny most of all: voluptuous trees towering over the roads that are too narrow in comparison with American streets; an overgrown orchard so thick and large I feel it embraces me; barking dogs; crowing roosters; talkative neighbors; constantly visiting friends and rattling trains piercing the silence of the night. Why do I love coming back? During my visits, when the initial excitement of seeing relatives and friends wears off, I look at Yuzhny with objective eyes and see a sleepy town where the electricity still goes off unexpectedly, sometimes for many hours, with every strong-ish gust of wind. After a while, I grow bored and feel guilty realizing my lack of productive activity contrasts with the busy schedules of people around me who continue working. But invariably, I grow sad and anxious as the time of my return approaches and people comment on how fast our visit has gone by. Perhaps it is the fact that I feel at home walking along the dusty and uneven roads with rugged edges where asphalt was thrown sloppily during construction many years ago? The fact that I never feel alone here, where I know every second person I meet on the street? Old houses, cozy and comforting with their harmonious imperfections, for which I long amidst the regularity and cleanness of American towns? Or perhaps it is the atavistic pull of my roots which gives me the illusion that the grass here is greener, the trees shadier and the sky bluer.

All these forces have infused my character, and the Soviet inheritance stamped it forever. I am not proud or ashamed of it—it is simply a part of me that cannot be washed away with time. In a popular Lviv restaurant, Kryivka, imitating an old Ukrainian bunker which housed independence fighters, visitors at the entrance are asked, jokingly, if they are Moscals[1] or Communists. Then they are offered a shot of vodka as a test: If a Communist drinks it, a red star will reveal itself on his forehead, according to Kryivka lore. I feel slightly nervous as I drink.

Chapter Notes

Propaganda and Life

1. The grades were assigned on the scale from one to five, five being the highest possible grade.

Teachers

1. The common way to address students in Soviet schools was by their last names. Frequently kids also called each other by the last name. The usage of the first name indicated the teacher's positive disposition towards the student or that she was simply in a benevolent mood.
2. The grades were given on a scale from one to five with one being the lowest.

Culture, Entertainment and Censorship

1. Lenin's middle name. It is a sign of affection and camaraderie to refer to a person by his or her middle name.
2. Don is the river where Cossacks settled to form an independent republic from the end of the 16th century until the Revolution.
3. Yerofeyev, Victor. Introduction. *Literary Almanac Metropol* Moscow: Text, 1991. In 1978, Yerofeyev and other fellow writers, in protest of the stagnation in all cultural spheres and in an attempt to win themselves "a shadow of independence," self-published a collection of their works reflecting the idea of aesthetic pluralism. The Union of Writers banned its publication in the Soviet Union and expelled Yerofeyev and many other authors from its ranks. The writers were further persecuted after the Almanac was published in the West.

4. Anna Akhmatova (1889–1966) used lyrical motifs in her poetry deemed as decadent and bourgeois by the Soviet censorship authorities. She also wrote a tragic cycle of poems called "Requiem," decrying the fates of the victims of the Stalinist purges. Her first husband Nikolai Gumilyov, also a poet, was executed by the Soviet secret police; her second husband died in Soviet prison, and her son, Lev Gumilyov, also spent many years in Gulag.
5. Mikhail Zoshchenko (1894–1958) satirized realities of the Soviet life in his short stories, which were very popular with different strata of society. After being denounced, he lived and died in extreme poverty.
6. The lady actually tried to say, "There is no sex in the Soviet Union on TV," but her last words were drowned in laughter, and later forgotten as the phrases became almost idiomatic.

Parties and Holidays

1. Many writers, musicians and artists based their works on the image of the Snow Maiden: Alexander Ostrovskiy wrote a play "Snow Maiden" in 1873; Nikolai Rimskiy-Korsakov wrote an opera in 1881; and such artists as Rerikh, Vrubel and Vasnezov painted this character.
2. According to old Slavic customs, on Christmas and Epiphany Eve nights, girls attempted to gain insight into who their future husband might be by way of different rituals, such as melting wax and trying to see the contour of their future groom's face or putting an object under the pillow and asking for a groom's image to appear in a dream.

The Church did not approve of such practices but they were very popular, especially with peasants. Russian poets, such as Alexander Pushkin, used the motif of divinations in their works. In more recent times, such rituals were sometimes practiced as a game.

3. In Russia, the tradition has been recently restored. In 2018, more than 100,000 people gathered for a May Day demonstration on Red Square.

4. The internal passport was used as a universal form of ID for various administrative domestic matters, including travel within the Soviet Union.

Community and Town

1. Communal flats still existed at the time of my childhood but were much rarer. I did not know anyone living in a communal flat.

2. My family was lucky to have such a close friendship with their neighbors. Residents of communal apartments did not always have such harmonious relationships, and conflicts were also frequent.

3. When apartment owners got married or divorced, they could exchange two small apartments for one bigger one, and a bigger apartment for two smaller ones. The process involved no money transactions, but placing an ad in the newspaper, strenuous search for adequate options and much bureaucracy.

4. "babushka"—literally "grandma"—is used to refer to any elderly lady.

School Fears

1. The grades were given on the scale from one to five with one being the lowest. The grade of one was rarely assigned since two was bad enough.

Exams

1. The golden medal used to be made of actual gold when it was introduced in the forties, but gold was eventually switched to some metal substitute, and used only as thin surface cover during my time.

Joys of Labor at the Soviet Schools

1. "Kolkhoz," the name for "Collective farm," was used metonymically to refer to both state and collective farms. On collective farms, people shared all the land, tools and products of their labor. State farms were run and financed entirely by the state. We actually worked at the state farm lying in the village of Berezivka, next to Yuzhny.

Bureaucracy

1. Gogol, Nikolai. "The Overcoat." Gibian, George, ed. *The Portable Nineteenth-Century Russian Reader*. New York: Penguin Books, 1993.

2. My imperfect translation. I did not include the entire text of the song.

The News

1. Samantha Smith died in an airplane crash in 1985. There was much speculation and conspiracy theories circulating in the Soviet Union about her death, but no proof of such has ever been found. She was greatly venerated in the Soviet Union, where a stamp was printed with her image, an asteroid named in her honor and a monument built in Moscow.

American Afterword

1. A popular, slightly derogatory name for Muscovites.

Index

Numbers in ***bold italics*** indicate pages with illustrations

ACTR/ACCELS 167, 201–203
Afghanistan 164, 201
Andropov, Yuri 164, 203
army 10, 27, 60, ***61***, 64, 83, 85, 87, 140
Artek 11, 12, 204

baptism 57, 69, 70, 72
Bolshevik 39, 62, 137, 140, 150
borsch 47, 48, 153
Brezhnev, Leonid 3, 26, 35, 37, 38, 137, 163, 164
bureaucracy 14, 69, 180, 183, 186, 187, 214

campus 206, 207
capitalism 27, 176, 188
Catholicism 52, 58, 139, 184
censorship 22, 24, 25, 34–39, 41, 164, 213
Chekhov, Anton Pavlovich 25, 97, 149
Chernenko, Konstantin 164
Chernobyl 3, 89, 90, 165, 199
Christmas 3, 52–54, 56, 139, 181, 206, 213
Chumak, Allan 199
church 5, 56, 68, 69, ***71***, 72, 76, 140, 184, 185, 200, 214
Cold War 82, 88, 150, 161
collective farm 117, 124–127, 143, 148, 164, 214; *see also* kolkhoz
Colorado beetle 148–151, 156
communal flat 92, ***93***, 96, 214
Communist party 4–6, 8, 9, 12–14, 35, 37, 56, 62, 63, 68, 71, 93, 117, 122, 141, 161, 162, 164, 188, 189
community 5, 9, 27, 29, 58, 60, 63, 72, 91, 92, 94, 96, 98, 102, 104, 109, 119, 142, 149, 158, 191, 207
Comsomol 5, 6, 14, 56
consumer card 195–197
corruption 137, 164, 189, 193, 202
coupon 76, 195
Crimea 11, 12, 94, 165, 171, 192

Crystal 42

democracy 167, 188

Easter 71, 72, 137
economy 4, 29, 43, 45, 76, 98, 106, 147–149, 189, 197
Engels, Friedrich 25, 62, 122
Epiphany 57, 213
Europe 3, 21, 33, 62, 165, 181
exam 25, 100, 119, 121–124, 140, 145, 147, 154, 158, 201, 202

fir tree 52–54, 64, 80
folklore 27, 29, 40, 52, 55–57, 64, 71, 73, 123, 141, 148, 152, 159, 166, 171, 175
funeral 161–163, 165

Gagarin, Yuri 27, 33
gas mask 82, 88
Gogol, Nikolai Vasilyevich 25, 153, 175, 180, 182, 214
Gorbachev, Mikhail 11, 161, 163, 165–167, 201, 203
graduation 79, 83, 88, 92, 98, 100, 121, 122, 128, 134, 139, 145–147, 157, 190, 194
Grandfather Frost 52–55, 64
grocery store 43, 44, 49, 116, 155, 163
Gulag 3, 213

Happy Pictures 27, ***28***
herring 49, 50
Holodez 50

International Women's Day 27, 61, 64; *see also* March 8
Iron Curtain 1, 35, 100, 200

Kalashnikov rifle 1, ***88***, 89
Kansas 25, 166, 167, 169, 201–203, 210

215

Index

kasha 47, 56, 57, 139, 163, 174, 177
KGB 34, 68, 72, 164
Kharkiv 12, 37, 42, 44, 45, 53, 84, 85, 93, 94, 96, 97, 101, 102, 107, 108, 122, 141, 146, 164, 171, 172, *174*, 176, 183, 184, 190, 194, 200, 206, 207
Kharkiv State University 93, **97**, 183, 194, 201, 207
Khrushchev, Nikita 36, 37, 117, 137, 164
Klin 159, 160
Knorosov, Yuri 97, 98
kum 70, 71, 78, 105, 107
Kupov'yanova, Rymma Aleksandrovna 158
Kyiv 56, 83, 84, 92, 136, 183, 184, 200-202; *see also* Kiev Rus

labor 6, 47, 50, 62, 84, 124, 126-129, 131, 143, 149-152, 154, 155, 166, 189, 190, 214
land 10, 20, 27, 48, 81, 97, 98, 148-150, 156, 181, 185, 189, 194, 210, 213
Lenin, Vladimir Ilyich 3-6, 8, 10, 25, 27, 62, 68, 77, 97, 100, 122, 137, 143, 162
Lycheva, Katya 204

Malanka 58
Marx, Karl 25, 62, 97, 101, 122
maternity 168. 169
May Day 62-64, 89, 100, 214; *see also* Labor Day; May 1
military training 1, 14, 82, 88, **89**, 90; *see also* military preparation
militia 52, 62, 104, 160, 161, 164, 182, 190
MMM 198
Moscow 3, 8, 10, 23, 26, 29, 33, 38, 45, 55, 68, 117, 122, 132, 157, 159, 162, 193, 196, 203, 213, 214
motherland 1, 5, 6, 8, 21, 72, 77, 88, 89, 100, 141, 143, 164, 181, 187
music school 116, 157, 158, 160
Myrhorod 175, 177, 178, 180

Neizvestny, Ernst 37
New Year 10, 27, 38, 52-56, 58, 64, 80, 164
Nu Pogodi! 38, 39, 42
nuclear 82, 83, 88, 89, *111*, 164, 203

October Revolution 19, 27, 64, 97, 139, 141; *see also* The Great October Socialist Revolution
Octobrist 4-6, 8, 27
Olympics 4, 116, 142, *172*
Orenburg 24, 29, 33, 92, 93, 96, 100
Orthodox 58, 68, *71*, 72, 76, 137, 139, 184, 185
OVIR 181-183, 185, 186

Palace of Pioneers 53, 57; *see also* Pioneer Palace
parade 1, 8, 13, 21, 80, 86, 88, 90, 91, 136, 137
perestroika 14, 35, 39, 116, 166, 171, 180, 192, 195, 201, 203
pickle 49, 151, 153, 154-156

Pioneer 1, 5-14, 27, 53, 101, 102, 117, 125, 127, 133, 143, 157, 202, 204
Pioneer camp 6, 11, 12, 101, 202, 204
Pioneer Truth 3, 12; *see also Pionerskaya Pravda*
pirogi 48; *see also* pies
potato 43, 47-49, 148-154
propaganda 2, 3, 12, 27, 61, 69, 115, 119, 141, 142, 203

Reagan, Roland 167, 201
religion 68, 69
resort 3, 12, 172, 174-177
Russia 9, 11, 15, 26, 29, 34, 35, 39, 49, 52, 57, 62, 76, 80, 83, 100, 108, 122, 135, 139-143, 148, 149, 153, 155, 159, 165-167, 171, 174, 175, 179, 180, 184, 185, 190-201, 207, 209, 210, 214

Sakharov, Andrey 164
salo 49, 50, 72, 151, 156, 197
sausage 26, 43, 45, 49, 56, 72, 95, 103, 107, 197
Shevchenko, Taras 77, 133
Slavic 63, 77, 84, 108, 119, 148, 207, 213
Smith, Samantha 204, 214
Snow Maiden 52, -55, 64, 213; *see also* Snegurochka
socialist 11, 14, 24, 25, 27, 29, 35-37, 61-63, 66, 92, 122, 125, 126-128, 130, 139, 140, 141, 157, 168, 189, 205
Soviet Union 1-4, 6, 8-11, 13, 14, 23-25, 27, 29-44, 52, 53, 55, 59-64, 68-70, 72, 82, 84-88, 90, 91, 93, 97, 98, 101, 102, 115, 116, 121, 122, 124, 126-129, 131, 135, 137, 138, 139, 140, 143, 146, 147, 149, 150, 155, 158, 159, 161, 162, 164, 165, 169, *172*, 174-176, 179-181, 185-189, 191, 193, 196, 198, 201, 203-206, 208, 210; *see also* USSR
speculant 145
sports 6, 11, 87, 101, 102, 113, 132, 139, 157, 164, 206
Stalin, Joseph 15, 25, 34, 35, 36, 38, 83, 96, 128, 161-164, 190
state 1, 2, 11, 12, 27, 34-36, 38, 39, 43-46, 56, 62, 63, 69, 72, 89, 90, 92, 93, **97**, 98, 116, 118, 121, 124-126, 128, 129, 132, 140, 141, 145, 149, 150, 161, 165, 167, 169, 174, 175, 182, 183, 184, 187-195, 198, 207, 214
stengazeta 9; *see also* wall newspaper

Tchaikovsky, Pyotr Ilyich 32, 158, 159, 163
telephone 21-24, 26, 42, 64, 65, 94, 95, 100, 104, 106, 107, 108, 119, 176, 179, 197, 202, 203, 208
television 22, 25, 32, 35, 39-41, 44, 64, 68, 142, 149, 157, 161, 163, 165, 167, 176, 177, 198, 199, 213
Texas 11, 50, 53, 58, 193, 211
theater 18, 32, 33, 35, 36, 92, 96, 101, 102, 158, 164, 172, 178
thimble dealer 197, 198

train 20, 24, 41, 46, 92, 102, 103, 105, 107, 122, 142, 159, 160, 171, 191, 197, 200, 207, 211

Ukraine 1, 9–12, 18, 21, 24, 25, 29, 35, 40, 44, *46*, 48, 49, 50, 54, 56–58, 67, *71*, 73, 74, 76, 77, 79, 83, 84, 89, 92–95, 96, 98, 101, 105–108, 116, 120, 121, 122, 125, 132, 133, 135, 141, 148, 150, 152, 153, 154, 155, 156, 157, 159, 170, 175, 178, 180, 182–187, 190, 192, 195, 196, 197, 199, 200, 201, 202, 205–211

uniform 1, 6, 87, 115, 116, 127, 129, 135, *136*, 137, 142, 168, 182

United States 1, 11, 21, 23, 25, 26, 31, 33, 34, 39–42, 44, 48–50, 52–54, *57*, 61–63, 65, 67, 79, 82, 95, 97, 103, *105*–108, 110, 112–114, 116, 121, 130, 133, 135, 138, 147, 148, 150, 153, 156, 164, 165, 167, 169, 176, 181–187, 192, 200–211

University of Dallas 1, 211

University of Kansas 200, 201, 203, 210

utrennik 38, 56; *see also* morning event

vacations 2, 4, 9, 11, 66, 126, 172, 178, 188

Victory Day 21, 27, 64, *80,* 83–87, 90, 91

voucher 11, 168, 171, 181, 184

vozhatye 6, *7*, 8

wedding *46*, 69–79, 128, 165, 181, 184, 185, 192, 193

West 1, 36, 39, 41, 44, 50, 72, 73, 107, 116, 117, 137, 139, 141, 165, 167, 172, 178, 181, 186, 192, 194, 200, 202, 206, 213

World War II 5, 10, 77, 82–*85*, 87, 90, 92, 99, 102, 122, 138, 152, 190, 205; *see also* Great Patriotic War

Yevtushenko, Yevgeniy 36, 37

Yuzhny 25, 31, 45, *57*, *75*, 84, 85, 88, 90, 91, 93, 94, 96–99, 101, 102, 104–106, 108, 125, 142, 147–149, 157, 158, 160, 171, 172, 175, 189, 207, 211, 214

Zarnitsa 87, 88

Zetkin, Clara 61, 62